SEPTEMBER 11

SEPTEMBER 11

THE 9/11 STORY, AFTERMATH AND LEGACY

REPORTS AND RECOLLECTIONS BY JOURNALISTS OF
THE ASSOCIATED PRESS

FOREWORD BY
ROBERT DE NIRO

INTRODUCTION BY TED ANTHONY
PREFACE BY MARK MITTELSTADT
AFTERWORD BY RICHARD DREW
DEVELOPED BY LES KRANTZ

STERLING
New York

Detail of *In Memoriam*, a photographic memorial exhibition at the National September 11 Memorial & Museum. The exhibition honors the 2,977 individuals killed as a result of the terrorist attacks of 9/11 at the World Trade Center, the Pentagon and in Shanksville. It also honors the six individuals killed in the terrorist bombing of the World Trade Center on Feb. 26, 1993.

STERLING
New York

ISBN: 978-1-4549-4359-4
ISBN: 978-1-4549-4360-0 (e-book)

Distributed in Canada by Sterling Publishing Co., Inc.
c/o Canadian Manda Group, 664 Annette Street
Toronto, Ontario M6S 2C8, Canada
Distributed in the United Kingdom by GMC Distribution Services
Castle Place, 166 High Street, Lewes, East Sussex BN7 1XU, England
Distributed in Australia by NewSouth Books
University of New South Wales, Sydney, NSW 2052, Australia

For information about custom editions, special sales, and premium and corporate purchases,
please contact Sterling Special Sales at 800-805-5489 or specialsales@sterlingpublishing.com.

Manufactured in Canada

2 4 6 8 10 9 7 5 3 1

sterlingpublishing.com

Cover design by Elizabeth Mihaltse Lindy
Interior design by Kevin Ullrich

Picture and Text Credits – see page 210

Pages ii–iii: Close-up of the bronze parapets edging the memorial pools at the
National 9/11 Memorial & Museum in New York, inscribed with the names of the 2,983 people
who were killed in the 2001 and 1993 terrorist attacks; OPPOSITE: Firefighters amid the smoking rubble
of the World Trade Center, Sept. 11, 2001; pages viii–ix: The top of the Freedom Tower
in downtown New York breaks through the clouds, April 21, 2015.

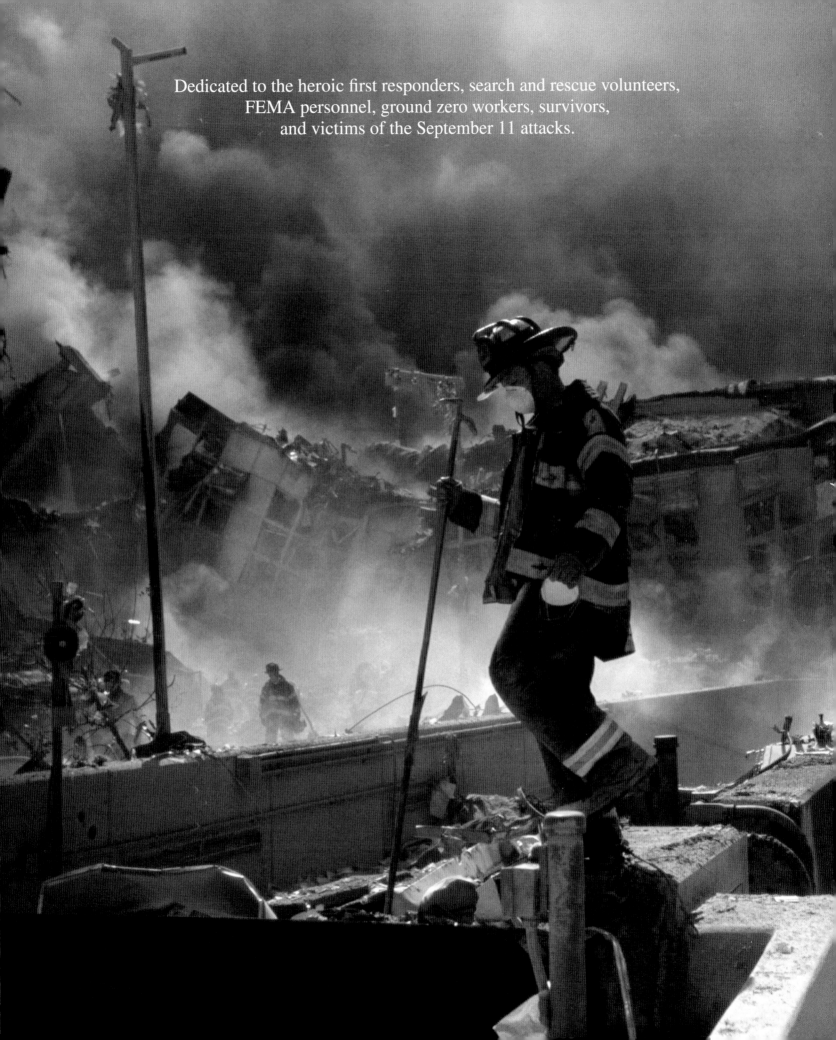

Dedicated to the heroic first responders, search and rescue volunteers,
FEMA personnel, ground zero workers, survivors,
and victims of the September 11 attacks.

CONTENTS

CHAPTER ONE
THE DAY
THE WORLD CHANGED

CHAPTER TWO
THE AFTERMATH

CHAPTER THREE
THE WORLD REACTS

CHAPTER FOUR
JUSTICE

When New York Came Back to Life

By ROBERT DE NIRO

I think those of us who lived and worked in downtown New York in 2001 felt the impact of the attacks on the World Trade Center most directly. You still can feel it today. Ground Zero is our neighborhood, so we were surrounded by devastation in the wake of 9/11.

That day I was in a meeting and about to head to the airport for a flight to Los Angeles when my son Raphael called me to say that a plane had hit the World Trade Center. I immediately went home.

From my apartment I could see the towers, about nine blocks away. I watched with binoculars as the flames and smoke rose from the buildings. When the south tower collapsed, the news was on and I had to turn from the window to the TV to confirm what I was seeing with my own eyes; it was surreal. Then the north tower went down. Watching this happen was beyond belief.

I didn't lose a relative or close friend when the towers fell but after the attacks, whatever I had done, whatever I was striving for, had no meaning; it all just stopped. I think 9/11 affected every New Yorker dramatically in some way.

A disaster brings out the best in people. I think about all those firefighters, policeman and citizens who responded. Many of them died heroically. It was human nature to respond, to want to drop what you are doing and help. When a terrible thing like that happens, people help each other. Whatever our differences, we forget them and join together.

Right after 9/11, Mayor Giuliani was saying that people should go back to living in the city as usual, as much as they could. To do that, we needed to get it started again—we needed to clean up and to go on living in our neighborhood. Giuliani's message made a lot of sense. We needed to rebuild what we had lost.

It was a difficult time. Downtown was only open to foot traffic, except for recovery operations. You had to show ID to get in. As days and weeks went by, the local businesses were struggling to survive. No one wanted to be downtown.

My business partner, Jane Rosenthal, her husband, Craig Hatkoff, and I started a program called Dinner Downtown, which was about bringing people back to help revive the neighborhoods. People came in on buses to Chinatown, Little Italy, Tribeca, Wall Street, wherever they could. We'd have dinner with them, and the program grew. It was a small thing we could do to help, and we were hoping to do more.

Before 9/11 we had entertained the idea of doing a film festival in New York. After the attacks it seemed to us that a film festival could bring more people back to the neighborhood. So we started calling people like Martin Scorsese, Meryl Streep, Ed Burns and many others. Everybody wanted to help.

From the start, the festival took on a life of its own. Mayor Bloomberg, who succeeded Giuliani, and Governor Pataki were very helpful. American Express, whose headquarters were downtown, became a sponsor. But we could never have made the festival happen without the thousands of volunteers.

Unlike a lot of other festivals, this one is about community and family: a true neighborhood film festival.

I'm especially proud of what brings everybody to the festival: The family street fair, the open screenings on the piers and all the events utilizing the local businesses, from restaurants to the Borough of Manhattan Community College—not to mention all the films. We wanted to help and we hope that we succeeded.

After the first festival we never thought we'd make it to the second one, but now 10 years later here we are. It's a tradition. The festival has become part of the city's cultural life, which is tremendously satisfying.

Some people think that the pace of the city's recovery has been slow, especially at Ground Zero, but New York has many moving parts and conflicting interests. Maybe we needed 10 years to put 9/11 into the kind of perspective that helps the city to rebuild in the right way.

People came to the festival from around the world. One of them was Sheikha Al Mayassa bint Hamad bin Khalifa al-Thani, daughter of Sheik Hamad bin Khalifa al-Thani, the ruling emir of Qatar. She wanted to help create a festival back home in Doha.

We thought the Doha festival was a good idea, and it gave us an opportunity to interact with a community in the Middle East. This partnership was a step in the right direction to help bring awareness. Both festivals would have an impact on culture, and not just locally: 9/11 was a world event.

In the end we can have our differences, even stereotypical attitudes toward each other, but once we are more aware, we get closer to realizing that we are no different from one another.

The Brooklyn Bridge and Manhattan skyline; One World Trade Center—the Freedom Tower—is seen at right, Jan. 3, 2016.

PREFACE
How AP Covered Sept. 11

By MARK MITTELSTADT

NEW YORK (AP)—Mounting an audacious attack against the United States, terrorists crashed two hijacked airliners into the World Trade Center and brought down the twin 110-story towers Tuesday morning. A jetliner also slammed into the Pentagon as the seat of government itself came under attack.

Thus did The Associated Press chronicle an unimaginable day of tumult and gore and heartache—the worst terrorist assault on American soil, the bloodiest moment in New York City's history, the biggest story in a generation, a day unlike any other since the AP began reporting the news in the middle of the 19th century. Altogether, AP would file 25 NewsAlerts, 18 Bulletins and two Flashes.

Over the hours and days to come, virtually all staffers in every AP outpost across the planet threw themselves into what one New York City reporter called "the story of our lives." They gave up weekends and vacations and sleep, some not going home for days. They stepped through rubble and inhaled the dust and smoke of the trade center's ruins; they worked on, even as some feared for the safety of friends and loved ones, even as some were forced from their homes by the calamity.

That day, and for months and years to come, they told the era's most important story to a world that hung on every image and word.

AP copy was quoted by broadcasters in every time zone, on every continent. Online news sites grabbed the latest developments from AP digital services. AP's online site at the time, The Wire, had 10 times the normal amount of traffic—near the capacity of its servers. Within hours, nearly 200 newspapers printed extra editions—many headlined simply "ATTACKED!" or "TERROR"—to report the extraordinary events to eager readers. Largely filled with AP stories and photos, those editions sold out quickly. Several papers printed rare, second "extras" with more details and photos.

"Your people in New York and D.C. did a hell of a job today," wrote Jack Ryan, publisher-editor of the *Enterprise-Journal* in McComb, Miss. And there was this from Chris Peck, former editor of the *Spokesman-Review* in Spokane, Wash., and then president of the Associated Press Managing Editors: "Your good work—no, your extraordinary work—over this last week has been a service to every newspaper, and every citizen of the nation." ■

—Mark Mittelstadt, former Executive Director,
AP Managing Editors Association

The World Trade Center twin towers burn, Sept. 11, 2001.

INTRODUCTION
Notes from a Jumbled World

By TED ANTHONY

Where were you the moment that everything changed? I was in a restaurant in the Chinese capital, eating grilled shrimp tails.

I had just moved to China from New York, weeks after getting married, to take up my new posting as an international correspondent for The Associated Press. I was ready to focus on the politics and culture of the world's most populous society as it took its place in the community of nations.

The world, though, had other plans.

The cataclysm of Sept. 11, 2001, its name in those early days not yet shortened to our current "9/11," summoned an entire generation of journalists whose career trajectories and lives were knocked onto an entirely new course by the biggest story of our era: covering the attacks and their aftermath as the unthinkable products of violence and rage reverberated across a reeling planet.

◆ ◆ ◆

From New York City and its newly named "ground zero" to Washington and the smoldering Pentagon, from towns across the United States to most of the world's capitals, committed AP journalists immediately mobilized and began doing what they do best: gathering information, telling stories, holding officials accountable, trying to advance the power of facts.

The goal, somehow even more urgent at this moment, was to give people the most fundamental service that the news can provide: the tools to help them make sense of what is happening.

For some of us, the coverage meant a chance at service, for others an unmatched professional opportunity. For many, like myself, it meant exposure to parts of the world we had never experienced firsthand and peoples we had never known.

For some journalists, the emotional toll of coming face-to-face with such death and destruction rippled out across the years. For still others, it meant unexpected endings, lives truncated tragically. Some of us died on a lonely road outside Jalalabad when a convoy of journalists en route to Kabul was ambushed in November 2001. One of us, Daniel Pearl of *The Wall Street Journal*, was kidnapped in January 2002 after being lured to an interview in Karachi, Pakistan's largest city, and brutally murdered shortly afterward.

As soon as it became clear that Afghanistan would be the focus, legions of us were sent in from all corners of the AP—from the Middle East and Africa, from Southeast Asia and the United States.

OPPOSITE: A view of the ruins through fragments of the World Trade Center facade, all that remained of the 110-story structures that once dominated the skyline of lower Manhattan, Sept. 21, 2001.

LEFT: AP journalist Kathy Gannon, far right, covers herself with a shawl so she can see her computer screen in Torkham, Afghanistan, Oct. 24, 2001. A Taliban commander is using a satellite phone to verify visa information for Gannon—then the AP's Pakistan bureau chief—and Athens-based AP photographer Dimitri Messinis, second from the right. At left is Amir Shah, an AP correspondent based in Kabul.

A U.S. Marine stands at parade rest following a memorial ceremony at the U.S. Embassy in Kabul, Sept. 11, 2002. Marines from the 4th Marine Expeditionary Brigade paid tribute to those who lost their lives on 9/11 by burying a piece of the World Trade Center and marking it with a specially made stone.

The first stop for so many of us was Pakistan, the "control bureau" for Afghanistan. That was where our knowledgeable colleague Kathy Gannon—her vivid dispatches already the stuff of legend within AP—briefed us about what might come next and about the complex politics of both Afghanistan and Pakistan.

Suddenly, many of us were submerged in a sea of political subtlety that, frankly, we barely understood. We buried ourselves in books and recent articles and background interviews with diplomats. We grabbed sleep when we could and, trying to get up to speed, took informal master classes in the AP's Islamabad bureau at the feet of Kathy and longtime AP editor Bob Reid, the role model for a generation of conflict correspondents. We said to ourselves: "Can we do this? Are we ready? Will we get this right? Will we survive?"

As the U.S. air war commenced and was completed, AP journalists converged on Afghanistan itself, coming in from Uzbekistan and Tajikistan and Iran, from Dubai and Islamabad, trying to see firsthand what the aftermath of 9/11 had wrought and what would take the place of the Taliban, overthrown by the United States after sheltering the attacks' mastermind, Osama bin Laden. We met the unforgettable Amir Shah, AP's courageous

Kabul correspondent, who had navigated Taliban rule and walked a tightwire to get the news out in the days after 9/11 without getting arrested or worse.

For many of the younger Western journalists among us, this all made for an almost unbelievable journalism experience. I remember having conversations with colleagues—people who, like me, had started our careers at small- and medium-sized newspapers covering cops and municipal government, hoping to one day travel the world as correspondents. Now we were, and it was dizzying.

✦ ✦ ✦

You'll note I am using the word "we" here quite liberally. Yet I do it carefully, and only with certain things. Because in truth, the "we" to which I refer—outsiders, usually Westerners, who came to these lands for a professional assignment and could go home anytime they needed to—was only a subset of the overall AP "we" that was creating the journalism used by the world to understand this massive event.

We outsiders, some of us veterans and some of us on our first big international assignments, realized how much more our colleagues who were actually from these countries knew about it all than we did. It was their brains that often contained the crucial context; it was their understanding that was more visceral and intimate. I'd like to think that in the months after the towers came down, by working alongside them we accumulated a better understanding of all the forces in the world that we didn't know enough about.

Together we set out to chronicle this era that was unfolding before us at top speed. The "scribblers" among us quickly learned the ways of photographers, and vice versa. Colleagues we had never met and knew only by their names on emails, we suddenly found ourselves living with. Stories were written to match photographs that had been taken. Late-night discussions over cheap cigarettes on dust-choked Kabul evenings begat story ideas that we'd rise at dawn to rush out and do. I believe that the "cross-format" journalism so common in the online news coverage of the 2020s—text and video and photography and audio working in lockstep to tell important stories—had roots in how journalists worked together so closely during those jumbled days when online journalism was first emerging.

And me? I kept going back. I ended up spending big chunks of my first 18 months of "living in China" working in either Afghanistan or Pakistan.

I walked the rutted streets of a refugee camp outside Kabul with a U.S. senator named Joe Biden, guarded by men with machine guns as we discussed foreign policy and talked to displaced Afghans. I visited a used book market in the Pakistani army's headquarters town and wrote about the divide between cultures as told by the publications for sale. I spent a day with

AP journalist Ted Anthony, left, and Sen. Joe Biden of Delaware, right, walk through a refugee camp in Kabul, Afghanistan, Jan. 11, 2002.

Afghans who had repurposed hundreds of abandoned Soviet shipping containers into stores and apartments—an entire neighborhood of commerce, street by salvaged street—as they tried to rebuild their capital. I crossed the war-scarred Shomali Plain, my mouth dry as I passed burned-out hulks of vehicles and roadside signs that said, in English and Dari, "BEWARE OF MINES."

I stood with Zalmay Horiakhail, one of Afghanistan's newest police officers, in a side alley as we dodged the sparks from soldering irons and watched a satellite dish, banned by the Taliban, being constructed out of a piece of salvaged sheet metal painted with Reddi-wip logos—waylaid, somehow, from its original destiny as a whipped-topping canister. "I'd be really interested in a good cop movie," Officer Horiakhail told me.

I spent an afternoon drinking tea with the newly minted minister of tourism, Abdul Rahman, as he passionately outlined his efforts to bring visitors back to a reborn Afghanistan. And then, back in town barely five months later, I interviewed his brother, who was trying to solve his brutal murder. I elbowed my way to the front of a bleary-eyed phalanx of regional Afghan officials after midnight at a *loya jirga*—a grand council—and held my first-generation digital camera aloft to grab a photo of Hamid Karzai moments after he was chosen as Afghanistan's president.

As I wrote all of this down in my notebook over the weeks and months, I thought often of my mother, who, when I decided to pursue journalism as a profession out of college, told me: "You'll be getting paid to get an education every day." I don't think she ever dreamed how right she'd be.

Almost two years after 9/11, as the Iraq invasion unfolded, U.S. Gen. Tommy Franks would famously say that embedded journalists there could see the story as if they were "looking through five, six hundred straws at one time."

When he said that, I realized: For AP journalists, that's essentially what covering 9/11 and its aftermath was.

We each could see what was in our narrow field of vision. We all felt entirely immersed in it all. But even at the time, we knew that there were always countless vantage points that we or our colleagues weren't seeing or covering. And often, the story that appeared under one or two bylines contained the work of many AP people around the world, each contributing a few filaments of news or context. No single vantage point—no single writer or photographer or video journalist—could have ever captured the story of 9/11, no matter how talented the journalist.

That's why a book like this must exist. This, in one volume, is a sampler of AP journalists at their best, crowdsourcing 9/11 for the world. Together and apart, day by day, interview by interview, image by image, paragraph by paragraph, we created a mural of the biggest story we'd ever known.

Twenty years later, the mural is still being painted. Here are some of its details.

—Ted Anthony,
Director of Newsroom Innovation

TIMELINE OF A NATIONAL TRAGEDY

The news came in a dizzying torrent. At first it was thought to be a freak accident when American Airlines Flight 11 crashed into the north tower of New York's World Trade Center at 8:46 a.m. on Sept. 11, 2001. But when United Airlines Flight 175 hit the south tower minutes later, the world knew a global war of terror had just begun.

The attacks rocked every notion that Americans had about wars. The war was no longer "over there"—it was going on right here, in New York City and in the nation's capital. Another one was somewhere in the sky over Pennsylvania, fought by rebellious passengers against a then-unknown enemy.

As panic gripped America, the sense of fear and shock spread around the globe: 2,977 victims had perished, and along with them, the world's sense of security from evil.

5:45 a.m.

All is normal along America's Eastern Seaboard and its airports before the plot unfolds.

Mohamed Atta and Abdulaziz al-Omari clear security at Portland International Jetport in Maine to catch a commuter flight to Boston. They soon connect to American Airlines Flight 11 on which three would-be hijackers await.

7:18 to 7:35 a.m.

At Dulles Airport in Washington, D.C., five other would-be hijackers pass through security to board American Airlines Flight 77. Similar scenes involving two more flights take place at the Newark and Boston Airports hours later as a total of 19 terrorists are inflight on California-bound airliners loaded with a combined total of approximately 250,000 pounds of jet fuel.

LEFT: Airport surveillance tape released Sept. 19, 2001, shows hijackers Mohamed Atta, right, and Abdulaziz al-Omari, center, pass through airport security at Portland International Jetport on Sept. 11 before boarding a commuter flight to Boston to connect to American Airlines Flight 11.

ABOVE: Hijacker Khalid al-Mihdhar, wearing a yellow shirt, foreground, passes through the security checkpoint at Dulles International Airport in Chantilly, Va., Sept. 11, just hours before American Airlines Flight 77 crashed into the Pentagon, in this surveillance video image.

TIMELINE OF A NATIONAL TRAGEDY

7:59 a.m.
American Flight 11 with 92 people leaves Boston's Logan Airport for Los Angeles.

Boeing 767 carrying 81 passengers (including five would-be hijackers) and 11 crew members, departs 14 minutes late from Logan International Airport in Boston, bound for Los Angeles International Airport. The aircraft is laden with 76,400 pounds of jet fuel.

8:19 a.m.
American Airlines Flight 11 attendant reports in-flight stabbing.

Moments after former Israeli army commando Daniel M. Lewin is stabbed—reportedly by hijacker Satam al-Suqami—Lewin becomes 9/11's first fatality. Betty Ong, flight attendant, calls ground personnel to report attack. Cohorts Mohamed Atta and Abdulaziz al-Omari are onboard and the first hijacking of four planes gets underway.

8:24 a.m.
Ringleader makes announcement of hijacking on AA Flight 11.

Mohamed Atta attempts to inform passengers of hijacking on in-flight PA system but instead mistakenly reaches ground control. News of the attack is overheard by United Airlines Flight 175 pilot, Capt. Victor J. Saracini, who informs FAA minutes before his plane is hijacked too.

8:15 a.m.
United Airlines Flight 175 with 65 people leaves Boston for Los Angeles.

Boeing 767 departs from Boston with 56 passengers (including five would-be hijackers), two pilots and seven flight attendants. The aircraft is laden with 76,000 pounds of jet fuel.

8:20 a.m.
American Airlines Flight 77 with 64 people leaves Washington's Dulles Airport for Los Angeles.

Boeing 757 with 58 passengers (including five would-be hijackers) and six crewmembers departs 10 minutes late. The aircraft is laden with 49,900 pounds of jet fuel.

BACKGROUND: Aerial view of the World Trade Center twin towers and the Hudson River taken several months before the 9/11 attacks.

8:37 a.m.
U.S. military put on alert.

Boston's air traffic control contacts U.S. Air Force Northeast Air Defense Sector (NEADS) in Upstate New York, which calls in the National Guard at Otis Air Force Base on Cape Cod and commands them to follow Flight 11.

8:42 a.m.
United Airlines Flight 93 with 45 people leaves Newark Airport for San Francisco.

After routine delay, Boeing 757—scheduled to depart at 8:01—leaves Newark, N.J. with two pilots, five flight attendants and 38 passengers (including four would-be hijackers). The aircraft is laden with 48,700 pounds of fuel.

8:46 a.m.
American Flight 11 crashes into north tower of World Trade Center in New York.

Aircraft slams into building instantly killing passengers and crew and hundreds of workers inside as it squarely hits floors 93 through 99. Hundreds are trapped above 91st floor due to three emergency stairways being destroyed. New York City's emergency squads rush to World Trade Center. NYFD Battalion Chief Joseph Pfeifer witnesses crash from 14 blocks away and issues alarms, dispatching units to the rescue and to begin evacuation.

The north tower shows the impact left by American Airlines Flight 11 moments after impact.
A person is just visible, standing at the bottom of the gaping hole.

TIMELINE OF A NATIONAL TRAGEDY

8:50 a.m.
President George W. Bush is alerted.

President Bush—who moments before had arrived at the Emma E. Booker Elementary School in Sarasota, Fla., to meet with grammar school children—is misinformed by aides who assumed that a "small aircraft" accidentally crashed into World Trade Center.

8:55 a.m.
South tower building assures workers they are safe.

Port Authority employee announces on PA system in south tower (Building Two) that it is "secure and there is no need to evacuate," an assurance that proved to be deadly wrong.

9:03 a.m.
United Flight 175 crashes into south tower of World Trade Center.

Now commandeered by hijackers, the aircraft smashes into 2 World Trade Center, making a direct hit on floors 77 through 85 and killing all onboard and hundreds in building. Force of explosion damages exits and elevator cables, trapping survivors. Many people trapped by intense heat and smoke jump from windows; along with victims in the north tower, up to 200 plunged to their deaths from the burning towers.

8:52 a.m.
Flight 175 flight attendant calls operator in San Francisco.

At 8:52, flight attendant Robert John Fangman announces hijacking to United Airlines operator in San Francisco; by 9:00, passengers Garnet Bailey, Peter Hanson and Brian Sweeney had all called their families. It would be the last phone conversations of their lives.

8:59 a.m.
Evacuations of north and south towers begin.

Sgt. Al DeVona of Port Authority Police Department orders evacuation of both towers; one minute later colleague Capt. Anthony Whitaker expands evacuation orders for entire World Trade Center. Workers scramble to exits.

Chief of Staff Andy Card whispers into the ear of President George W. Bush to give him word of the plane crash at the World Trade Center, during Bush's visit to the Emma E. Booker Elementary School in Sarasota, Fla.

United Flight 175 about to make impact with the south tower.

9:05 a.m.

President gets news of second hit at World Trade Center and makes plan to leave Sarasota and take charge of national emergency.

President Bush, amid listening along with a group of second graders to a story about a pet goat being read, is interrupted by White House Chief of Staff Andy Card, who walks into the room and whispers in the president's ear: "A second plane has hit the World Trade Center. America is under attack."

9:12 a.m.

Flight 77 crewmembers and passengers call family and ground personnel to inform them of hijacking.

With passengers now forced to rear of aircraft, flight attendant Renée May calls her mother, Nancy May, to report situation, and moments later calls American Airlines. Minutes pass and passenger Barbara K. Olson phones her husband, Theodore Olson, at his office at Department of Justice, relating that hijackers brandishing knives and box cutters are in control.

9:17 a.m.

Federal Aviation Administration shuts down all New York City–area airports.

New York City is first metropolitan area to ground all flights before FAA spokesman Les Dorr announces nationwide shut down that cancels 36,000 to 40,000 daily flights in the U.S., including all general aviation flights and incoming flights from foreign destinations.

9:06 a.m.

President Bush begins the scramble to take action.

Bush, now in a holding room at the school, contacts Vice President Dick Cheney, New York Gov. George Pataki and FBI Director Robert Mueller III; they begin assessing the situation and evaluating next steps. The back-and-forth with government officials continues for 25 minutes.

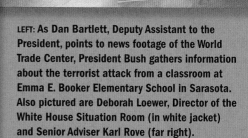

LEFT: As Dan Bartlett, Deputy Assistant to the President, points to news footage of the World Trade Center, President Bush gathers information about the terrorist attack from a classroom at Emma E. Booker Elementary School in Sarasota. Also pictured are Deborah Loewer, Director of the White House Situation Room (in white jacket) and Senior Adviser Karl Rove (far right).

ABOVE: President Bush watches television coverage of the attacks during a briefing in the Emma E. Booker classroom.

9:21 a.m.

All bridges and tunnels to Manhattan closed.

New York Mayor Rudy Giuliani, recently rushed to his first temporary command post near the World Trade Center, begins plans to clear access for emergency vehicles. He orders city to shut off all access to Manhattan, including subway, and orders evacuation of Wall Street and the United Nations. Cell phone services in area crippled; children kept in school for safety before parents can take their charge.

9:30 a.m.

President Bush makes first public statement on terrorist attack.

"Today we've had a national tragedy," Bush announces in the school gymnasium. "Two airplanes have crashed into the World Trade Center in an apparent terrorist attack on our country. . . . [I've] ordered that the full resources of the federal government go to help the victims and their families, and to conduct a full-scale investigation to hunt down and to find those folks who committed this act." President remains at school for another 30 minutes as he continues his information gathering and plans his response.

9:36 a.m.

Vice President Cheney rushed to bunker.

Dick Cheney is ushered by U.S. Secret Service into Emergency Operations Center, a secure underground shelter beneath the White House, where he authorizes fighter jets to shoot down hijacked airliners.

BELOW: Vice President Cheney strategizes with senior staff in the Emergency Operations Center bunker under the White House, Sept. 11.

ABOVE: President Bush makes his first public remarks on the attack, from the Emma E. Booker school in Sarasota.

9:37 a.m.
American Airlines Flight 77 crashes into Pentagon.

With five hijackers in command of aircraft, it smashes into southwest side of U.S. military headquarters in Arlington County, Va., killing all onboard, including 53 passengers. Among the military personnel and civilians at scene, 125 more will perish.

9:45 a.m.
U.S. Capitol and White House West Wing evacuated.

All U.S. Senate and House of Representatives activity is halted and all congressional personnel and their support persons begin evacuating. The White House takes similar action. Soon after, bridges, buildings and all public spaces in U.S. begin closing down.

9:58 a.m.
Passengers on Flight 93 use cell phones to make distress calls.

Huddled in the rear of the aircraft, passengers try to reach loved ones on cell phones, logging 37 known calls made from airspace near Pittsburgh. As aircraft descends toward ground, passenger Edward P. Felt makes one of last-known calls from plane, dialing 911 from aircraft's lavatory where he locks himself in for safety. He succeeds in reaching emergency operator to report hijacking.

9:42 a.m.
U.S. airspace ordered closed.

Federal Aviation Commission orders closure of all civilian aviation in U.S. and orders that all aircraft land immediately, cancels all scheduled departures and grounds all civilian aviation.

9:54 a.m.
President Bush leaves Sarasota.

Air Force One departs with no announced destination. Washington, feared to be too dangerous for President Bush, is ruled out. Barksdale Air Force Base in Louisiana, manned with military personnel and air power, is deemed more secure. Airbase traffic control gets word the president is on his way there.

ABOVE: A monitor displaying US Airways flight arrivals at Bradley International Airport in Windsor Locks, Conn., Sept. 11, shows all flights canceled after the FAA grounded all planes in the United States following the terrorist attacks.

RIGHT: The Pentagon's southwestern side burns after it was hit by American Airlines Flight 77 on Sept. 11.

10

9:59 a.m.
South tower of World Trade Center collapses.

Now a flaming inferno for 56 minutes, the first hit of the twin towers is in chaos with workers escaping from the exits and jumping from windows while first responders rush in. With smoke billowing amid the towers and expanding into nearby office and residential buildings, witnesses hear deafening rumbling and cracking sounds. Within 10 seconds, the south tower collapses, killing 800 civilians and emergency personnel.

RIGHT: The south tower of the World Trade Center collapses as smoke billows from both towers.

LAST WORDS FROM VICTIMS: "LET'S ROLL"

By JOANNE LOVIGLIO
The Associated Press

PHILADELPHIA, Sept. 17, 2001 (AP)—"Are you guys ready? Let's roll!" is an expression Todd Beamer used whenever his wife and two young sons were leaving their home for a family outing.

The businessman and Sunday-school teacher said the same thing before he and other passengers apparently took action against hijackers aboard United Airlines Flight 93 on Tuesday, shortly before the plane crashed in a western Pennsylvania field.

The jetliner, which government officials suspect was headed for a high-profile target in Washington, was the fourth to crash in a coordinated terrorist attack that killed thousands and the only one that didn't take lives on the ground.

Todd Beamer, 32, placed a call on one of the Boeing 757's onboard telephones and spoke for 13 minutes with GTE operator Lisa Jefferson, said Beamer's wife, Lisa. He provided detailed information about the hijacking and—after the operator told him about the attacks on the World Trade Center and Pentagon—said he and others on the plane were planning to act against the terrorists aboard.

Before the call ended and with yelling heard in the background, Beamer asked the operator to pray with him. Together, they recited the 23rd Psalm. Then he asked Jefferson to promise she would call his wife of seven years—who is expecting a third child—and their two sons, 1 and 3.

After receiving clearance from investigators, Lisa Beamer said, Jefferson kept her promise Friday. Bobbi Hennessey, a spokeswoman for GTE parent company Verizon Communications, declined comment yesterday. A telephone number for Jefferson could not be found.

"People asked me if I'm upset that I didn't speak with him, but I'm glad he called [Jefferson] instead," Lisa Beamer said. "I would have been helpless. And I know what his last words would have been to me anyway."

Beamer said her husband placed the call at 9:45 a.m. Tuesday and told Jefferson there were three knife-wielding hijackers on board, one who appeared to have a bomb tied to his chest with a belt. The other two hijackers took over the cockpit after forcing out the pilot and co-pilot.

"They realized they were going to die. Todd said he and some other passengers were going to jump on the guy with the bomb," Lisa Beamer said.

Several other passengers made phone calls from the jet before it crashed southeast of Pittsburgh: Jeremy Glick, 31; Mark Bingham, 31; and Thomas Burnett Jr., 38. Glick and Burnett said they were going to do something.

Todd Beamer dropped the phone after talking to Jefferson, leaving the line open. It was then that the operator heard his words: "Let's roll."

Then silence. Shortly afterward, the plane crashed, killing all 44 aboard. ∎

Todd Beamer's wife, Lisa, with their sons David and Andrew, in their New Jersey home, Sept. 16, 2001; Todd Beamer, seen in the framed photograph, right, led other passengers aboard Flight 93 to take action against the hijackers, according to an operator who talked to Beamer just before the plane crashed in a field in western Pennsylvania on Sept. 11.

10:03 a.m.

Flight 93 crashes amid passenger revolt over Somerset County, Pa.

Minutes earlier, hijacker Ziad Jarrah, manning the aircraft controls in the cockpit, rolled plane left and right, up and down, in attempt to knock revolting passengers off balance. Another hijacker blocked cockpit door after passenger Todd Beamer yelled "Let's roll." As passengers try breaking into cockpit, hijackers decide to nosedive plane. The aircraft, reportedly intended to crash into the White House or the U.S. Capitol—now just 20 minutes flying time away—crashes onto a field near Shanksville, Pa., killing all onboard, including 33 passengers and seven crewmembers.

10:15 a.m.

Pentagon section crashes to ground.

A portion of the west-facing outer E Ring, afire now for over 30 minutes reaches 2,000 degrees Fahrenheit and collapses while surviving Pentagon workers remain at work in unaffected areas. Secretary of Defense Donald Rumsfeld, who was in his office on the other side of the building, rushed to the crash.

10:28 a.m.

North tower of World Trade Center collapses.

With upper-level stairwells blocked and scores of trapped workers having jumped to their death, the structure finally collapses after burning for 102 minutes. Seconds before the fall, a loud, screeching roar—similar to that heard seconds before the south tower had collapsed—jolts onlookers and survivors trapped within the structure, estimated at 1,800 persons, most of whom perished.

LEFT: Firefighters and emergency personnel at the fatal crash scene near Shanksville, Pa., Sept. 11.

BELOW: A helicopter flies over the Pentagon as smoke billows over the building.

VILLA RICA WOMAN DESCRIBES ESCAPE FROM WORLD TRADE CENTER

ATLANTA, Sept. 18, 2001 (AP)—A Villa Rica woman working in New York last week escaped from a burning World Trade Center tower after it was struck by a hijacked plane, only to fear she would be killed by debris from the collapsed towers.

Teresa Tryba, 36, said it took an hour to negotiate 70 flights of stairs and reach the street Sept. 11 after the jets struck.

"I'm going to die. This is it, this is the end of my life," she recalled thinking. "You heard this incredible noise—that sound—and you knew the building was falling. It was getting closer and closer and closer." . . .

Tryba went to New York in April for her job with a computer-consulting firm hired by the Port Authority of New York and New Jersey, which owns the 16-acre World Trade Center property. She said she sat down at her desk about 8:40 a.m. on the 70th floor of the north tower. Less than 10 minutes later, she heard a boom and felt the building shake.

"It was swaying, it was just shaking," Tryba said. "I've never been in an earthquake before, but I think that's what it would have felt like."

Hearing that a plane had just crashed into the building, Tryba followed other frightened office workers who rushed to the stairs. Walking down the stairs, as firefighters rushed the other way to help people, people didn't know that a second plane had struck the other tower. The pace slowed as the descent continued, with more panic-stricken employees joining the evacuation in a scene of "controlled chaos," Tryba said.

"It was extremely hot," she said. "People who had water were giving out water to people who needed it."

Tryba eventually reached the basement, which connects to a subway terminal and an underground mall. The sprinklers had stopped and the air felt cooler, she said. Tryba walked a block and a half from the towers and then heard a rumbling noise. She dived between two parked cars, which were quickly engulfed by a shroud of dust and ash.

"At that particular moment, I thought I was going to be crushed to death," she said. "I thanked God for my life because I had a good life." ■

14

11:02 a.m.
New York mayor orders evacuation of Lower Manhattan.

Mayor Rudolph Giuliani—who, along with his staff, was temporarily sheltering from falling debris in an office building near the World Trade Center complex—is approached by reporters. Giuliani urges all present in Lower Manhattan to stay calm and evacuate. The press begins to spread the word.

12:16 p.m.
U.S. Airspace clear.

With all aircraft having been ordered two and a half hours earlier to cease operation over the continental United States, the last plane lands. Trains and buses, having canceled departures all morning, leave American travelers stranded around the country.

LEFT: The south tower begins to collapse following the terrorist attack. The Millennium Hilton hotel is in the foreground.

ABOVE: Craig McFarland of Los Angeles holds his head at the American Airlines ticket counter at Logan International Airport in Boston on Sept. 11. McFarland, who had exchanged his ticket, said he was originally booked on the hijacked American Flight 11 that crashed into the World Trade Center.

FIREFIGHTER BURIED IN RUBBLE JUST WANTED TO DIE FAST

12:30 p.m.
14 Survivors at north tower discovered in stairwell B.

GOSHEN, N.Y., Sept. 15, 2001 (AP)—New York City Fire Department Battalion Chief Rich Picciotto just wanted it over quickly.

Picciotto, 50, buried in debris when the first World Trade Center tower collapsed Tuesday morning following the terrorist attacks on the twin towers, was trapped for more than four hours.

"I was praying to die fast," Picciotto told the *Times Herald-Record* of Middletown in Friday's edition. The father of two from Chester, Orange County, was buried with five other firefighters and an elderly woman named Josephine they stopped to help.

Slowing down to save the woman is what saved their lives, said Capt. Jay Jonas, 43, of Goshen. "A little quicker, and we would've been in the lobby," said Jonas, a father of three. "We would have been killed. . . . She was probably our guardian angel."

The firefighters, stationed at Ladder 6 in the Chinatown section of Manhattan, rushed to the scene before the alarm after one of them saw the first plane crash into the World Trade Center. They had made it up to the 27th floor when the other tower came down in a rumbling roar. "It was like an earthquake," said firefighter Bill Butler of Ladder 6, a father of four from Greenville.

"We're out of here," Jonas told them, before meeting up with Picciotto.

They met Josephine in the stairwell at the 12th floor, fatigued and unable to continue.

"We never left her," Jonas told the paper. Ironically, he said, it was pausing to help the woman that placed them in a pocket between the second and fourth floors.

The building then collapsed. Jonas called the sound "the most horrific noise I ever heard." As tons of rubble was being cleared from all sides, the men could hear others calling for help. They tried to make radio contact, repeating their position in stairway B over and over.

Butler called his wife on a cell phone. "Don't cry," he told her. "We need help."

Then, a light appeared overhead through the dust. "There's sunlight!" Picciotto said. "That's our way out!"

Though they had thought they were buried beneath 110 stories, they found themselves near the top of the twisted pile.

Jonas called to his men, "Your wives and kids are on the other side of that ridge. Keep climbing." ∎

Miraculously, stairwell B in lower section of north tower remains undamaged after structure implodes. Thirteen first responders emerge from the rubble and summon help for the lone civilian trapped with them.

Survivors covered in ash and dust after the World Trade Center collapse, Sept. 11

12:30 p.m.–3:00 p.m.

Rescue crews in New York and Washington in full force as president stays on the move.

President Bush and entourage continue looking for secure command post outside the Capitol while vigil to detect new attacks goes on. At 1:04 p.m., Bush says he has put the U.S. military on high alert in taped remarks at Barksdale. U.S. Navy dispatches missile destroyers bound for New York and Washington. Unbeknown to public, Bush team settles on Offutt Air Force Base in Bellevue, Neb. as temporary command post, remaining in midair—the lone U.S. travelers—until 2:50 landing. Frantic efforts at twin towers focus on finding open stairwells and elevators with trapped survivors, while 300 search and rescue dogs aid first responders. Press coins term "ground zero" for impact zone, a moniker that sticks. Early reports of 10,000 or more casualties in New York and D.C., but later revised downward to near 3,000 as "missing persons" are tallied and eventually presumed dead.

3:15 p.m.

President Bush Arrivesy at Offutt Air Base in Nebraska.

At approximately this time, President Bush meets with his team via teleconference in the U.S. Strategic Command bunker at Offutt Air Force Base in Bellevue, Neb. National Security Advisor Condoleeza Rice said Bush began the meeting with the words, "We're at war."

5:20 p.m.

Empty 47-story 7 World Trade Center collapses.

Having been in flames all day, building is fully evacuated when a wall of dust spreads over ground zero as structure comes tumbling down, the third building in complex that is totally destroyed in attack.

Firefighters and emergency rescue workers on the scene at ground zero, Sept. 11.

6:54 p.m.

President arrives at White House.

On Air Force One almost all day and escorted by F-16 fighters, President Bush and entourage arrive safely at White House, where president begins preparing message to American public while juggling critical logistics.

LEFT: President Bush and his staff look out the windows of Air Force One at their F-16 escort on 9/11 while en route to Barksdale Air Force Base in Bossier Parish, La.

ABOVE: After departing Offutt Air Force Base in Nebraska for Washington, President Bush talks on the phone with Vice President Dick Cheney from Air Force One.

BACKGROUND: An F-16 escorts Air Force One on Sept. 11 from Offutt Air Force Base to Andrews Air Force Base near Morningside, Md.

OPPOSITE, LEFT: U.S. National Security Advisor Condoleezza Rice waits at the South Portico of the White House for President Bush to arrive, Sept. 11.

8:30 p.m.

President addresses nation; vows to "find those responsible and bring them to justice."

In a calm, controlled speech from White House, President Bush assures nation of its safety and security and cites support from nations throughout the world. He finishes address with excerpt from 23rd Psalm: "Even though I walk through the valley of the shadow of death, I fear no evil, for You are with me."

10:30 p.m.

Trapped Port Authority officers saved.

It is learned that Port Authority police officers John McLoughlin and William Jimeno are trapped beneath the rubble at ground zero. After hours of digging in an exhausting rescue, first Jimeno and then McLoughlin are both rescued—the last successful ones of the day. One more survivor remains, Port Authority worker Genelle Guzman, discovered the next day by rescue dogs.

11:08 p.m.

President Bush and First Lady Laura Bush are rushed to White House Bunker by the Secret Service, due to reports of an unidentified plane nearby.

After Bush retired for the night after several hours of meetings with his National Security Council, he and the First Lady were awakened by Secret Service agents who thought White House was under attack. The Bushes were rushed down to White House bunker, but it proved to be a false alarm. In his diary Bush recorded: "The Pearl Harbor of the 21st century took place today. . . . We think it's Osama bin Laden."

LEFT: Counselor to the President Karen Hughes and White House Counsel Alberto Gonzales follow President Bush into the Oval Office after his return to D.C. on 9/11.

BELOW: The president delivers an address to the nation regarding the terrorist attacks at 8:30 p.m.

CHAPTER 1
THE DAY THE WORLD CHANGED

On Sept. 11, 2001, a fiery and deafening explosion at 8:46 a.m. changed the world forever.

American Airlines Flight 11 smashed into the upper floors of the north tower of the World Trade Center in New York City. A chaotic scramble for the exits ensued, punctuated by the chilling realization that hundreds, maybe thousands, were trapped inside.

The street—what you could see of it, at least—was a montage of ashen faces, twisted wreckage and terror. Swaths of the numbed and dazed wandered aimlessly, still ignorant of what had actually happened.

Then, at 9:03 a.m., United Airlines Flight 175 crashed into the adjoining south tower. The jolt was deadly and deafening. Far louder was the message it instantly sent around the globe: *This is war.*

America had seen many wars and mourned many war deaths. None had been like this.

Blindsided, the United States' next move was uncertain. But many Americans, however confused and caught off guard, were immediately sure of two things: a defense had to be mounted and an offense had to be engaged.

The real danger was that the unknown enemy already had its next move planned and in gear. That turned out to be true: Even as the towers burned, five would-be hijackers sat quietly in their coach seats on American Airlines Flight 77, bound for California but soon to be forcefully redirected to Washington, D.C. By 9:37 a.m., all on board would be dead, along with over 100 people at the Pentagon.

The recently inaugurated chief executive, George W. Bush, suddenly found himself a wartime president—not in command in the War Room, but ensconced at a grammar school in Florida, his lecture to schoolchildren abruptly interrupted. Vice President Dick Cheney was whisked to a bombproof shelter under the White House, where he ordered the U.S. military to shoot down any passenger aircraft that might be under the control of the unknown enemy.

To some, that enemy's identity was not so elusive.

Well-known to U.S. intelligence sources was a Saudi expatriate and millionaire named Osama bin Laden, on the FBI's Ten Most Wanted list as of 1999 after he was tied to bombings overseas, including attacks on U.S. embassies in 1998 in two East African cities. Bin Laden went from being relatively unknown to the world's most-sought criminal—and the face of evil to much of the world.

At 9:59 a.m., the seemingly impossible happened. The south tower collapsed, killing the trapped office workers and first responders inside. Almost simultaneously, a passenger revolt quashed the hijackers' plan to crash United Airlines Flight 93 into the White House, but the scuffle made the pilot lose control and the aircraft went down at 10:03 a.m. near Shanksville, Pennsylvania, sparing the White House but killing all on board. By 10:28, the north tower had collapsed. With it, hundreds more of the trapped people perished. That afternoon, 7 World Trade Center also fell; it had been evacuated hours before.

By day's end, the United States was in a state of confusion and distress, and its citizens faced many more questions than answers. As chaos gripped New York and Washington and fear engulfed the whole country, the questions were more personal and heartbreaking for the families of those who were missing.

In clouds of smoke and disarray, in the wreckage of aircraft and architecture, the post-9/11 era of American history had begun.

A view of Lower Manhattan and the twin towers of the World Trade Center, six weeks before the Sept. 11 attacks, July 29, 2011.

AP Wire, Tuesday, September 11, 2001

TERRORISTS ATTACK N.Y., WASHINGTON

By DAVID CRARY and JERRY SCHWARTZ
The Associated Press

NEW YORK (AP)—In the most devastating terrorist onslaught ever waged against the United States, knife-wielding hijackers crashed two airliners into the World Trade Center on Tuesday, toppling its twin 110-story towers. The deadly calamity was witnessed on televisions across the world as another plane slammed into the Pentagon, and a fourth crashed outside Pittsburgh.

"Today, our nation saw evil," President Bush said in an address to the nation Tuesday night. He said thousands of lives were "suddenly ended by evil, despicable acts of terror."

Said Adm. Robert J. Natter, commander of the U.S. Atlantic Fleet: "We have been attacked like we haven't since Pearl Harbor."

Establishing the U.S. death toll could take weeks. The four airliners alone had 266 people aboard and there were no known survivors. At the Pentagon, about 100 people were believed dead.

In addition, a firefighters union official said he feared half of the 400 firefighters who first reached the scene had died in rescue efforts at the trade center—where 50,000 people worked—and dozens of police officers were believed missing.

"The number of casualties will be more than most of us can bear," a visibly distraught Mayor Rudolph Giuliani said.

"We have entire companies that are just missing," said firefighters union vice president Mike Carter. "We lost chiefs. . . . We're going to have to bury a lot of people."

A police source said some people trapped in the twin towers managed to call authorities or family members, but it was not clear how many people or when all the calls were made. In one of the calls, which took place in the afternoon, a businessman called his family to say he was trapped with police officers, whom he named, the source said.

No one took responsibility for the attacks that rocked the seats of finance and government. But federal authorities identified Osama bin Laden, who has been given asylum by Afghanistan's Taliban rulers, as the prime suspect. Aided by an intercept of communications between his supporters and harrowing cell phone calls from at least one flight attendant and two passengers aboard the jetliners before they crashed, U.S. officials began assembling a case linking bin Laden to the devastation.

U.S. intelligence intercepted communications between bin Laden supporters discussing the attacks on the World Trade Center and Pentagon, according to Utah Sen. Orrin Hatch, the top Republican on the Senate Judiciary Committee.

The people aboard planes who managed to make cell phone calls each described similar circumstances: They indicated the hijackers were armed with knives, in some cases stabbing flight attendants. The hijackers then took control of the planes.

At the World Trade Center, the dead and the doomed plummeted from the skyscrapers, among them a man and woman holding hands.

Shortly after 7 p.m., crews began heading into ground zero of the attack to search for survivors and recover bodies. All that remained of the twin towers by then was a pile of rubble and twisted steel that stood barely two stories high, leaving a huge gap in the New York City skyline.

"Freedom itself was attacked this morning and I assure you freedom will be defended," said Bush, who was in Florida at the time of the catastrophe. As a security measure, he was shuttled to a Strategic Air Command bunker in Nebraska before leaving for Washington. "Make no mistake," he said. "The United States will hunt down and pursue those responsible for these cowardly actions." . . .

Officials across the world condemned the attacks but in the West Bank city of Nablus, thousands of Palestinians celebrated, chanting "God is Great" and handing out candy. The United States has become increasingly unpopular in the Mideast in the past year of Israeli-Palestinian fighting, with Washington widely seen as siding with Israel against the Arab world.

At the Pentagon, the symbol and command center for the nation's military force, one side of the building collapsed as smoke billowed over the Potomac River. Rep. Ike Skelton, briefed by Pentagon officials, said, "There appear to be about 100 casualties" in the building.

The first airstrike—on the trade center—occurred shortly before 8:45 a.m. EDT. A burning, 47-story part of the trade center complex, long since evacuated, collapsed in flames just before nightfall. . . .

For the first time, the nation's aviation system was completely shut down as officials considered the frightening flaws that had been exposed in security procedures. Financial markets were closed, too.

Top leaders of Congress were led to an undisclosed location, as were key officials of the Bush administration. Guards armed with automatic weapons patrolled the White House grounds and military aircraft secured the skies above the capital city. National Guard troops appeared on some street corners in the nation's capital.

Evacuations were ordered at the tallest skyscrapers in several cities, and high-profile tourist attractions closed—Walt Disney World, Mount Rushmore, Seattle's Space Needle, the Gateway Arch in St. Louis. The Federal Reserve, seeking to provide assurances that the nation's banking system would be protected, said it would provide additional money to banks if needed.

In Afghanistan, where bin Laden has been given asylum, the nation's hardline Taliban rulers rejected suggestions he was responsible.

Bin Laden came to prominence fighting alongside the U.S.-backed Afghan mujahedeen—holy warriors—in their war against Soviet troops in the 1980s.

Destroyed mullions, the vertical struts that once faced the soaring outer walls of the World Trade Center towers, are the only thing left standing behind a lone fireman, Sept. 11.

But former followers say he turned against the United States during the 1991 Gulf War, seething at the deployment of U.S. troops in Saudi Arabia during the Gulf War campaign to oust Iraq from Kuwait. He has repeatedly called on Muslims worldwide to join in a jihad, or holy war, against the United States.

Abdel-Bari Atwan, editor of the *Al-Quds Al-Arabi* newspaper, said he received a warning from Islamic fundamentalists close to bin Laden, but had not taken the threat seriously. "They said it would be a huge and unprecedented attack, but they did not specify," Atwan said in a telephone interview in London.

Eight years ago, the World Trade Center was a terrorist target when a truck bomb killed six people and wounded about 1,000 others. Just the death toll on the planes alone could surpass the 168 people killed in the 1995 bombing of the federal building in Oklahoma City.

This is how Tuesday's mayhem unfolded:

At about 8:45 a.m., a hijacked airliner crashed into the north tower of the trade center, the 25-year-old, glass-and-steel complex that was once the world's tallest.

Clyde Ebanks, an insurance company vice president, was at a meeting on the 103rd floor of the south tower when his boss said, "Look at that!" He turned to see a plane slam into the other tower.

"I just heard the building rock," said Peter Dicerbo, a bank employee on the 47th floor. "It knocked me on the floor. It sounded like a big roar, then the building started swaying. That's what really scared me."

The enormity of the disaster was just sinking in when 18 minutes later, the south tower also was hit by a plane.

"All this stuff started falling and all this smoke was coming through. People were screaming, falling, and jumping out of the windows," said Jennifer Brickhouse, 34, from Union, N.J.

The chaos was just beginning. Workers stumbled down scores of flights, their clothing torn and their lungs filled with smoke and dust. John Axisa said he ran outside and watched people jump out of the first building; then there was a second explosion, and he felt the heat on the back of his neck.

Donald Burns, 34, was being evacuated from the 82nd floor when he saw four people in the stairwell. "I tried to help them but they didn't want anyone to touch them. The fire had melted their skin. Their clothes were tattered," he said.

Worse was to come. At 9:50, one tower collapsed, sending debris and dust cascading to the ground. At 10:30, the other tower crumbled.

Glass doors shattered, police and firefighters ushered people into subway stations and buildings. The air was black, from the pavement to the sky. The dust and ash were inches deep along the streets.

Dark smoke billows from the north tower as flames explode from the south tower soon after it was hit by United Flight 175.

RIGHT: **Smoke rises from the Pentagon in Arlington County, Va. on Sept. 11, as members of the Fairfax Co. Search and Rescue team approach after the terrorist attack.**

OPPOSITE LEFT: **Firefighters gather outside the Pentagon on Sept. 11, 2001.**

OPPOSITE BOTTOM: **Flames shoot out of the damaged outer E Ring of the Pentagon.**

OPPOSITE RIGHT: **Front cover of the Sept. 11, 2001, edition of the *Journal News* of Westchester, Putnam, and Rockland counties in New York.**

Bridges and tunnels were closed to all but pedestrians. Subways were shut down for much of the day; many commuter trains were not running.

Meanwhile, at about 9:30 a.m., an airliner hit the Pentagon—the five-sided headquarters of the American military. "There was screaming and pandemonium," said Terry Yonkers, an Air Force civilian employee at work inside the building.

The military boosted security across the country to the highest levels, sending Navy ships to New York and Washington to assist with air defense and medical needs.

A half-hour after the Pentagon attack, United Airlines Flight 93, a Boeing 757 jetliner en route from Newark, N.J., to San Francisco, crashed about 80 miles southeast of Pittsburgh.

Airline officials said the other three planes that crashed were American Airlines Flight 11, a Boeing 767 from Boston to Los Angeles, apparently the first to hit the trade center; United Airlines Flight 175, also a Boeing 767 from Boston to Los Angeles, which an eyewitness said was the second to hit the skyscrapers; and American Airlines Flight 77, a Boeing 757 en route from Washington-Dulles to Los Angeles that a source said hit the Pentagon. . . .

Giuliani said it was believed the aftereffects of the plane crashes eventually brought the buildings down, not planted explosive devices. Hyman Brown, a University of Colorado civil engineering professor and the construction manager for the World Trade Center, speculated that flames fueled by thousands of gallons of aviation fuel melted steel supports.

"This building would have stood had a plane or a force caused by a plane smashed into it," he said. "But steel melts, and 24,000 gallons of aviation fluid melted the steel. Nothing is designed or will be designed to withstand that fire."

At mid-afternoon, Giuliani said 1,500 "walking wounded" had been shipped to Liberty State Park in New Jersey by ferry and tugboat, and 750 others were taken to New York City hospitals, among them 150 in critical condition.

Well into the night, a steady stream of boats continued to arrive in the park. "Every 10 minutes another boat with 100 to 150 people on it pulls up," said Mayor Glenn Cunningham. "I have a feeling this is going to go on for several days."

Felix Novelli, who lives in Southampton, N.Y., was in Nashville with his wife for a World War II reunion. He was trying to fly home to New York when the attacks occurred.

"I feel like going to war again. No mercy," he said. "This is Dec. 7 happening all over again. We have to come together like '41, go after them."

The attack on Pearl Harbor claimed the lives of 2,390 Americans, most of them servicemen. ∎

EXTRA!

The Journal News

Tuesday, September 11, 2001   Serving Westchester, Rockland and Putnam counties since 1850   50 cents

United States UNDER ATTACK

- Thousands hurt, killed in New York City, **2A**
- Pentagon attacked; White House evacuated, **3A**
- Color images from today's devastation, **8A**
- **Editorial:** 'United States must pull together,' **6B**

TERROR

Trade Towers collapse; D.C. hit

In a horrific sequence of destruction this morning:

- Terrorists crashed two planes into the World Trade Center. Within an hour, the twin 110-story towers collapsed.
- Explosions also rocked the Pentagon and the State Department and spread fear across the nation.
- Islamic Jihad claimed responsibility, citing American involvement in the Mideast, CNN reported.
- Police said casualties could be in the thousands.
- One of the two planes that crashed into the World Trade Center was reported hijacked from Boston — American Airlines Flight 11, en route to Los Angeles.
- The Federal Aviation Administration stopped all takeoffs nationwide, and the Capitol and the White House were evacuated.
- Bridges, tunnels and subways were shut.
- "Today we've had a national tragedy," President Bush said in Sarasota, Fla.
- International flights bound for the United States were ordered to U-turn or find landing sites outside America.
- A flood of emergency vehicles poured into lower Manhattan, as black smoke engulfed the neighborhood.

EDITOR'S NOTE:
This extra edition contains four pages of breaking news on today's attacks. Coverage of the explosions can be found inside on pages 2A, 3A and 8A. Pages 4A and 5A contain the front page and page 2B from this morning's edition. For detailed coverage of this tragic day, see our Web site at www.thejournalnews.com and read tomorrow's paper for all the latest details.

Anyone with information about today's events can call our special hotline at 914-696-8218.

Smoke pours from the World Trade Center towers this morning after two planes crashed into the upper floors of both 110-story buildings minutes apart.   Patrick Sison/The Associated Press

AP Wire, Tuesday, September 11, 2001

I JUST SAW THE TOP OF TRADE TWO COME DOWN

By HELEN O'NEILL
The Associated Press

Americans watched in horror Tuesday as New York turned into a crumbling, smoking nightmare in the wake of an apparent terrorist attack.

"I just saw the building I work in come down," said businessman Gabriel Ioan, shaking in shock outside City Hall a cloud of smoke and ash from the World Trade Center behind him. "I just saw the top of Trade Two come down."

Nearby a crowd mobbed a man on a pay phone, screaming at him to get off the phone so that they could call relatives. Dust and dirt flew everywhere. Ash was 2 to 3 inches deep in places. People wandered dazed and terrified.

"I was in the World Financial Center looking out the window," said one woman. "I saw the first plane and then 15 minutes later saw the other plane just slam into the World Trade Center."

Another eyewitness, AP newsman Dunstan Prial, described a strange sucking sound from the trade center buildings after the first building collapsed.

"Windows shattered. People were screaming and diving for cover. People walked around like ghosts, covered in dirt, weeping and wandering dazed."

"It sounded like a jet or rocket," said Eddie Gonzalez, a postal worker at a post office on West Broadway. "I looked up and saw a huge explosion. I didn't see the impact. I just saw the explosion."

Morning commuters heading into Manhattan were stranded as the Lincoln Tunnel was shut down to incoming traffic. Many left their cars and stood on the ramp leading to the tunnel, staring in disbelief at the thick cloud of smoke pouring from the top of the two buildings.

On the streets of Manhattan, people stood in groups talking quietly or watching on television at ground-level network studios.

Joan Goldstein, communications project leader for The Associated Press, was on a bus from New Jersey at about 8:50 a.m. when she saw "smoke pouring out of the World Trade Center building. We said, 'Oh, my God! The World Trade Center's on fire!'"

Perhaps 10 minutes later, "All of a sudden, there was an orange plume, a huge explosion. It shot out the back of the building. Everybody on the bus was just moaning and gasping," said Goldstein, who wept and trembled as she spoke.

The plume was from the second plane, but she didn't see the plane because of the thick smoke.

She tried to call friends who work there, but couldn't get through.

"It was the most horrible thing I've ever seen in my life," said Goldstein. ∎

People in front of New York's St. Patrick's Cathedral react with horror as they look down Fifth Avenue toward the collapsing World Trade Center, Sept. 11.

The south tower of
New York's World
Trade Center begins to
collapse; 9:59 a.m.,
Sept. 11.

"It's Not Safe, It's Not Safe"

By SUZANNE PLUNKETT
Former AP Photographer

It's less than a minute before the south tower of the World Trade Center collapses on the morning of September 11, 2001. I'm a block away trying to get closer, waving my press card in a cop's face. He stands his ground, barking: "It's not safe, it's not safe." Then all hell breaks loose. Someone pelts past us screaming, "It's coming down!" as billows of dust and smoke punch high into the sky over the end of the street. Adrenaline kicks in and I start to run across Broadway and down Fulton, chased by the debris of the collapsing south tower. That obstinate cop on the barricade at Fulton and Broadway probably saved my life.

About 65 feet down the block I skid to a stop, thinking: "Shit, I've got to take a picture." I spin around, grab one of my Nikons and position the shot. As people sprint toward me, I fire off 13 frames—among them, one that will become famous.

I run some more. Aware I can't escape the advancing cloud, I pick up my camera again and photograph the debris as it whooshes past, blotting out the sunlight and plunging us into a silent, twilight world of lurching, dust-covered people and tumbling ash.

"This is it, I'm going to die," I think as I struggle to breathe. That sends me into automatic mode. I'm a photographer for The Associated Press. I've got to send my photos. I'm on deadline and the seconds are counting down like an incessant drumbeat.

I dive into the lobby of an office building where others are already taking shelter, but the noise of wailing and panicking voices unnerves me, and I need to get out. I tie my cardigan around my face as a mask and head back out into the dust.

For a while I stumble around, dazed, inside the muffled quietness of the cloud, photographing others in the same state. At some point

RIGHT: Suzanne Plunkett's iconic photograph of petrified pedestrians running up Fulton Street as the north tower collapses on Sept. 11, 2001.

OPPOSITE: Plunkett's photograph from a 20th-floor apartment balcony overlooking the World Trade Center site on Sept. 11; smoke from the collapsed towers shrouds Lower Manhattan.

I call my dad, leaving him a voicemail to tell him I love him—it's a message he later says he listens to again and again for weeks.

Twenty-five minutes have gone by since the south tower went down and I've still got to send those photos. I squeeze through the door of a tiny shop farther down Fulton where about 15 people are taking shelter. The owner locks the door behind me as other people hammer on the glass. We don't know it, but the north tower is now crashing to the ground.

The people in the shop crowd around as I hook up my laptop to my clunky Nokia cellphone and start transmitting my photos. September 2001 is still pre-iPhone, pre-Wi-Fi, pre-4G, even pre-3G, and sending images from a remote computer is a novelty. One woman giggles awkwardly as she spots herself in one of the photos.

In the AP office located at Rockefeller Center, my editors see the images appear on their feed. It's the first contact they've had with me since the day before. Relieved I'm OK, they call and ask if I can head to an apartment block overlooking the site of the towers to take an overhead shot.

On a balcony about 20 stories up, the turmoil is still unfolding beneath. More buildings are groaning and collapsing, throwing new clouds up into the blue sky. Sirens blaze through the streets.

Inside the apartment, a three-year-old watches *The Lion King* on TV, the volume on high. His mother is on the phone complaining about her broken dishwasher. It's an absurd scene, but they're just blotting out the carnage in the same way I am—by going through the motions.

Back on street level, a passing firefighter asks to use my Nokia to call his family. He can't get through so he dashes off toward ground zero. The number lingers on my phone for weeks after. I'll often think of calling it to see if he came back alive, but I never work up the nerve.

I'm assigned to the hospital watch for the rest of the day, told to photograph the injured as they are brought in. It's quiet at St. Vincent's so I trek over to Chelsea Piers, where a vast entertainment complex has become an emergency triage center.

It's one of the most chilling scenes of my day. Ambulances and medics have raced here from far-flung places like Rhode Island to help, but they're all standing idle. Rows of beds are empty. It slowly becomes apparent that no one caught up in the collapse got out alive.

Later in the night, I walk home across Manhattan. Around the world my photo is rolling off the presses and being circulated online. Colleagues are praising me for standing firm when others around me were running. I feel numb, the uncontrollable sobbing still days away.

For years afterwards I thought that photo had nothing of me in it—I'd simply held a mirror up to other people caught in a horrific event. But that's not true. Today I look at that image and see myself as I was 20 years ago. A young photographer, turning toward a scene of terrible destruction. Snatching 1/200th of a second of clarity from the chaos to come. ∎

AP Wire, Tuesday, September 11, 2001

PENTAGON ATTACK CAME MINUTES AFTER RUMSFELD PREDICTED: "THERE WILL BE ANOTHER EVENT"

By ROBERT BURNS
The Associated Press

WASHINGTON (AP)—Inside the Pentagon, Defense Secretary Donald H. Rumsfeld had just raced to his office after hearing of the World Trade Center attack. On a house porch a little more than a mile away, Ralph Banton, 79, was enjoying a crystal-clear morning. Then Banton heard a jet flying directly overhead, very low. "It sounded like it was jetting instead of slowing down," he said.

Seconds later, American Flight 77, hijacked while carrying 64 people from Washington to Los Angeles, tore into the side of the Pentagon in a shocking terror attack aimed at the building that represents America's military power around the world.

The Pentagon burst into flames, sending into the blue sky a huge cloud of smoke visible for miles. And a part of the western side of the five-sided building in suburban Arlington, Va., collapsed.

By Tuesday night, firefighters were just gaining control of the fire, and searchers were preparing to enter the wing to search for dead and injured inside.

They had no clear idea how many casualties would be found, Rumsfeld said at a briefing inside the Pentagon. But he added: "It will not be a few." Nevertheless, "The Pentagon is functioning," Rumsfeld said. "It will be in business tomorrow."

The area hit by the aircraft was under renovation, and thus some offices may not have been occupied, officials said. Overall, 24,000 people work in the Pentagon.

A priest prays over a wounded man outside the west entrance of the Pentagon as emergency workers help the injured, Sept. 11.

When the attack came at 9:40 a.m. EDT, "the whole build-ing shook" with the impact, said Terry Yonkers, an Air Force civilian employee at work inside the Pentagon at the time. "There was screaming and pandemonium."

Outside, Alan Wallace, one of three firefighters to be regularly assigned to the Pentagon, saw the airplane approaching and dived beneath a van for protection. Then he began working to help get people from the building. His fire truck was on fire.

On a nearby road, debris hit several cars. Cab drivers watched, stunned, as hundreds of people poured out the doors of the huge building.

Rumsfeld was in his office when the aircraft hit on the opposite side of the building. He had just run there after hearing of the trade center attack while at a meeting on missile defense in his private dining room.

U.S. Rep. Christopher Cox, R-Calif., also at the meeting, said Rumsfeld had just predicted that the United States would face another terrorist incident at some point.

"He said, 'Let me tell ya, I've been around the block a few times. There will be another event.' And he repeated it for emphasis," Cox said. "And within minutes of saying that, his words proved tragically prophetic."

Rumsfeld said he "felt the shock of the airplane hitting the building," then went running down to the site where the aircraft hit. "They were bringing bodies out that had been injured, most of which were alive and moving but seriously injured," he said.

The defense secretary then went to the National Military Command Center in the lower floors of the Pentagon. ■

Fire engines working to dowse the flames at the Pentagon, Sept. 11.

CHAOS, FEAR GRIP WASHINGTON

WASHINGTON, Sept. 11, 2001 (AP)—A frantic guard out-side the Supreme Court shouted at strolling passers-by: "You don't have time to stay in this area!" Why, he was asked, what happened? "Explosions! Leave!" Secret Service agents similarly yelled at White House tourists to get away. At the Capitol, stunned congressmen huddled under the shade of trees outside. Some officers who typically keep firearms out of sight made a show of toting pump-action shotguns.

Across Washington, people left work and jammed streets and subways to try to get home as the seat of government was evacuated after devastating terrorist attacks at the Penta-gon and the World Trade Center in New York. Sirens wailed. Cars packed the streets, and bomb-sniffing dogs patrolled the Washington Monument. . . .

Outside, Senate President Pro Tem Robert Byrd, D-W. Va., talked to reporters until a loud boom sounded behind the Capitol. An aide grabbed his arm and tried to drag him away. "Some people in the world are bent on destruction," Byrd said. Despite the evacuation, some lawmakers stayed put.

"They tried to throw me out three times, but they didn't suc-ceed," said Rep. Bob Stump, R-Ariz., chairman of the House Armed Services Committee. "I figured I was safer in the build-ing than out on the street."

Some Congress members insisted on more symbolic acts, singing "God Bless America" on the Capitol steps. Congres-sional leaders kept the Capitol Dome bathed in floodlights all night to reinforce the message that the light of democracy shines on. . . .

Dozens of stranded passengers sat in the lounge of Washington Dulles International Airport, trading stories and trying to determine how they would get to their loved ones, but the room fell silent when President Bush's address came on television. And when Bush promised to "make no distinction between the terrorists who committed these acts and those who harbor them," the room broke out in applause.

"There is no panic, no fear—just anger," said Lisa Newton, a philosophy professor at Fairfield University who was headed to Miami for a conference on ethics. "There must be retaliation for this act, and I think that is what Americans will want to see in the coming days." ■

AP Wire, Wednesday, September 12, 2001

PASSENGERS MAY HAVE THWARTED HIJACKERS

By MARTHA RAFFAELE
The Associated Press

SHANKSVILLE, Pa. (AP)—Just before United Flight 93 crashed, some of the passengers learned of the attacks on the World Trade Center and may have tried to overpower their hijackers and keep the jetliner from hitting another landmark.

Authorities have not disclosed whether there was a struggle aboard the plane, and have not said what caused the airliner carrying 45 people to plunge into a Pennsylvania field. But some of the victims telephoned relatives from the plane and said that they had resolved to wrest control of the flight back from their captors.

Passenger Jeremy Glick, 31, telephoned his wife, Liz, after terrorists took over, Glick's uncle Tom Crowley said Wednesday. She conferenced the call to a 911 dispatcher, who told Glick about the New York attacks.

"Jeremy and the people around them found out about the flights into the World Trade Center and decided that if their fate was to die, they should fight," Crowley said.

"At some point, Jeremy put the phone down and simply went and did what he could do" with the help of an unspecified number of other passengers.

Among them was Thomas Burnett, a 38-year-old business executive from California. In a series of four cellular phone calls, Burnett had his wife, Deena, conference in the FBI and calmly gathered information about the other hijacked flights.

Burnett said "a group of us are going to do something," his wife said, and he gave every indication that sacrificing the passengers wasn't part of their plan. "He was coming home. He wasn't leaving. He was going to solve this problem and come back to us," she said at her home in San Ramon, Calif.

The three other hijacked planes in Tuesday's attacks destroyed New York's twin towers and severely damaged the Pentagon.

U.S. officials have said the Secret Service feared the target of the United flight was Camp David, the presidential retreat in Maryland about 85 miles from the crash site. Others speculated that the White House or Pentagon could have been targets.

"It sure wasn't going to go down in rural Pennsylvania. This wasn't the target; the target was Washington, D.C.," said Rep. John Murtha, D-Pa. "Somebody made a heroic effort to keep the plane from hitting a populated area."

He added: "I would conclude there was a struggle and a heroic individual decided 'I'm going to die anyway, I might as well bring the plane down here.'"

During the flight, other passengers screamed and shouted through cell phones to share final words with their loved ones. Not Burnett, who seemed unshakable from his first call.

"He said, 'I'm on the airplane, the airplane that's been hijacked, and they've already knifed a guy. They're saying they have a bomb. Please call the authorities,'" his wife said. She called 911, who patched her through to the FBI. She was on the phone with agents when his second call came.

"I told him in the second call about the World Trade Center and he was very curious about that and started asking questions. He wanted any information that I had to help him," she said.

By the third phone call, "I could tell that he was formulating a plan and trying to figure out what to do next," she said. "You could tell that he was gathering information and trying to put the puzzle together."

In his last call, Burnett said he and some other passengers had decided to make a move. "I told him to please sit down and not draw attention to himself and he said no. He said no," Deena Burnett said, shaking her head with a half-smile.

In Washington, Attorney General John Ashcroft said each of the planes was seized by three to six hijackers armed with knives and box cutters.

Photograph of Thomas E. Burnett Jr., CEO of a California heart pump manufacturer; Burnett, along with other Flight 93 passengers, formed the brave plan to take back the plane from the hijackers to prevent it from being used as a weapon.

Crowley said Glick described the terrorists as "looking and speaking Arabic" and reported that they were armed with knives and had a "large red box" they said contained a bomb.

The plane had left Newark, N.J., at about 8 a.m. for San Francisco. But it banked sharply as it approached Cleveland and headed back over Pennsylvania, losing altitude and flying erratically.

It slammed nose-first into a field about 80 miles southeast of Pittsburgh at 10 a.m.—an hour after the trade center crashes and about 20 minutes after the Pentagon attack. Hundred of investigators were at the scene Wednesday, hoping to recover the plane's cockpit voice recorder and other clues.

Deena Burnett is sure her husband had something to do with the fact that with this plane, at least, no one on the ground was hurt.

"We may never know exactly how many helped him or exactly what they did, but I have no doubt that airplane was bound for some landmark and that whatever Tom did and whatever the guys who helped him did they saved many more lives," she said.

"And I'm so proud of him and so grateful," she said, breaking off to choke back a sob. ■

EDITOR'S NOTE: Associated Press Writer Michelle Locke in Berkeley, Calif., and D. Ian Hopper in Washington contributed to this report.

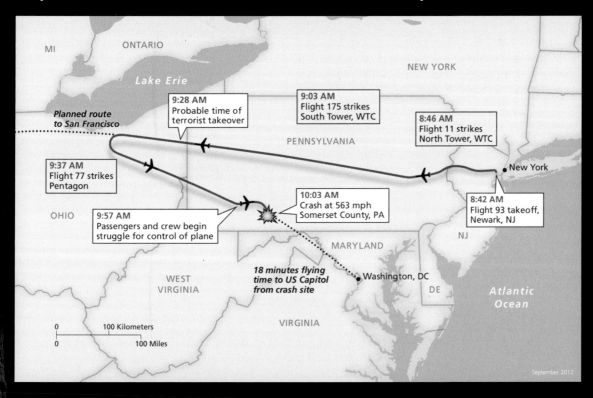

LEFT: A National Park Service map showing the route of United Flight 93 on Sept. 11, from its takeoff at 8:42 a.m. to its crash at 10:03 a.m.

BELOW: Investigators and police probe the site where United Flight 93 crashed onto a field near Shanksville, Pa., Sept. 11.

"What's Happening to My City?"

By HOWIE RUMBERG
Deputy Sports Editor

Seventeen minutes. Twenty years later, unraveling the morning of Sept. 11, it feels like an eternity.

About 17 minutes passed between the time I stepped out of the subway station at Canal Street to rush hour shouts of disbelief and horror seconds after American Airlines Flight 11 struck the north tower, and the shocking boom of United Airlines Flight 175 crashing into the south tower as I stood one block north of the World Trade Center complex.

Just off an overnight shift in the AP Sports department, a night that began by catching a glimpse of Michael Jackson emerging from Madison Square Garden into a shower of flashing strobe lights from fans and photographers, all I could think of was sleep—until I saw the jagged, burning hole in tower one. The explanation seemed implausible: A plane had flown right into the building. It had just happened. I didn't even hear sirens yet, just the chorus of "Oh, my God!" from people instantly halted in their morning hustle. I sprinted the 100 yards or so home, woke my girlfriend and breathlessly told her to look out the window. I then took her cell phone—I didn't even have one then—and called the office. Do they need help?

"Yes. Go!" I was told by a voice I didn't know.

I sprinted down Hudson Street, shouting at stunned people looking up at the building that we took for granted each day as it loomed over our neighborhood, "Did anyone see what happened?"

Ambulances buried under rubble at ground zero in the aftermath of the attacks, Sept, 11, 2001.

A construction worker tried to describe the white bottom of a low-flying plane, but he was too shaken to focus.

The closer I got to the scene, the more intense the emotions became. Groups of gawkers formed on corners. Others raced away at the urging of just-arriving police. People on phones tried to explain where they were and what was happening.

As I approached the World Trade Center, it became apparent that it wasn't debris falling from the higher floors but people overcome by the smoke and heat. It was shattering. But I focused on what I felt I needed to do.

Remembering the pictures from the first attacks on the World Trade Center in 1993, I ran for West Street, the western edge of the trade center and a large thoroughfare where many emergency vehicles gathered during those attacks. And there it was: a growing hive of flashing lights a few blocks south. I didn't think it was a smart place to be if I wanted to remain close by, with all the police around, so I turned to walk back toward a more pedestrian-focused area.

Then an explosion jerked my attention back up to the sky. The building was not in view, but you could see the flames, black cloud and debris bursting out from what was certainly the south tower.

In an instant, the tone changed.

The shock—a plane hit the World Trade Center!— turned to terror and chaos once that emphatic strike made it obvious that New York City was under attack. Commuters turned scared gawkers became sprinters. One woman ran right out of her shoes. A man in a suit and tie dropped his briefcase and took off. I thought, "Why'd he have to leave the briefcase?" The silver case sat on Greenwich Street as people scrambled for safety. I'm not sure anything felt safe in that moment, in a place most likely crushed not too much later by the debris of the collapsed north tower.

On a corner just two blocks north of the towers, a woman paused. Through sobs, she screamed: "What's happening to my city?" Then she ran off.

Twenty years later, with almost an entire generation gone by, I'm still not sure whether I have her answer. ∎

Survivors of the World Trade Center terrorist attacks make their way through smoke, dust and debris on Fulton Street, about a block from the collapsed towers, Sept. 11, 2001.

CHAPTER 2
THE AFTERMATH

On Tuesday, Sept. 11, 2001, officials estimated that 10,000 to 20,000 people were in the twin towers of New York City's World Trade Center when the first plane crashed into its north tower. Thousands more worked at the Pentagon, the U.S. military headquarters in Washington, which was also attacked. The number of people initially reported as missing two days later by New York City's mayor, Rudolph Giuliani, was staggering: an estimated 4,763 people, among them nearly 400 firefighters and police officers. And that horrific tally did not include the 266 reported passengers and crewmembers who died aboard the planes that crashed into the three attack sites. Also unimaginable was the number of injured, 2,300. As statistics mounted, each report of carnage rocked a bruised nation anew.

New York, Washington and the nation at large were multitasking at a feverish pace. The priorities were, above all, to rescue those trapped in the wreckage at the World Trade Center, now referred to as "ground zero," a moniker that stuck. Casualties at the Pentagon were easier to determine but no less painful to tally; the building

was smaller and less damaged, but the early estimate of over 100 dead hardly assuaged the grief. And then there were more grim tasks: burying the victims, saluting the first responders, investigating the crime, and keeping national and international travel locked down. Those and more were the issues at hand in what was shaping up to be one of the most difficult weeks in 225 years of U.S. history.

With so much to be despondent about, New Yorkers found courage and inspiration by looking to the bravery of their public servants. Entire engine companies and multitudes of first responders were lost in New York the day of the attack. Those still on the job, many of whom had taken no rest at all, were loudly cheered. Throngs, hundreds strong, lined the highways leading to ground zero, wildly applauding them. "Don't mess with the U.S." became a rallying cry—and, eventually, a point of division—and signage visible to the rescuers proclaimed to them: "You're the Brave" and "Thank You!"

For some, there was little good feeling. Muslims around the nation began to feel uneasy. When it was revealed the 19 hijackers were all

from Middle Eastern countries and affiliated with Saudi millionaire and wanted terrorist Osama bin Laden, a new word, "Islamophobia," entered the American lexicon. Middle Eastern and Arab American men were detained from California to Germany. Mosques and Islamic schools in U.S. cities felt threatened and tightened security, as verbal abuse of Muslims was reported. But Arab Americans vocalized their patriotism, publicly condemning the attacks; groups organized blood drives, flew American flags and cooperated with the investigations.

President Bush made a plea to the nation in a nationally televised call with Mayor Giuliani and New York governor George Pataki: "Our nation must be mindful that there are thousands of Arab Americans that live in New York City who love the flag just as much" as other Americans. And mincing no words, he proclaimed later that bin Laden—believed to be operating from a hidden location in Afghanistan—was wanted "dead or alive."

By Thursday, Sept. 13, with uncounted human beings still missing—and most likely among the dead—vigils and silent prayers sprouted around the nation. President Bush designated the following day a "National Day of Prayer and Remembrance" and called for noon memorial services and candlelight vigils in the evening. But most painful of all were the funerals, and there were far too many.

Among the nation's chief consolers were the president and New York City Mayor Rudolph Giuliani. President Bush, donning a fire helmet, made his first official visit to ground zero to thank the rescuers on Friday, Sept. 14. The mayor had a special connection to the damage, having narrowly escaped himself when ensconced in a building not far from the twin towers as they were under siege. Even among the controversial mayor's detractors, he was loudly praised. Some called the aftermath of the onslaught "his finest hour," and he would soon earn an unofficial title: "America's Mayor."

Sun faintly streams through the dust cloud over the wreckage of the World Trade Center as first responders survey the damage, Sept. 13, 2001. Visible at bottom right, directly below the standing shards of the facade, is part of a destroyed bronze sculpture called *The Sphere*. Created in 1967–71 by German sculptor Fritz Koenig, it stood on the plaza between the twin towers. It was later reinstalled in Liberty Park at the rebuilt World Trade Center site (see page 201).

AP Wire, Thursday, September 13, 2001

MAYOR: MORE THAN 4,700 MISSING IN NEW YORK; RESCUERS CONTINUE DIGGING THROUGH RUBBLE

By LARRY MCSHANE
The Associated Press

NEW YORK (AP)—Five rescue workers were pulled alive from the ruins of the World Trade Center on Thursday, two days after terrorists toppled the skyscrapers. The city said more than 4,700 people were still missing.

Authorities said three of the five Fire Department workers were able to walk away from the sport utility vehicle in which they had been trapped for more than 48 hours. They had rushed to the scene on Tuesday when the towers were stuck by hijacked airliners.

It was rare good news on a day when Mayor Rudolph Giuliani had said 4,763 people had been reported missing in the devastation.

"It could turn out we recover fewer than that; it could be more," he said. "We don't know the answer." . . .

In a call to Giuliani and New York Gov. George Pataki, President Bush said he would visit the nation's largest city on Friday.

"I weep and mourn with America," he said, describing Tuesday's attacks as "the first war of the 21st century."

The president will find a reeling metropolis. A vast section of the city has been sealed off, as emergency workers struggled to cope with the unprecedented destruction. Work was slowed by hellish bursts of flame and the collapse of the last standing section of one of the towers taken out by suicide jets. The effort was mirrored at the Pentagon, where 190 people were feared dead and 70 bodies had been recovered. . . .

A thick cloud of acrid, white smoke blew through the streets Wednesday after the four-story fragment of the south tower fell. Gusts of flame occasionally jumped up as debris was removed from the smoldering wreckage. "The volunteers are literally putting their lives at risk," Giuliani said.

The vast search to uncover the terrorist plot stretched from Miami to Boston to Portland, Maine, and on to Canada and Germany. Up to 50 people were involved in the attack, the Justice Department said, with at least four hijackers trained at U.S. flight schools. Saudi fugitive Osama bin Laden remained a top suspect. . . .

In Washington, Bush worked with Congress on legislation authorizing military retaliation, and officials disclosed that the White House, Air Force One and the president himself had been targeted Tuesday. America's NATO allies bolstered Bush's case for military action, declaring the terrorist attacks an assault on the alliance itself. . . .

Three financial companies with offices in the complex had nearly 1,400 workers unaccounted for. Marsh & McLennan, an insurance firm, said it had not been able to account for 600 of 1,700 employees; Keefe Bruyette & Woods, a securities firm, said 69 of 172 employees were missing. Cantor Fitzgerald, a bond firm, said 730 people of its 1,000-person staff were missing, according to *The New York Times*.

Giuliani was among those who escaped Tuesday's attack uninjured, bolting from a building barely a block from the site when the first of the towers collapsed.

More than 3,000 tons of rubble was taken by boat to a former Staten Island garbage dump, where the FBI and other investigators searched for evidence, hoping to find the planes' black boxes with clues to what happened in the final terrifying minutes before the crashes. . . .

Insurance industry experts say the attack could become the nations most expensive manmade disaster ever, with payouts ranging from $5 billion to $25 billion.

The densely packed bottom tip of the island, an area roughly five square miles, remained off-limits to everyone but emergency workers. Volunteers emerged from the search-and-rescue mission with grisly tales as they cleared away the twisted steel and glass wreckage of the twin towers. One body was carried out wrapped in an American flag.

When workers hung another American flag from a piece of a transmission tower that apparently survived the collapse, "everybody stopped and saluted," said Parish Kelley, a firefighter from Ashburnham, Mass. Kelley spent the day working in a crater left by the towers' collapse. . . .

"We're looking at a pile of rubble 30 to 40 feet high. Where do you start?" said sheriff's Sgt. Mike Goldberg of Hampden County, Mass. ∎

LEFT: Dust and debris cover the ground and cloud the air near the site of the terrorist attack on the World Trade Center, Sept. 11, 2001.

BELOW: Flags fly at half-staff in Bayonne, N.J., as smoke rises from lower Manhattan following the collapse of both towers of the World Trade Center in New York, Sept. 12, 2001.

People line up to buy newspapers on the corner of New York's Astor Place the day after the attacks, Sept. 12, 2001.

New York Gov. George Pataki, left, New York City Mayor Rudolph Giuliani, center, and Sen. Hillary Rodham Clinton, D-N.Y., tour the site of the World Trade Center disaster, Sept. 12, 2001.

President George W. Bush examines the devastation at the Pentagon in Washington, D.C., Sept. 12, 2001. At left is Secretary of Defense Donald Rumsfeld.

President Bush, center, looks down during a meeting with Joint Congressional Leadership in the Cabinet Room at the White House, Sept. 12, 2001. From right to left are, Senate Republican leader Trent Lott, R-Miss., Senate Majority Leader Tom Daschle, D-S.D., Secretary of Defense Donald Rumsfeld, President Bush, Speaker of the House Dennis Hastert, Rep. Dick Gephardt, D-Mo., CIA Director George Tenet and Rep. Dick Armey R-Texas.

RIGHT TOP: **An American flag flies over the rubble of the collapsed World Trade Center buildings in New York, Sept. 13, 2001.**

RIGHT BOTTOM: **People pose with pictures of their missing loved ones who were last seen at the World Trade Center, Sept. 13, 2001.**

OPPOSITE PAGE: **This undated photo of ground zero was taken by acclaimed photographer Joel Meyerowitz, who was granted unparalleled access to the site as the official photographer creating an archive for the Museum of the City of New York.**

AP Wire, Thursday, September 13, 2001

AFTER THE ATTACKS: THE VIGILS; IN SILENCE AND PRAYER, REMEMBERING THE VICTIMS

BOSTON (AP)—Thousands of people waved the American flag today, sang "America The Beautiful" and listened to words of peace and tolerance at a vigil for victims of the terrorist attacks.

"What we must fear most is not evil, it is becoming evil ourselves," said Rabbi Barry Starr of Temple Israel in Sharon, Mass., and one of the Jewish, Muslim and Christian clerics leading the multidenominational service. He cautioned against seeking revenge against other religious groups or foreign nationals.

American flags sprouted everywhere among the crowd, estimated at 10,000 to 15,000.

The service provided a chance to show solidarity and to pray for friends killed or missing Tuesday, when four airliners—including two originating in Boston—were hijacked and crashed in New York, the Pentagon and rural Pennsylvania.

"It's not so much a religious feeling, it's just paying respects, and being thankful that you're still alive," said Matt Tipple, 25, of Boston, whose friends worked on the 104th floor of New York's World Trade Center.

Similar scenes have been repeated in many states, and more services are planned over the next few days around the country. President Bush designated Friday a National Day of Prayer and Remembrance and called for noon memorial services and candlelight vigils in the evening.

Today, Boeing workers worldwide bowed their heads in a moment's silence. Three of their colleagues died on American Airlines Flight 77, which rammed into the Pentagon.

"What about all the children that were in day care yesterday—nobody to come pick them up?" asked Charles Grieser, a Boeing employee in Seattle.

Some 350 Las Vegas cabdrivers lined the Strip in a show of solidarity with the victims and their families, and raised $1,000 for the American Red Cross.

Residents in Phoenix held an interfaith prayer service at downtown Patriots Square. The Islamic Center of Tucson co-sponsored a memorial service for victims and their families.

In Nashville, a crowd gathered in Centennial Park before the Parthenon statue, a full-scale replica of the one in Athens.

Kirvin Hodges, 65, a Vietnam War veteran, said he wanted to do more than just attend the service. "I wish I was young enough to join the military again," he said. ■

On Sept. 14 and 15, 2001, candlelight vigils and memorials for the victims of the Sept. 11 attacks took place in New York City and around the world. The Sept. 14 vigil was part of a national day of prayer activities held across the U.S. Here, candles are lit at a vigil in New York.

LEFT: On Sept. 15, 2001, people light candles at a memorial in front of a wall covered with flyers depicting pictures and descriptions of the missing, and prayers for their safe returns—one of many such walls seen in New York after the attack.

BELOW: Two girls hold American flags and candles as a memorial to the victims of 9/11, New York, Sept. 14, 2001.

ABOVE: Angelenos gather outside St. Agatha Catholic church in Los Angeles for a candlelight vigil honoring the victims of Tuesday's terrorist attacks, Friday, Sept. 14, 2001.

RIGHT: People stream to Seattle Center International Fountain, Sept. 15, 2001, at a city-sponsored flower vigil for victims of 9/11. Thousands of people carrying bouquets of flowers flocked to the fountain in the shadow of the Space Needle. So many people showed up—some 10,000 by noon—that what was supposed to be a three-hour ceremony turned into a weekend-long memorial.

the world will remember
September 11th 2001
love & prayers to all

FLAG SHORTAGE

SAN FRANCISCO, Sept. 14, 2001 (AP)—A show of patriotism in the days following the terrorist attacks in New York and Washington, D.C., has left one flag manufacturer fresh out of Old Glorys.

Doublet Manufacturing, Inc., a leading provider of flags to events such as the 1996 Atlanta Olympics, the U.S. Open golf championship and the World Figure Skating Championships, is all out of American flags. The company says it won't be able to get any more in stock for another two weeks.

The flags have been cropping up from big to small cities around the country, popping up on street lamps and fastened to vehicle antennas throughout the United States.

Many of those flags atop local, state and federal buildings were flown at half-staff Friday in remembrance of those who lost their lives in Tuesday's attack. ■

RIGHT: **People buy flags after standing for hours in line outside the AAA Manufacturing Co. flag store in Hollywood, Sept. 14, 2001.**

BELOW: **Military and fire personnel unfurl a large American flag on the roof of the Pentagon, Washington, D.C., Sept. 12, 2001.**

9/11: Memory and Beyond

By RICHARD PYLE
AP Correspondent

Everyone within a few miles of the World Trade Center that morning had a story to tell.

They were pieces of a 10,000-part mosaic. At the center, the people jumping 90 stories, at the outer edge, people lined up 12 or more deep at pay phones in a city where communications had broken down. In days to follow, posters of the missing covered walls and lampposts in the brave hope that personal details such as height and hair color would help bring back someone buried under seven stories of debris.

Sincere as they were, the candles, letters and flowers outside the city's firehouses could not do justice to 100 fire trucks and 343 firefighters obliterated in less than an hour. My first task as a reporter was to get to the scene. I made it to the subway, and soon realized that most of the Manhattan-bound passengers were unaware of anything having happened, until the conductor announced that due to an "emergency," service was being suspended at the last stop in Brooklyn. Fortunately we were near the Brooklyn Bridge, which suddenly had become the only way to get to Manhattan.

I found myself with two companions—Ann, a young *Newsweek* magazine employee who was carrying a camera, and Mike, a big demolition worker. Not knowing what to expect, we headed across

People flee Lower Manhattan across the Brooklyn Bridge in New York, the morning of Sept. 11, 2001,
following the terrorist attacks on the World Trade Center.

the bridge on foot. We were soon like salmon swimming upstream against a crush of people coming the other way—thousands of them, scared, stunned, angry, crying. Covered with gray ash, they looked as if they'd aged 30 years in five minutes. Maybe some of them had.

On the bridge, we learned the south tower had fallen at 9:59 a.m.—while I was on the train—but the smoke from that collapse was still so thick that one couldn't see it was no longer standing. We also learned then that the Pentagon had been hit by a hijacked jetliner.

The north tower still stood but just as we reached the halfway point, it suddenly caved in, falling straight down, right before our eyes. The sound was not loud, but a hollow rumble, like a rockslide combined with breaking glass. It lasted all of 10 seconds, and as the 110-story skyscraper with its 35-story TV tower vanished in billowing dust and smoke, there was a vast, collective moan, pierced by cries, on the bridge. Some people panicked and tried to run through the crowd ahead. It was, as one of my colleagues said, "like a Godzilla movie."

Ann, the *Newsweek* girl, was suddenly overcome with fear. "I can't go on," she said. She wasn't a reporter, but I told her she might be the only *Newsweek* person at the scene with a camera and the magazine would be desperate for her pictures. Momentarily, she wavered—then headed back to Brooklyn. I have often wondered whether she later came to regret her lost opportunity. The truth was that no one knew what was ahead. But Mike the demolition man, a Marine veteran of Vietnam, was determined to continue. He had a hard hat, goggles, mask and a canvas satchel of tools. I asked why he was making this trip. He said, "I just want to go over there and maybe I can help some people."

Mike was worried that we'd be stopped by police at the end of the bridge. I showed him my NYPD press pass and said that with all that gear, he could pretend to be a photographer. In the end it didn't matter. Nobody was there, throwing up barricades. Surreal hardly begins to describe the scene. The streets around City Hall were nearly deserted. No pedestrians, no cars. It was a strange, yellowish darkness, nuclear winter, a volcanic eruption, the end of the world. The air was filled with dust and several inches of gray powder covered everything. All sound was muffled, as if by a winter snowstorm.

On Broadway, a group of cops stood in military ranks like soldiers, awaiting deployment orders. . . . A block further on toward the trade center we found a working phone booth. While talking to an editor at AP, I turned around, and Mike was gone. I didn't know what became of him, but he had his own mission. I had to assume he knew what he was doing—and that he would survive.

One can't adequately describe the effect of a place as familiar as the trade center suddenly becoming a scene from another planet.

The wide plaza itself was 16 acres of utter destruction, smoking and strangely quiet. Human figures were vague shapes moving about the fringes of the physical chaos, as if reality had not yet gained a foothold. I saw nobody I recognized as a fellow journalist. Unknown to me then, some of my colleagues had been forced to run for their lives.

My instructions by phone had been to get to police head-quarters, but 1 Police Plaza was surrounded by cops in riot gear, with automatic weapons and orders to admit no one. A senior officer suggested I head for the police academy, 20-some blocks to the north, where Mayor Rudolph Giuliani, having escaped from the trade center area himself, was setting up a fallback command post.

It was a trek through a paralyzed city. Stores were closing, streets were eerily empty of vehicle traffic, but filled with a vast army of people walking, the only way to get home. Cell phones did not work and every public phone had a line of people waiting. A Franciscan priest in a brown cassock was acting as a pedestrian traffic cop, directing people toward the East River bridges. Hospitals had activated emergency outdoor triage centers to handle casualties. As it turned out, very few people had gotten away alive.

Doctors in blue scrubs stood on the sidewalks, looking for ambulances that never came. At the command center, we first learned the estimate of missing—more than 300 firefighters and dozens of city and Port Authority police. I called AP and dictated a story from my notes. My editors clarified reports I had heard only in brief snatches of street talk—more planes had been hijacked, one had crashed in Pennsylvania, possibly shot down. Like most disasters, this one was full of such rumors, along with ironic touches and curious coincidences.

As a young newspaper reporter in Michigan in the late 1950s I had become acquainted with a promising Japanese-American architect named Minoru Yamasaki, who was designing schools and other buildings in the Detroit area. Years later he was chosen over more prominent architects to create the new World Trade Center, and it was his design for the world's tallest buildings that was tested on 9/11. Yamasaki had built them to withstand the impact of a Boeing 707, the biggest commercial aircraft of the day, and to collapse straight downward rather than topple to the side and take out several blocks of Manhattan.

Among the thousands of pieces of paper that floated across to Brooklyn, our next-door neighbor found on his sidewalk a one-page letter from an insurance company. Dated April 13, 2001 and scorched along the edges, it itemized $3 million worth of jewelry owned by Randolph A. Hearst and Veronica Hearst— the late father and stepmother of Patricia Hearst. I still marvel that within that blizzard of papers and documents from the towers, you could randomly come across one with a recognizable name on it. ■

AP Wire, Friday, September 14, 2001

HUNDREDS OF FAMILY MEMBERS SEARCH ON FOR LOVED ONES

By LARRY MCSHANE
The Associated Press

NEW YORK (AP)—The gruesome search through the mass graveyard of the World Trade Center yielded no survivors Thursday, and hopes dimmed for the 4,700 who are still missing. President George W. Bush was to visit New York today to "hug and cry" with its shaken citizens.

Two days after the World Trade Center was hit and destroyed by two hijacked passenger planes, swirling dust kept visibility limited, and sanitation trucks waged a losing fight against the residue of the blast. Hundreds of family members searched for signs of their loved ones.

Tens of thousands of residents still could not return to their homes in a closed-off lower Manhattan. Nerves were frayed by bomb scares and false alarms. And the city brought in 30,000 body bags for pieces of human remains.

"Even scary movies do not happen like this," said Enver Kesti, 42, a pizza chef who returned to clean up a lower Manhattan gourmet shop that once sat in the shadows of the towers.

Bush declared Friday a "national day of prayer and remembrance." He asked Americans to spend their lunch breaks taking part in services at their chosen places of worship, said White House spokesman Ari Fleischer.

The president praised New Yorkers for showing "the compassion of America and the bravery of America."

New York was not alone in counting its missing and dead. At the Pentagon—also a target of terrorist hijackers Tuesday—126 people were believed to be dead and 70 bodies had been recovered. Among those assumed dead was a three-star Army general.

Add the 4,763 missing reported by Mayor Rudolph Giuliani, plus the 266 passengers and crew members who died aboard the planes that hit the trade center, the Pentagon and a field southeast of Pittsburgh, and the total dead in Tuesday's carnage could be more than 5,000. The death toll from those reported missing in the attacks in New York and Washington could exceed 5,000. A total of 2,390 Americans died at Pearl Harbor nearly 60 years ago.

The missing in New York included nearly 400 city firefighters and police officers. Another 2,300 people were injured.

The lone bit of bright news was the recovery of two firefighters who slipped into an underground pocket beneath the rubble while searching for survivors on Thursday. The two radioed for help and were rescued by fellow firefighters several hours after they fell.

At One Liberty Plaza, an office building near the trade center site, volunteers were evacuated when the top 10 stories of the complex appeared unsteady.

At a grief center set up for families with missing relatives, Jeanine Nardone arrived to look for her brother, Mario, who worked on the 83rd floor of the World Trade Center. She had hung his photo in a Brooklyn subway station, hoping someone would recognize him. "He's a strong person," Nardone said. "He would not give up on us. And I'm not going to give up on him."

Many family members stopped by the armory-turned-counseling center established by the city. Looking south from there, the seemingly endless plume of acrid, white smoke from the wreckage still corkscrewed above the Manhattan skyline.

At Bellevue Hospital, a blue wall erected around a construction site was covered with pictures and descriptions of the missing, and prayers for safe returns.

New Yorkers did take some small steps toward normal life. While everything south of 14th Street remained closed, the northern part of Manhattan became busier. Office buildings reopened, restaurants put out sidewalk tables and hawkers handed out flyers. Traffic on the streets and subways was up sharply.

The government gave the go-ahead for commercial flights to resume and some did, but schedules were expected to be in disarray, and heavy security was the rule. Bond trading resumed, while Wall Street officials said the stock markets were expected to open again on Monday. . . .

New Yorkers also remained edgy. On Staten Island, parents pulled children off school buses after a report that a car possibly linked to the terrorists had driven into the borough. At LaGuardia Airport, passengers were briefly evacuated from the just-reopened facility after a man said something about a device in a bag. Buildings around Manhattan were evacuated as authorities erred on the side of caution. "Right now, a lot of people are panicking," said Police Commissioner Bernard Kerik. "And they really have to be as cautious as possible." ■

LEFT: James Symington and his German shepherd, Trakr, search through rubble at the World Trade Center site, Sept. 13, 2001. Trakr, who died in 2009, was named one of history's most heroic animals by *Time* magazine. Trackr and Symington, a retired Canadian police officer, were among the first K9 search and rescue teams to arrive at ground zero after the attacks.

BELOW LEFT: A FEMA first responder rappels down a girder into the depths of the wreckage as members of his team at the bottom look on, Sept. 19, 2001.

BELOW: A FEMA search and rescue specialist with her K9 partner beneath the rubble at ground zero, Sept. 13, 2001.

RIGHT: **FEMA urban search and rescue specialists strategizing among the wreckage at the World Trade Center, Sept. 13, 2001.**

BELOW: **Rescue workers remove their hats and bow their heads as they circle a body recovered at the World Trade Center site, Sept. 27, 2001. It didn't take long after the attacks of Sept. 11 for the realization to set in that there would be no more survivors. Hope gave way to the grim process of recovering victims, all while picking apart a hopelessly complicated pile of steel that, if handled incorrectly, could have shifted, collapsed and killed someone.**

LEFT: An area is marked as "SEARCHED" at the ruins of the World Trade Center, Sept. 29, 2001.

BELOW: Concerned New Yorkers gather around missing person flyers on a telephone booth, Sept. 13, 2001.

ABOVE: A woman looks at the Wall of Prayers—flyers of missing persons and prayers papering a construction fence at Bellevue Hospital in Kips Bay, New York, Sept. 14, 2001.

RIGHT: A man and woman comfort each other in front of one of the walls in New York covered with missing person notices, Sept. 14, 2001.

A New York City mailbox covered with missing person notices, Sept. 14, 2001.

HUNDREDS CHEER THOSE HEADING FOR WTC DUTY

By VERENA DOBNIK
The Associated Press

NEW YORK, Sept. 13, 2001 (AP)—It was a thumbs up for the rescuers, and for those with the job of carting away piles of debris that were once two of the tallest buildings in the world.

Hundreds of New Yorkers on Wednesday lined the highway leading to the World Trade Center site, cheering on emergency workers, police officers and volunteers as they headed to work. "DON'T MESS WITH THE U.S.," said the letters scrawled in white paint on Luke Littell's black T-shirt.

Littell, a 27-year-old television producer, started the effort with his girlfriend. Within hours, hundreds had joined in, waving signs on plywood lifted from a construction site, yelling their thanks.

Littell didn't know he would end up next to the highway when he woke up Wednesday in his Greenwich Village apartment. First, he gave blood at a hospital and donated clothes. But he decided he wanted to do more. So he painted the slogan on his T-shirt, got a can of paint, found the wood, and headed to a vantage point close to the convoy of heavy trucks, police cruisers and ambulances slowly motoring down the highway.

Only a day earlier, the site near the Hudson River had a stunning view of the twin towers. Soon, a crowd had developed, holding signs telling the workers, "You're the Brave" and "Thank You!" ■

With smoke still drifting from the site of the World Trade Center attacks one week earlier, a truck carries New York City police officers to ground zero, Sept. 18, 2001.

Volunteers line up to help the search and rescue efforts at the World Trade Center, Sept. 15, 2001.

AP Wire, Friday, September 14, 2001

PRESIDENT BUSH URGES PEOPLE NOT TO TAKE VENGEANCE AGAINST ARAB AMERICANS, MUSLIMS

By MELANIE COFFEE
The Associated Press

Arab Americans and Muslims have been attacked, threatened and harassed in a backlash over the terrorist bloodbath, prompting President Bush to urge people not to take vengeance.

"Our nation must be mindful that there are thousands of Arab Americans that live in New York City who love the flag just as much" as other Americans, Bush said in a nationally televised telephone call Thursday to New York City's mayor and New York's governor.

Wednesday night, police in Bridgeview, Ill., turned back 300 marchers—some waving American flags and shouting "USA! USA!"—as they tried to march on a mosque in the Chicago suburb. Three demonstrators were arrested. There were no injuries and demonstrators were kept blocks from the closed Muslim house of worship.

"I'm proud to be American and I hate Arabs and I always have," said 19-year-old Colin Zaremba who marched with the group from Oak Lawn.

Federal authorities said they had identified more than a dozen hijackers of Middle Eastern descent in Tuesday's terror attacks in New York and Washington and have gathered evidence linking them to Saudi-born terror mastermind Osama bin Laden and other extremist networks.

Ziad Asali, president of the American-Arab Anti-Discrimination Committee, expressed concern about both the bias incidents and Tuesday's terror attacks.

"Arab Americans, in addition to feeling the intense depths of pain and anger at this attack we share with all our fellow citizens,

An employee of the Islamic Society of Boston holds a flag while listening to a prayer during an interfaith vigil of prayer and solidarity at Boston City Hall, Sept. 13, 2001. Jewish, Christian, Muslim and other religious leaders joined thousands of participants in the prayer vigil for victims of Tuesday's fatal terrorist attacks.

Members of the Omar Mosque in Paterson, N.J., put up a sign condemning the Sept. 11 terrorist attacks as a worshipper arrives for the afternoon service, Sept. 14, 2001.

A woman carrying a sign supporting Arabs argues with a man during a rally at New York's Union Square, Sept. 15, 2001.

are feeling deep anxiety about becoming the targets of anger from other Americans," he said. "We appeal to all Americans to bear in mind that crimes are the responsibility of the individuals who committed them, not ethnic or religious groups."

In a show of patriotism, 45 people from the Islamic community in Tampa, Fla., registered with blood services to donate Wednesday, and 30 members of the Muslim Students Association at the University of South Florida signed up.

"You feel the pain twice: once because of what has happened and once because of the looks you get," said Sami Al-Arian, an engineering teacher at the University of South Florida.

In Dearborn, Mich., Issam Koussan said he bought large U.S. flags to fly in front of his home and outside his supermarket after men pulled into his parking lot and yelled threats and racial slurs at his customers.

"I just feel I needed to show my loyalty to this country," Koussan told the *Detroit News*.

Early Thursday, a Molotov cocktail was thrown against the side of the Islamic Society of Denton, Texas, causing an estimated $2,500 in damage, said Kiersten Dieterle, a spokeswoman for the Dallas suburb. The building was empty and there were no injuries.

In Chicago, a firebomb was tossed Wednesday at an Arab American community center. No injuries were reported.

In nearby Palos Heights, a man who used the blunt end of a machete to attack a Moroccan gas station attendant was charged with a hate crime, police said. The attendant did not seek treatment.

"The terrorists who committed these whorrible acts would like nothing better than to see us tear at the fiber of our democracy and to trample on the rights of other Americans," Illinois Gov. George Ryan said.

In Huntington, N.Y., a 75-year-old man who was drunk tried to run over a Pakistani woman in the parking lot of a shopping mall, police said. The man then followed the woman into a store and threatened to kill her for "destroying my country," authorities said.

A man in a ski mask in Gary, Ind., fired an assault rifle at a gas station where a Yemen-born U.S. citizen born was working Wednesday, the *Post Tribune* of Merrillville, Ind., reported. Police were investigating it as a hate crime.

In Tulsa, Okla., police said a Pakistani native was beaten by three men late Tuesday in a hate crime. The victim was in a fair condition at a hospital Thursday.

Tamara Alfson, an American working at the Kuwait Embassy in Washington, spent Wednesday counseling frightened Kuwaiti students attending schools across the United States.

"Some of them have already been harassed. People have been quite awful to them," said Alfson, an academic adviser to about 150 students. ■

MUSLIMS WARY OF REPRISALS IN WAKE OF DEADLY ATTACKS

By MICHAEL MELLO
The Associated Press

PROVIDENCE, R.I., Sept. 12, 2001 (AP)—As police led a handcuffed, bearded man in a green turban away from an Amtrak train station Wednesday, a crowd cheered and one woman yelled "burn in hell!" Less than an hour later, Providence Police Chief Richard Sullivan said the man was arrested for carrying a medium-sized knife and did not appear to be connected to this week's deadly terrorist attacks.

Sher Singh, 28, of Leesburg, Va., was released on his own recognizance later that night. Singh is a member of the Sikh religion, and he said he carries a knife as a symbol of strength.

The incident marked heightened tensions across the state and country, with Muslims fearing reprisals as authorities investigate whether Muslim terrorists orchestrated the attacks along the East Coast.

"Some people just want to blame the Muslim groups," said Issan Chagil, 35, owner of a Cranston restaurant, Kabob To Go. "My customers know we have nothing to do with this," he said. . . .

Mohammed Sharif, a board member of the Islamic Council of New England, says Muslims are vulnerable to harassment or attack as long as Muslim terrorists are being investigated. "Even my wife, Ayesha, who works in a Providence daycare called me to say one of her co-workers said all (Muslims) are bad people, terrorists," he said. . . . Sharif is appealing to the media and others not to rush to judgment about those responsible for the attacks and said Muslims are suffering along with everyone else.

"This is tragic to everybody, not only non-Muslims," he said. "One of my friends worked in the World Trade Center. I'm really concerned because there's no way I can reach him, and he's a Muslim," Sharif said. "The people who did this are crazy, Islam does not condone these type of acts," he said.

Even some family members of victims of the attacks are concerned about displaced anger toward local Muslims.

"Everybody should not misdirect their anger right now," pleaded Richard DelleFemine, 46, of East Providence. His sister Carol Bouchard, of Warwick, was on one of the planes that crashed into the World Trade Center. "We should help the living by giving blood and pray for the dead," he said. ■

Sen. Joe Lieberman, D-Conn., center, sits in prayer with Iman Nasif Muhammad, right, from the Al-Aziz Islamic Center of Bridgeport, during a prayer and remembrance service at the Hartford Islamic Center in Hartford, Conn., Sept. 17, 2001.

AP Wire, Saturday, September 15, 2001

BUSH VISITS RESCUERS

By LARRY MCSHANE
The Associated Press

NEW YORK (AP)—Sopping-wet search crews slogged through the rubble of the World Trade Center on Friday under gray skies that mirrored their dwindling hopes for miracle rescues.

Though President Bush made a morale-boosting visit to the site in the afternoon, the grim reality was that for a second straight day, no survivors were found in the debris.

Bush, after working his way through a throng of rescue workers, donned a fire helmet and later addressed the cheering crowd through a megaphone. "Thank you for your hard work," he said. "USA! USA!," the firefighters and volunteer workers shouted in return. "God bless America!" screamed one man.

Earlier, the rescuers operated in a quieter mode. Occasionally, the crews halted all work to listen for any noise—a sharp knock or muffled voice—that might lead them to a survivor. "When they call for silence on the pile . . . (it) caused me to say a prayer every time," said volunteer Richard Coppo. "It meant there was a possibility a hope that we had found something."

But all they heard was silence. And then they resumed moving rubble—10,425 tons and counting.

President Bush stands with firefighter Bob Beckwith on a burnt fire truck in front of the World Trade Center during a tour of the devastation, Sept. 14, 2001.

President Bush greets Mayor Rudolph Giuliani of New York City, left, and New York Gov. George Pataki, right, at McGuire Air Force Base, Burlington County, N.J., Sept. 14, 2001.

More than 4,700 people remained missing. Just five people have been pulled alive from the ruins since two hijacked jetliners toppled the twin towers Tuesday. The official death toll remained at 184, while the number of people injured including those injured in the rescue efforts climbed to 4,300, Giuliani said.

New York City's two airports, where a dozen people of Middle Eastern descent were detained and then released overnight, reopened Friday after an 18-hour shutdown. One person was still being questioned but was not charged, said Barry Mawn, head of the FBI's New York office.

"We are running down hundreds, if not thousands, of leads around the country," Mawn said.

Newark International Airport, close to New York, also reopened. Work at ground zero—the enormous mass of wreckage created when the two skyscrapers crumbled—was complicated by a ferocious overnight downpour that turned dust into mud and made even the simplest tasks more difficult and dangerous.

Workers who have battled fatigue and choking smoke were slowed by the muck. One worker reported finding mud-caked body parts.

The mayor did offer some good news: the Wall Street financial district—closed off since the terror attacks—should be back in business Monday. The stock markets, closed for the longest stretch since the crash of 1929, also are due to resume operations Monday.

The Staten Island ferry will start running again the same day, and city officials hope to reopen another slice of downtown to thousands of displaced residents, Giuliani said.

An overflow of response led the city to temporarily suspend its call for volunteers and donated goods for victims and rescue workers. ∎

CAVE EXPLORER RUSHED TO GROUND ZERO

By J. M. HIRSCH
The Associated Press

CONCORD, N.H., Sept. 19, 2001 (AP)—By the time a second airliner slammed into the World Trade Center, Russell Keat knew his mind was urgently needed. There would be rubble and wreckage. There would be bodies as twisted and broken as the debris that buried them. Somebody would need to crawl through it, finding and mapping safe paths for other rescuers to follow. And that is Keat's specialty.

Keat, 40, is a rarity when it comes to search and rescue missions, of which he has participated in hundreds, from airliner crashes to collapsed buildings to people trapped in caves. He is trained to work underground, to map the crevices, tunnels and holes in the debris that could fall several stories. He makes the search for survivors possible.

"In some ways my whole life was leading up to this," he said in a telephone interview from his Grantham home Tuesday.

After the attacks, Keat didn't wait for a call. He grabbed his gear, stopped by the elementary school to say goodbye to his 5- and 6-year-old daughters, then headed for New York.

Though his mission was mapping, Keat went in with 350 pounds of gear, including enough food and water for him to stay with a trapped survivor for up to a week, if necessary.

"We're looking for human life, we're looking to support and evacuate. Or if they're trapped, to stay there with them. Once we can make a life sign that's trapped, we never leave."

Keat didn't find anyone alive, though he found plenty of remnants of lives.

"You'll pick up a picture that somebody obviously had in their office of their kids or a loved one," he said. "In some ways one of the hugest feelings is a sense of reverence. You are walking in the personal spaces of people and even as you're wriggling through stuff that is awful, this is still their space."

It was his love of exploring caves that got Keat interested in underground rescue missions. . . .

By the time Keat and his team finished mapping the pile Thursday, he had endured some close calls, from dangerous precipices to clouds of noxious asbestos dust. He was treated four times for smoke inhalation.

"The worst moment was when we were probing the voids," he said. "I was going pretty much near vertical. I got to the bottom of it and there's this buckled over piece of concrete. I was looking straight down into eight stories of empty." ∎

AP Wire, Saturday, September 15, 2001

CITIES HOLD FUNERALS FOR VICTIMS

By DAVID CRARY
The Associated Press

In the heart of Manhattan, in Washington's suburbs, in saddened towns elsewhere, mourners grieved and reminisced Saturday at the first wave of services for the terror attacks' victims—a fearless priest, a feisty TV commentator, parents and their preschool daughters.

A Supreme Court justice spoke at one service, a U.S. senator and former president attended another. Mourners for a 3-year-old girl sang her favorite song, "I Love You," from the TV show *Barney*."

The wistful tributes from relatives, friends and civic leaders will be echoed over and over, at hundreds of churches across the nation, in the coming days, weeks and perhaps months.

In New York City, at a Roman Catholic church across from a grief-stricken firehouse, bagpipers played the national anthem before the service for the Rev. Mychal Judge, chaplain of the city's fire department. Sen. Hillary Rodham Clinton, former President Clinton and their daughter, Chelsea, were among the mourners.

Supreme Court Justice Clarence Thomas delivered a eulogy in Arlington, Va., for Barbara Olson, a lawyer, an unabashedly conservative TV commentator and the wife of U.S. Solicitor General Theodore Olson. She was aboard the jetliner that crashed into the Pentagon on Tuesday.

"Barbara strode boldly through life, full of cheer and verve, shying from no challenge or obstacle," Thomas said. "She was irrepressible in the fullest sense . . . ignoring all torpedoes and charging full speed ahead."

"This is indeed a sad occasion," the justice added. "One to be repeated thousands of times by our fellow citizens across the country."

Congressmen, federal judges and others from Washington's political elite were among about 1,500 people gathered for the memorial service at Arlington's St. Thomas More Cathedral.

Judge, 68, died Tuesday as he was administering last rites to a firefighter mortally injured in the attack on the World Trade Center. The Franciscan priest had removed his fire hat to pray when he was hit by falling debris. "He was a saint, a wonderful man," said Mayor Rudolph Giuliani.

The funeral Mass for Judge took place at St. Francis of Assisi Church, across from the firehouse of Engine Co. 1/Ladder Co. 24, which lost seven firefighters in the disaster.

Visiting the firehouse after the service, Bill Clinton said Judge's vocation was "a rebuke to the act of hatred" that killed so many Americans.

"So all of us who were here this morning feel a special loss," Clinton said. "We should live his life as an example of what has to prevail."

On any other day, a firefighter killed in the line of duty would draw hundreds of colleagues in dress blue uniforms and white gloves. But as a testament to the round-the-clock work proceeding in the disaster zone, the firefighters attending Judge's service numbered perhaps 200.

The Fire Department's losses, estimated at 300, included many of its top leaders. Funeral services were held Saturday for William Feehan, the department's first deputy commissioner, and chief of department Peter Ganci.

In California, family and friends held memorials for two men believed to have helped thwart hijackers aboard United Flight 93, the plane that crashed in Pennsylvania before reaching a target. Both men had called relatives to tell them of the danger, and to say goodbye.

In Pleasanton, Calif., nearly 2,000 mourners remembered Thomas Burnett Jr., 38, an executive at a medical device company. In San Francisco, mourners gathered for Mark Bingham, 31, who owned a public relations firm and played on the San Francisco Fog, a gay men's rugby team.

Two services were held in Connecticut towns—both involving parents and children killed together when United Flight 175 smashed into the trade center.

In East Lyme, Conn., mourners grieved for Ruth McCourt, 45 and her daughter, Juliana Valentine McCourt, 4. A service was held in Easton, Conn., for Peter Hanson, 32, his wife, Susan, 35, and their 3-year-old daughter, Christine.

It was during the Hanson service that mourners sang "I Love You" in memory of Christine. Friends said the child would often ask guests at her home to sing the purple dinosaur's anthem with her.

In Batesville, Ark., a service was held for Sara Low, a flight attendant aboard American Flight 11, which also struck the World Trade Center.

An overflow crowd packed a Landover, Md., church at a service for James Debeuneure, a teacher at Ketcham Elementary in Washington. He was one of three teachers and three students heading to California on a field trip when their flight from Washington-Dulles was hijacked and crashed into the Pentagon. ■

A crowd watches as the coffin of New York City Fire Department chaplain Rev. Mychal Judge is escorted by members of the FDNY after his funeral service at St. Francis of Assisi Church in Midtown South, Sept. 15, 2001. Judge died after being struck by debris after the collapse of the south tower while giving the last rights to a fireman.

A portrait of Rev. Judge is part of the memorial to firemen missing or killed on 9/11, displayed at the Engine 1/Ladder 24 firehouse in New York City, Sept. 14, 2001. The fire company had seven missing firefighters commemorated in the memorial.

First Lady Laura Bush, right, attends a memorial service with Gov. Tom Ridge of Pennsylvania, center, and his wife, Michelle Ridge, left, in Indian Lake, Pa., Sept. 17, 2001. Families of the victims of United Flight 93 were present following a visit to the crash site.

A little girl watches as the funeral procession for firefighter Gerard Schrang, who was one of the victims of the World Trade center attack, enters the Good Shepherd Catholic Church in Holbrook, N.Y., Sept. 28, 2001.

LEFT: Airline employees console each other at the official funeral ceremony for American Airlines Flight 77 pilot Charles Burlingame at his burial site in Arlington National Cemetery, Dec. 12, 2001. The former Navy pilot was killed after the jetliner he was piloting was hijacked on Sept. 11, 2001, and crashed into the Pentagon.

BOTTOM: Sen. Dianne Feinstein, D-Calif., left, presents an American flag that had flown over the U.S. Capitol the week of 9/11 to Keith Grossman, CEO of Thoratec Corporation, Sept. 17, 2001, during Day of Remembrance ceremonies in San Francisco. Thoratec was the employer of Thomas Burnett, who, along with other passengers, confronted the hijackers of United Flight 93.

AP Wire, Monday, September 17, 2001

NEW YORK CLEANUP JOB UNPARALLELED

By RICHARD PYLE
The Associated Press

NEW YORK (AP)—From tall, telescoping cranes, bulldozers and power shovels to bucket brigades, the cleanup at the shattered World Trade Center is as basic as it gets in the demolition industry. The difference: Ground zero is also a crime scene—the site of the biggest mass murder in American history.

Working behind the machines digging into layers of debris, hard-hat workers, firefighters, police officers and volunteers proceed cautiously to avoid collapsing gaps in the 150-foot heap of rubble where survivors might be trapped.

The crews must also preserve potential evidence for FBI investigators, such as debris from the two jetliners that hijackers crashed into the 1,300-foot twin towers last Tuesday.

Even with the heavy equipment, it is a labor-intensive operation to rival the pyramids of Egypt. Never in history has one 110-story skyscraper fallen down, let alone two, at the same time and place. Workers use power saws, crowbars and their hands to slice and pry at the wreckage.

Officials were close Sunday to finalizing contracts with four New York construction companies to do the heavy lifting.

At the scene, Mark Loizeaux, a Maryland-based demolition expert, was running the operation for one of the companies, Tully Construction. At his command was a battalion of power tools: a

On Sept. 16, 2001, workers in a crane basket are suspended over a pit of rubble as they inspect the debris at ground zero in New York; the debris was being moved at a rate of about 3,000 cubic yards a day.

TOP: Contractors stand on a beam in the pit at ground zero, Oct. 4, 2001. BOTTOM: Members of the New York Fire Department remove debris and continue to search for survivors among the wreckage around the clock, Sept. 16, 2001.

RIGHT: **Rubble covers the tracks of the New York City subway 1 and 9 train lines in the Cortland Street station under the World Trade Center, c. Sept. 20, 2001. The station, which was destroyed, did not reopen until 2018.**

BELOW: **Firefighters make their way over the ruins of the World Trade Center through clouds of smoke, Oct. 11, 2001.**

OPPOSITE: **Chief John W. Norman, FDNY Search and Rescue manager at the World Trade Center site, Oct. 4, 2001.**

110-ton hydraulic crane, a 250-ton hydraulic crane, two 300-ton "crawler" cranes and eight hydraulic excavators with attachments that can "grab steel, cut steel and rip out debris," Loizeaux said.

In the course of the day, he said, workers penetrated for the first time into the lowest level below the towers, a commuter railroad station 80 feet underground. They found some "voids"—pockets in the rubble—but no one alive.

"We are basically opening up voids to support fire department and government search and rescue operations," Loizeaux said by phone from the site. "We take a layer of debris off, let them go in and search, take another layer of debris off.

"Everybody is doing whatever it takes to support the search and rescue, to stabilize the situation and to assist the utility crews."

Several building experts have said the towers collapsed because blazing jet fuel melted steel braces, causing outer walls to peel away in a shower of steel pillars and glass. The floors—unsupported by internal pillars—"pancaked" downward, gaining momentum from ever-increasing weight.

The towers were built to withstand a strike by a Boeing 707—the largest aircraft at the time, but much smaller than the jets that struck Tuesday.

Within hours after the mortally wounded monoliths vanished in vast, opaque clouds of cement dust, bulldozers, excavators and other heavy-duty construction machines were converging on the scene.

A flatbed truck carrying a huge crane trundled down Second Avenue under police escort, past the city morgue where the first Trade Center dead were arriving. Scores of other machinery lined the streets near the disaster site.

At night powerful floodlights, some borrowed from a film studio in Queens, illuminate the scene, silhouetting other financial district buildings in an eerie tableau visible from the boroughs of Brooklyn and Staten Island, up to five miles away.

Dump trucks take the rubble to Staten Island, where it is spread out in a field near the city's recently closed Fresh Kills landfill. There, teams of FBI agents and New York City detectives sort through the debris by hand, seeking anything that might add to the file of criminal evidence. The debris was being moved at a rate of about 3,000 cubic yards a day. How long it would take to clear the estimated 2 million cubic yards covering 16 acres of lower Manhattan is unknown.

To Tom Rowe, a New Jersey firefighter working as a volunteer, the material collected by the bucket brigades seemed insignificant. "It's like if you filled your backyard with sand, and you tried to empty it with a teaspoon."

All across the country, people in the building industry—architects, engineers, construction and demolition experts—have watched the World Trade Center operation with eyes that see more than just the television pictures of workers dwarfed by their project.

ABOVE: **A worker wearing a respirator sifts through debris from the World Trade Center as it passes by on a conveyor belt at the Fresh Kills landfill in the Staten Island borough of New York, Jan. 14, 2002. They were searching for human remains, personal items, identification cards, jewelry and other items.**

OPPOSITE PAGE: **An aerial view shows a portion of the World Trade Center wreckage. Surrounding buildings were heavily damaged by the debris and massive force of the falling twin towers, Sept. 17, 2001.**

"I would say it takes a task and multiplies it by 100 times in terms of the level of care," said Bill Walsh, operations manager for Engineered Demolition, an Idaho firm that specializes in bringing down large buildings.

"It's most unusual," said Jay Lubow, a New York architect who has done work at the World Trade Center. "People seem to think you can just start picking up the rubble. But because it fell randomly, it's like 'pick up sticks'—you pick up a stick on top, which will then move sticks on the bottom." ■

WTC GIULIANI PRAISED FOR "FINEST HOUR"

By BETH J. HARPAZ
The Associated Press

NEW YORK, Sept. 18, 2001 (AP)—Mayor Rudolph Giuliani has been quoting Winston Churchill to help New York get through its darkest hour. Now, even the mayor's usual critics say his steady leadership since the terrorist attack on the World Trade Center has been Giuliani's finest hour.

After barely escaping with his own life from a building adjacent to the twin towers, he gently, calmly informed his fellow New Yorkers that the death toll would be "more than any of us could bear." He lost personal friends and officiated at funerals; he has worked around the clock, holding news conferences in between visits to the disaster site and meetings to coordinate the response; he has pledged to rebuild and prosper, and he even found time to officiate at a wedding, saying, "This is what life is all about."

Many New Yorkers are wishing they could undo a term-limits law that prevents, the lame-duck mayor—who has just three months left in office—from running for office again.

"Ten more years!" shouted a rescue worker Monday as Giuliani toured the site of the World Trade Center disaster.

Giuliani's new admirers include die-hard Democrats who never voted for him, activists who have long lambasted him as insensitive to minorities, and people in other countries who may not have known his name a week ago. Political consultants say Giuliani could run for anything now and win.

Giuliani deflected the acclaim. "What I should do is do the job until Dec. 31, and prepare someone else as the next mayor," he said.

Ordinary New Yorkers disagree. "I wish he could stay on and that we didn't have term limits," said Linda Yarwood, a Manhattan paralegal. "I would vote for him again. He is a pillar of strength for our community and our nation."

Rachel Biern, who works as an online-researcher, did not support the mayor until now. "I think he's been amazing under crisis," she said. "He was calm and he kept people together. He was just the right balance of sadness and determination. He really does care about New York."

The mayor ran for U.S. Senate from New York last year against Hillary Rodham Clinton, but dropped out of the race six months before the election amid revelations that he had prostate cancer and a girlfriend. He is now in the middle of a nasty divorce.

Nelson Warfield, a Republican political consultant and former press secretary to Bob Dole, predicted that "whoever becomes mayor will beg him to stay on in some role to oversee the rebuilding of the city. But I think Rudy Giuliani goes wherever he wants from here. If he chooses to seek political office, I can't imagine anybody stopping him."

ABOVE: Mayor Rudolph Giuliani is seen at the World Trade Center disaster site after a short interfaith memorial service at the disaster area, Oct. 11, 2001. Soon after, Oprah dubbed him America's mayor, Queen Elizabeth knighted him, and *Time* named him Person of the Year.

OPPOSITE TOP: Mayor Giuliani, center, gives a thumbs-up on the floor of the New York Stock Exchange, Monday, Sept. 17, 2001, where he helped ring the opening bell of the exchange. Stock prices plummeted but stopped short of collapse in the emotional reopening of Wall Street, closed since 9/11. The Dow Jones industrial average lost 684.81 points and ended the day at 8,920.70—a record one-day point drop and the first close below 9,000 since Dec. 21, 1996.

Four Democrats and two Republicans are running for mayor. The primary was supposed to have taken place Sept. 11, the day two hijacked jets crashed into the trade center. The primary was rescheduled for Sept. 25.

Former Mayor Ed Koch, a Democrat who wrote a book about Giuliani called "Nasty Man," said the mayor "over the last eight years has often been petty and insensitive. But there's no question he has risen to the occasion here. The challenge of leading the city when it's under attack, comparable to war, has been met."

Koch suggested that Giuliani be kept on as a reconstruction czar. Asked Monday if he would consider being an anti-terrorism czar, Giuliani said: "I've never been big on czars."

On Sunday, Giuliani presided at a promotion ceremony for the Fire Department to fill its leadership ranks after hundreds of firefighters were lost Tuesday.

He quoted Churchill during the ceremony, saying: "Courage is rightly esteemed the first of human qualities because it's the quality which guarantees all others."

Asked Monday if he would consider being an anti-terrorism czar, Giuliani said: "I've never been big on czars." ■

LEFT: **Secretary of Defense Donald Rumsfeld and Mayor Giuliani hold a joint media conference at the site of the World Trade Center disaster in Lower Manhattan, Nov. 14, 2001.**

AP Wire, Tuesday, September 18, 2001

FBI SLOWLY PIECES TOGETHER TERRORISTS' PLOT, SUPPORT

By JOHN SOLOMON
The Associated Press

WASHINGTON (AP)—The FBI has meticulously pieced together a broad terrorist plot, securing evidence the hijackers trained for months or years without raising suspicions in the United States, received financial and logistical support from others and identified additional targets for destruction.

Law enforcement and other officials familiar with the evidence said the FBI is investigating whether the terrorist network behind Tuesday's attacks targeted more flights for hijacking beyond the four that crashed.

Authorities have grown increasingly certain—from intelligence intercepts, witness interviews and evidence gathered in hijackers' cars and homes—that a second wave of violence was planned by collaborators. They said Sept. 22 has emerged as an important date in the evidence, but declined to be more specific.

Tuesday's attacks were "part of a larger plan with other terrorism acts, not necessarily hijacking of airplanes," said Sen. Bob Graham, D-Fla., chairman of the Senate Intelligence Committee. "Those acts were going to occur in the United States and elsewhere in the world."

The FBI said it has issued an advisory to fire departments across the country to increase security and guard against the theft of any ambulances or fire trucks, which could be used in bombing attacks. The bureau said the warning was precautionary.

The investigation, the largest in American history, has engulfed the full resources of the FBI, Justice Department, Customs Service, Treasury Department agencies that track assets and the CIA, National Security Agency and other spy agencies.

Officials from several of those agencies described developments in the investigation to The Associated Press on condition of anonymity. Most of the evidence remains sealed by court orders. A federal grand jury in White Plains, N.Y., was convened last week to weigh evidence and issue subpoenas.

U.S. officials have made no secret they believe exiled Saudi millionaire Osama bin Laden masterminded the plot from Afghanistan and organized his and other terrorist groups to carry it out. In President Bush's words, bin Laden is wanted "dead or alive."

The FBI has hinted at the magnitude of the collaboration, sending airlines, local police and border patrol agencies a list of about 200 people it believes may have information or assisted the attacks. The government has detained 75 people for questioning and on immigration charges, from California to Germany.

At least four people on the list have been arrested as material witnesses, law enforcement officials said Tuesday. That means they are believed to have critical information about the plot and are at risk to flee.

Authorities have explored whether the hijackers may have had help from people with access to airlines. On Tuesday, authorities arrested and charged three men in the Detroit area with possessing false documents after searching a house where agents found airport-related diagrams and documents about a military base and the "American foreign minister," according to an FBI affidavit. It did not explain the reference to "foreign minister."

Authorities said they believe some of the men may have worked at one time for a company that provides food service to airlines at the Detroit airport.

Several detainees have been flown to New York, where the grand jury is working and where prosecutors have significant anti-terrorism experience from earlier cases involving bin Laden.

These detainees include Ayub Ali Khan, 51, and Mohammed Jaweed Azmath, 47, two men who left the Newark, N.J., airport aboard a flight headed for Texas about the same time as the hijackings. The men were grounded in St. Louis and then took a train toward Texas, where they were taken into custody. They had $5,000 cash and box cutters like those used by the hijackers, immediately drawing the attention of law enforcement.

Authorities also have flown to New York a French-Algerian man who was detained last month after he sought flight training in Minnesota. The school where he offered to pay for the training was suspicious, and called authorities.

The government has held Zacarias Moussaoui on immigration charges since Aug. 17.

Two weeks before Tuesday attacks, agents had already gathered evidence tracing Moussaoui to an effort to get flight training as early as fall 2000 in Norman, Okla., officials said.

Similarly, the FBI has traced the steps of the 19 known hijackers to flight schools across the country, from Maryland to Florida.

The FBI is seeking as many as a dozen others who fit this profile: Middle Eastern men who came to the United States, got pilot licenses or sought flight training, like the men who flew jetliners into the World Trade Center and Pentagon.

"We want to know whether there were other pilots, other teams who were supposed to take down airliners or strike Americans in other ways," one law enforcement official said.

Agents are investigating whether some associates of the 19 hijackers planned or did board other planes, possibly with similar plans for suicide hijackings that weren't carried out.

Vice President Dick Cheney hinted at such additional hijackings during a TV appearance Sunday when he said U.S. authorities believed six planes were targeted by the hijackers last week.

Law enforcement has gathered evidence suggesting the plot was patiently hatched over many months and years, and that the terrorists spent significant time training for it and grooming supporters.

Many of the hijackers trained or sought training in flight schools as early as 1999, and most entered the United States with legal visas. Some of the hijackers met with supporters overseas, in places like Germany and Malaysia, before returning to carry out their plan, officials said.

"One of the keys to understanding this is the length of time these hijackers spent here. These weren't people coming over the border just to attack quickly. . . . They cultivated friends, and blended into American society to further their ability to strike," one investigator said.

Authorities said the fact that some of the men claimed to have connections to Middle Eastern countries friendly to the United States—Saudi Arabia, Egypt and United Arab Emirates—may have lessened suspicion. Some of the pilots carried identification suggesting they were connected with Saudi Arabia's national airline.

The FBI has pressed for evidence across the globe as to who may have assisted the hijackers, seizing bank and computer records and studying credit cards used to pay for plane tickets, rental cars and the like.

A doctor in San Antonio, where the two Newark, N.J., passengers were heading, has been detained, as has a man in California who has been linked through financial transactions to hijackers Khalid al-Mihdhar and Nawaf al-Hamzi, authorities said.

Al-Mihdhar and al-Hamzi were placed on a watch list this summer after U.S. intelligence received information they might have been meeting with suspected terrorists. By the time they were added to the watch list, they'd already entered the United States, officials said.

On the financial trail, the Securities and Exchange Commission has received information from other U.S. regulators about possi-

A New York City police officer stands guard at a checkpoint on the corner of Nassau and Liberty near the New York Stock Exchange in the Financial District of Manhattan, Sept. 18, 2001. Visible on the barrier is the front page of the *New York Post* with a photograph of Osama bin Laden and the headline reading: "WANTED DEAD OR ALIVE."

bly suspicious trading ahead of the attacks. European regulators are looking to see if bin Laden's network sought to profit off investments related to the attacks.

The potential collaborators are also being linked by communication intercepts—some of which have occurred since the attacks, authorities told AP. ∎

CHAPTER 3
THE WORLD REACTS

It did not take long for the world to react to the attack on the United States. Among the first responses was a strong condemnation of America from Iraqi president Saddam Hussein, who boldly stated the day after the attack: "Those who do not want to harvest evil should not plant evil." He claimed that America was being punished for the U.N. sanctions that it supported against Iraq since Baghdad's invasion of neighboring Kuwait in 1990.

Saddam had little company. Support for the United States was building. On Sept. 12, NATO and the United Nations endorsed the U.S. call to battle terrorism. NATO Secretary-General Lord Robertson pronounced that "An attack on one is an attack on all." The U.N. Security Council called the attacks "a threat to international peace and security" and promised to combat terrorism "by all means."

Individual nations stepped up to the plate, too. Canada offered its airports as a refuge while American flights were grounded. More than 200 airliners were diverted toward Canadian airports, and passengers slept on concourses, in schools, church halls, lodges—any place they could find respite.

In Berlin, over 200,000 people gathered at the Brandenburg Gate in solidarity. In South Korea, sirens blared in a one-minute tribute to America and schoolchildren knelt outside the U.S. Embassy. British shoppers and pedestrians stood at attention to honor fallen firefighters; European stock exchanges stopped business transactions in a three-minute tribute; fishermen in Iceland stood in silence at the Reykjavík docks.

Some Middle Eastern countries were also quick to condemn the attack. In Yemen, prominent officials and journalists gathered at the U.S. Embassy to offer condolences. Even Iran, longtime adversary of the U.S., exhibited solidarity, as 60,000 sports fans participated in a moment of silence during the World Cup qualifying matches in Tehran.

On Sept. 20, President Bush spoke before Congress to assure the legislature and the nation that a plan of action was already in motion, including a new cabinet-level office to fortify what was being called "homeland security." Tom Ridge, the governor of Pennsylvania, was slated to be the first director of the Office of Homeland Security. The U.S. response would go much further, Bush announced. America's armed forces were to "be ready" for battle, proclaiming: "The hour is coming when America will act, and you will make us proud." And his demand to the Taliban religious militia, the ruling party in Afghanistan, was clear: Surrender all of the leaders of al-Qaida that hide in Afghanistan and hand over every terrorist, release all imprisoned foreign nationals and give the U.S. access to the terrorist training camps to make sure they are closed.

They refused. The campaign dubbed "Operation Enduring Freedom" would soon be underway.

On Sunday, Oct. 7, Tomahawk cruise missiles began to fire on terrorist targets in Afghanistan. The capital, Kabul, was bombarded relentlessly. To its south, the city of Kandahar—the headquarters of the Taliban and home to its leader, Mullah Mohammed Omar—was also struck and badly damaged. Despite the encouraging news, it was also reported that Omar and bin Laden had survived the onslaught. In nearby Pakistan, influential clerics declared America's response was an attack against Islam and grounds for a holy war.

At home, on Oct. 26, President Bush signed the USA Patriot Act, an antiterrorism bill that gave unprecedented power for federal authorities to "search seize, detain or eavesdrop in the pursuit of possible terrorists." It was a controversial move in a nation built on civil liberties, but to many Americans it mattered little and the president correctly predicted that the nation at large would be supportive. The previous week it was reported that his approval rating hovered at 90 percent, with bipartisan political support, and it seemed to be in little jeopardy of falling.

On Dec. 10, news broke that bin Laden had been located in Afghanistan's Tora Bora cave complex, where al-Qaida troops were hiding him deep within the White Mountains. Days of constant bombing by high-flying B-52s proved to be dramatic television, but bin Laden escaped and was suspected to have fled to Pakistan.

A memorial gate erected at the crash site of United Airlines Flight 93 in Shanksville, Pa., is covered with mementos from people from all over the world in honor of the victims of the 9/11 attacks, c. 2002.

AP Wire, Thursday, September 13, 2001

NATO, U.N. SAY ATTACK ON U.S. IS ATTACK ON ALL

By *CONSTANT BRAND*
The Associated Press

BRUSSELS, Belgium (AP)—Building support in its battle against terrorism, the United States won key endorsements from NATO and the United Nations for punishing those responsible for the attacks against symbols of American financial and military power.

NATO's governing council declared Wednesday night that if the attacks were directed from abroad, they would be considered an attack against all 19 NATO member nations.

The unprecedented NATO decision was taken after the U.N. Security Council in New York unanimously condemned the terrorist attacks "as a threat to international peace and security" and vowed to combat terrorist acts "by all means."

Although the council resolution gave no explicit authority for an armed attack, international law provides for military intervention to combat threats to "international peace and security."

The UN flag flies at half-staff above UN headquarters in Geneva, Switzerland, Sept. 13, 2001. All the flags along the road leading to the Palais des Nations were removed; as is customary, when the United Nations flag is at half-mast, no other national flags are flown.

The two decisions represented diplomatic victories for the United States as it tries to determine who was responsible for the biggest terrorist attacks in American history. Suspicion has fallen on Saudi billionaire Osama bin Laden, who lives in Afghanistan.

In taking its decision, the 19 NATO ambassadors agreed to allow Washington to invoke Article 5 of NATO's charter—a first in the alliance's 52-year history. Article 5, designed to respond to a Cold War offensive, declares an "armed attack" on any member to be an attack on all. That means the United States will be able to count on support from its 18 NATO partners for any potential military response.

"An attack on one is an attack on all," NATO Secretary-General Lord Robertson said, while emphasizing that no military action had yet been decided upon.

U.S. Secretary of State Colin Powell said invoking the solidarity principle would not necessarily mean using NATO forces against terrorists and their protectors. Rather, Powell said, NATO allies could provide support such as overflight rights. NATO said that America's allies "stand ready to provide the assistance that may be required as a consequence of these acts of barbarism."

Following NATO's action, major European leaders underscored their personal support for the United States in the face of the crisis.

"They were not only attacks on the people in the United States, our friends in America, but also against the entire civilized world, against our own freedom, against our own values, values which we share with the American people," German Chancellor Gerhard Schroeder said in Berlin. "We will not let these values be destroyed—in Europe, America or anywhere in the world," Schroeder added. "I am convinced that together we will weather this criminal challenge."

French Prime Minister Lionel Jospin said governments that encourage terrorism must be made to act responsibly. "It is obvious that it is their responsibility to fight terrorism in their own territory, not to encourage terrorist ideas," Jospin said in a television interview. "If not, they risk paying the consequences, and that is logical."

In a separate show of allied solidarity, the European Union pledged Wednesday to help U.S. authorities track down and punish those responsible for Tuesday's attacks.

The EU foreign ministers, at a special meeting, asked all Europeans to observe three minutes of silence at noon Friday.

"There will be no safe haven for terrorists and their sponsors," the EU ministers said in a statement. "The Union will work closely with the United States and all partners to combat international terrorism." ∎

SADDAM SAYS AMERICA IS HARVESTING ITS THORNS

BAGHDAD, Iraq, Sept. 12, 2001 (AP)—The United States is harvesting the thorns that it has planted around the world, Iraq President Saddam Hussein said Wednesday.

The official Iraqi News Agency quoted Saddam as speaking to his top generals about Tuesday's terror attacks in New York and Washington.

State-run media have portrayed the catastrophe as the United States receiving due punishment for the U.N. sanctions that it has supported against Iraq since the 1990 invasion of Kuwait.

"Those who do not want to harvest evil, should not plant evil," Saddam said. "Those who think that their people's lives are dear to them, must think that the lives of the world's people are dear too. America is exporting evil, not only wherever their army lands, but even where their movies land too."

Wearing a gray suit, Saddam was shown on Iraqi television talking to his chief military advisers at a long table.

"Despite the contradictory humanitarian feelings on what happened in America yesterday, America is harvesting the thorns that its rulers have planted in the world."

"There is no place without a statue pointing to American criminal acts," he added.

"Nobody has crossed the Atlantic carrying weapons against America. [But] it has crossed the Atlantic carrying death and destruction to the whole world." ∎

Iraqi President Saddam Hussein holds up a rifle during a military parade in Baghdad, Dec. 31, 2000.

AP Wire, Friday, September 14, 2001

PEOPLE AROUND THE WORLD UNITE IN SYMPATHY AND FRIENDSHIP WITH GRIEVING AMERICANS

By AUDREY WOODS
The Associated Press

LONDON (AP)—Millions of people gathered in silence around the world Friday to express sympathy and friendship for an American nation grieving for the victims of Tuesday's fiery airborne strikes on New York and the Pentagon.

Many reached back half a century to the still-fresh memory of American help received in time of need, and declared their continuing commitment to that old friendship.

More than 200,000 Berliners filled the broad boulevard leading to the Brandenburg Gate in a heartfelt demonstration of solidarity with the country that helped rebuild post-war Germany and sustained the divided city with an airlift during the Soviet blockade.

"No one knows better than the people here in Berlin what America has done for freedom and democracy in Germany," President Johannes Rau said.

"Therefore we say to all Americans from Berlin: America does not stand alone."

The global day of mourning for thousands who died in Tuesday's suicide attacks on the World Trade Center and the Pentagon began in Asia.

Sirens blared for one minute in South Korea and young children appeared outside the American Embassy in Seoul. Some knelt before the building and prayed silently.

In Iran, antipathy toward the United States was briefly set aside as 60,000 spectators sat quiet in their seats at Tehran stadium and players stood silently on the field for one minute before a World Cup qualifying match.

In the Arabian Peninsula nation of Yemen, more than 100 journalists, intellectuals and government officials gathered at the U.S. Embassy in Sana'a to offer condolences.

In Europe, stock exchanges from Norway to Austria stopped business for three minutes. In Britain, people stood silently in shopping centers and firefighters stood at attention outside their stations as a mark of respect for the American firefighters lost in rescue efforts. In Finland, cabbies pulled to the side of the road. In Iceland, fishermen stood in silence at the Reykjavik docks.

Passengers stand in front of a television screen at the main train station in Frankfurt, Germany, Sept. 13, 2001. The display reads: "Ladies and Gentlemen, the American people were hit by an act of terror on September 11. We feel sorrow for the victims of the attack. We empathize with the relatives of the victims, their friends and with all American people. We ask our employees and customers to observe a minute of silence."

LEFT: **Traffic and pedestrians come to a complete standstill at Parliament Square in London, for three minutes of silence for the victims of the terrorist attacks on the United States, Sept. 14, 2001. As described by the Archbishop of Canterbury, the moments of silence—observed by millions across Europe—served as a "a message of love and solidarity, a message also of hope" toward the American people.**

BELOW: **British ambassador William Farish (center) is flanked by U.S. Marines, police officers, fellow employees, and Londoners during three minutes of silence for the victims of the terrorist attacks on the United States, Sept. 14, 2001, at the American embassy in Grosvenor Square.**

CANADIANS SCRAMBLE TO PUT UP PASSENGERS FROM DIVERTED FLIGHTS

OTTAWA, Sept. 13, 2001 (AP)—Some stayed in their planes overnight, while others slept in hotel corridors, in the beds of strangers, on cots in school gyms and anywhere else Canadians could find for thousands of unexpected guests.

More than 200 jetliners heading for the United States on Tuesday were diverted to Canada after the terrorist attacks in New York and Washington, overwhelming services at airports and communities across the nation.

The U.S. and Canadian governments said Wednesday that the planes would be allowed to proceed to their U.S. destinations, but officials said they doubted all the planes could take off by Wednesday night. Busloads of passengers already had left some cities for the U.S. border.

In Gander, Newfoundland, a remote town connected to an international airport built before World War II, 38 planes carried in 6,500 passengers; the town's population is 10,000.

Most had to sleep on the airliners Tuesday night because of the problems of clearing so many people through customs and finding them lodging. The planes were finally emptied Wednesday morning.

More than 300 people on a charter flight from Manchester, England, to Orlando, Fla., were taken to St. Paul's Intermediate School after spending 22 hours on the tarmac without being told why.

"We were really in the dark. We did not know how serious it had been until we got off," George Gemmell of Ayr, Scotland said.

With Gander's hotels occupied mostly by flight crews, passengers were taken to schools, the community center, fire stations, camps, lodges and church halls. A military transport flew in 5,000 cots. Stores donated blankets, coffee pots, plastic foam cups, cases of coffee and food, and grills were set up to cook hot dogs and hamburgers. Residents took some people home for showers.

In Halifax, Nova Scotia, about 7,000 people on 44 planes endured waits on the aircraft of up to six hours while sniffer dogs checked the planes and baggage, then stood in 90-minute lines for immigration and luggage. Planes also landed at Toronto, Montreal, Moncton, New Brunswick, Vancouver, British Columbia, and Whitehorse, Yukon Territory. ∎

The story of Gander, Canada and 9/11 was turned into a popular, award-winning musical called *Come from Away*, which premiered on Broadway in New York in 2017. Here, the marquee of the touring version of the show at the Comedy Theatre in Melbourne, Australia, Sept. 26, 2019.

Several hundred Bosnian Muslims attend Friday prayers at the newly opened mosque in the Bosnian town of Bugojno, Sept. 14, 2001. Bosnia's Muslims devoted their prayers this day to the victims of the terrorism attacks in the United States.

Thousands of people, many of them Americans, filled St. Paul's Cathedral in London and overflowed into the surrounding plaza for a prayer service attended by Queen Elizabeth II and Prime Minister Tony Blair.

Tariq Muhammad Dhamial, a native of Pakistan, stood out in traditional Sunni Muslim black garb, a green head band and long beard. "I am here to show as a Muslim that we condemn these acts," he said.

Inside, Archbishop of Canterbury George Carey said that although the World Trade Center had disappeared in smoke and carnage, "another, older, American icon was not submerged. The September morning sun continued to shine on the Statue of Liberty, her torch raised like a beacon . . . a symbol of all that is best in America."

French President Jacques Chirac stood to attention in front of a military honor guard at the Élysée Palace in Paris, and the Republican Guard played "The Star-Spangled Banner."

Most European nations observed a three-minute silence in the morning or at noon as banks of floral bouquets swelled outside American embassies.

In Serbia, an exception, authorities called no period of mourning.

In Greece, many observed three minutes of silence, but others continued their argument that America had brought this evil upon itself through its political and military actions. Many Greeks hold Washington responsible for a litany of regional troubles that runs from the Greek civil war in the late 1940s to the bombing of Yugoslavia two years ago.

More than 2,000 people carrying candles marched in the rain to the American Embassy in Warsaw, where they left candles and flowers. Many banners read "America, We are with you."

South Africans people lined up to sign books of condolence outside the U.S. Embassy in Pretoria, and President Thabo Mbeki said those responsible had demeaned whatever cause they stood for.

"All human beings . . . will surely be engulfed by a deep sense of shame that human society is still capable of producing people who can deliberately plan and execute a crime as heinous as the crime that was perpetrated in the United States earlier this week," Mbeki wrote in a letter carried on the ruling African National Congress Internet site.

In Havana, two dozen workers filed out of the Spanish Embassy, standing solemnly on the sidewalk to observe three minutes of silence while the Spanish flag flew at half-staff. Several other European embassies in Havana did the same at noon.

Cuban President Fidel Castro has condemned the attacks and expressed sympathy for the American people.

Colombian President Andrés Pastrana attended a Mass at the presidential palace in Bogota and invited all Colombians to observe a minute of prayer to coincide with a prayer service in the National Cathedral in Washington.

In Ottawa, tens of thousands of Canadians gathered under bright midday sunshine for a nationwide ceremony attended by Prime Minister Jean Chrétien and U.S. Ambassador Paul Cellucci. ■

AP Wire, Thursday, September 20, 2001

BUSH TO CONGRESS AND THE NATION: AMERICA AWAKENED TO DANGER, CALLED TO DEFEND FREEDOM

By SANDRA SOBIERAJ
The Associated Press

WASHINGTON (AP)—President Bush cautioned a shaken nation Thursday that there are "struggles ahead and dangers to face" as American combats global terrorism. He announced that Pennsylvania Gov. Tom Ridge will direct a new cabinet-level office to fortify homeland defenses.

Addressing a joint session of Congress nine days after suicide hijackers are believed to have killed more than 6,000 Americans, Bush clasped the badge of a slain policeman in his fist.

"I will not forget this wound to our country, or those who inflicted it. I will not yield. I will not rest," he said. The Sept. 11 attacks had put the United States on notice that the world's only superpower was not immune to attack, Bush said.

He blamed Osama bin Laden and demanded that Afghanistan's ruling Taliban militia surrender the suspected terrorist and give the United States full access to terrorist training camps. Bush directed U.S. military forces to "be ready" for the gathering battle: "The hour is coming when America will act and you will make us proud."

Bush asked every nation to take part, by contributing police forces, intelligence services and banking information.

With British Prime Minister Tony Blair watching from a House gallery seat at First Lady Laura Bush's right arm, Bush said: "The civilized world is rallying to America's side. They understand that if terror goes unpunished, their own cities, their own citizens may be next. Terror unanswered cannot only bring down buildings, it can threaten the stability of legitimate governments and we will not allow it."

Bush entered the House of Representatives chamber to rousing applause from both sides of the aisle, Democrats and Republicans alike.

Unprecedented security shrouded his address in the Capitol one week after it was evacuated for the second time because of suspected threats. Vice President Dick Cheney stayed away, due to security concerns. Speaker Dennis Hastert, R-Ill., third in line for the presidency, was in the vice president's customary seat behind Bush on the speaker's rostrum. Sen. Robert C. Byrd, D-W.Va., next in line as the Senate president pro tempore, sat beside Hastert.

Bush compared the terrorists to the 20th century world's evil forces: "By sacrificing human life to serve their radical visions—by abandoning every value except the will to power—they follow in the path of fascism and Nazism and totalitarianism. And they will follow that path all the way to where it ends, in history's unmarked grave of discarded lives."

In a nationally televised address, his fourth prime-time speech since taking office, Bush tried to explain to a horrified nation the anti-American hatred of its enemies.

Bush blamed last week's attacks on suspected terrorist Osama bin Laden and his followers—the same forces suspected of bombing American embassies in Tanzania and Kenya and last year's bombing of the USS *Cole*.

"The terrorists' directive commands them to kill Christians and Jews, to kill all Americans and make no distinctions among military and civilians, including women and children," Bush said.

Bush condemned the Taliban religious militia that rules most of Afghanistan and gives bin Laden refuge. He demanded that the Taliban turn over to the United States all the leaders of bin Laden's network "who hide in your land," and to release all foreign nationals, including American citizens who have been imprisoned in Afghanistan.

Further, Bush demanded that the Taliban "close immediately and permanently every terrorist camp in Afghanistan and hand over every terrorist and every person in their support structure to appropriate authorities."

Moreover, Bush demanded full U.S. access to terrorist training camps in Afghanistan "so we can make sure they are no longer operating."

These demands are not open to discussion, Bush said. "They will hand over the terrorists or they will share in their fate."

Even as he spoke of wiping out terrorism, Bush conceded that the violent extremists had already extracted a heavy toll. "Great

President George W. Bush holds the badge of a Port Authority police officer killed in the Sept. 11 attacks during his address to a joint session of Congress at the U.S. Capitol, Sept. 20, 2001.

harm has been done to us. We have suffered great loss and in our grief and anger we have found our mission and our moment. Freedom and fear are at war," he said.

While cautioning that Americans need remain on alert, Bush said, "It is my hope that in the months and years ahead, life will return almost to normal."

He asked for patience. He warned of more casualties. This war against elusive terrorists, he said, "will not look like the air war above Kosovo two years ago, where no ground troops were used and not a single American was lost in combat."

He said it would be a war unlike any in history. "It may include dramatic strikes, visible on television, and covert operations, secret even in success."

Still, he assured the nation, "We'll go back to our lives and routines, and that is good. Even grief recedes with time and grace. But our resolve must not pass."

Before leaving the White House for Capitol Hill, Bush gathered international and spiritual support. He separately huddled with Blair and Saudi Foreign Minister Saud al-Faisal, who delivered his country's support.

A Methodist himself, Bush welcomed two dozen religious leaders—Catholics, Protestants, Orthodox Christians, Jews, Muslims, Sikhs, Hindus and Buddhists—to pray with him and give counsel and sing together "God Bless America." Archbishop Demetrios C. Trakatellis, whose Greek Orthodox Church of New York was destroyed in last week's bombing, called the private meeting with Bush "a religious ceremony in front of God." ■

President Bush receives a standing ovation during his address to Congress, Sept. 20, 2001.

AP Wire, Monday, September 24, 2001

NATIONS BACK U.N. IN TERRORISM FIGHT

By EDITH M. LEDERER
The Associated Press

UNITED NATIONS—(AP) Secretary-General Kofi Annan's call Monday for the United Nations to play a major role in the long-term international fight against terrorism won immediate support from the United States, Russia and China. But the world body still struggled over what it can and should do.

Addressing a scaled-down meeting of the General Assembly, Annan declared that only the United Nations can give "global legitimacy" to the long-term struggle against "the unspeakable horror" of terrorism. He urged all countries to work together to strengthen international peace and security "by cementing the ties among nations, and not subjecting them to new strains." . . .

Backing Annan, [Russian Foreign Minister Igor] Ivanov told the General Assembly that the United Nations should lead any global action against terrorism and warned against moves that could erode international law.

"It is necessary to strengthen and enhance the role of the United Nations as an indispensable instrument for maintaining international peace and security and for mobilizing people of the world against new, unprecedented threats," he said.

China's U.N. Ambassador Wang Yingfan urged all countries to strengthen cooperation "and make joint efforts for the sake of their common interests to prevent and combat all forms of terrorist activities."

"The United Nations should play an important role in this regard," he said.

Cameron Hume, the third-ranking U.S. diplomat, said "the entire (U.N.) membership has a new and overarching challenge after Sept. 11," which must be met by a global response.

Supporting the secretary-general, he said: "The U.N. must play an international role in marshaling the international community's long-term efforts to defeat this scourge."

"This is a crucial moment for the United Nations," Hume said. "It has a chance to live up to the ideals on which it was founded. The United States pledges its support to the United Nations."

The new U.S. ambassador, John Negroponte, who presented his credentials last week, was on the list of speakers, but U.S. officials said he had a previously scheduled appointment with the New Zealand ambassador.

The secretary-general did not address specific measures in his speech, but last week he said U.N. member states must stop providing shelter and logistical support for terrorists, halt the laundering of money used to finance terrorist acts, and share information on terrorists and their organizations.

Annan said Monday he expects the General Assembly at its Oct. 1 plenary meeting on international terrorism to stress the urgency for all nations to ratify, and above all implement, a dozen legally binding conventions and protocols to fight terrorism and to consider new ones.

Hume said the United States hopes next week's meeting "will promote unity of purpose and strong steps that the U.N. can take to combat terror." He gave no indication of what steps Washington was seeking.

"These efforts will also require absolute clarity that the international community condemns and rejects any effort to offer false justification for the attack or to protect those who committed it," he said.

In somber tones, Annan told diplomats in the hushed General Assembly chamber that the attacks struck at everything the United Nations stands for: "peace, freedom, tolerance, human rights, the very idea of a united family." ■

United Nations Secretary General Kofi Annan signs a book of condolences in the lobby of the U.N. headquarters building for the victims of the World Trade Center attack, Sept. 24, 2001, before leading a scaled-down meeting of the General Assembly.

AP Wire, Sunday, October 7, 2001

BUSH ANNOUNCES STRIKE ON AFGHANISTAN

By SCOTT LINDLAW
The Associated Press

WASHINGTON (AP)—Bundled against Sunday's unseasonable cold, President Bush bowed his head in prayer for wisdom, for the salvation of firefighters killed in the crumble of the World Trade Center. He had already, in secret the night before, ordered retaliation for their deaths.

"We did not ask for this mission, but we will fulfill it," Bush told the nation. At midmorning Sunday, the president had returned to the White House from an outdoor service at the National Fallen Firefighters Memorial in rural Maryland. He strode into the Oval Office knowing that, within two hours, Tomahawk cruise missiles would fire upon terrorist targets in Afghanistan.

"I gave them fair warning," he told one adviser. He reached for the phone to alert Russian President Vladimir Putin.

Military action under Operation Enduring Freedom was "imminent," Bush told French President Jacques Chirac.

At 12:30 p.m. EDT, 26 days of horror, grief, investigation and ultimatums culminated in a shower of missiles over Kabul, the Afghan capital and headquarters of its ruling Taliban militia. The Taliban had refused Bush's demands to surrender prime terror suspect Osama bin Laden.

White House press secretary Ari Fleischer described the president's mood as resolute. There were signs of anxiousness, as well.

Minutes before he addressed the nation from the Treaty Room, Bush could be heard over an open audio feed impatiently ordering his personal aide to empty the room. "Clear 'em out, Logan," Bush barked. To the country, Bush announced, "The battle is now joined on many fronts." His speech, in the works for at least 36 hours, had gone through a half-dozen drafts. He acknowledged that many Americans fear the terrorists will strike again.

Underscoring that possibility, Vice President Dick Cheney was removed from his official residence to a secret, safer place. The street in front of the State Department was closed. . . .

Bush, his piece said to the public, hunkered down inside to monitor military operations. He paused for lunch with senior advisers in the Roosevelt Room. It was then that bin Laden's videotaped statement first aired, thanking God that America was "full of fear."

Bush, Cheney and Secretary of State Colin Powell divided up a call list, together reaching more than a dozen foreign leaders from Canada to Israel to Egypt to Pakistan. The windup was methodical—and held secret over several days. On Wednesday, the United States told Britain which of its air bases, aircraft and submarines would be needed. At 8:30 a.m. Saturday, Defense Secretary Donald Rumsfeld, just off the plane from grueling military consultations in the Middle East and Central Asia, briefed Bush by teleconference. Within hours, a small circle of advisers knew the operation would begin in the next day or two.

Bush gave House and Senate leaders the heads-up on Saturday night, telephoning senior Democrats and Republicans just after he gave the Pentagon his go-ahead order to strike as soon as strategic and intelligence officials knew the time was right.

It was 12:34 p.m. EDT Sunday when word came that explosions over Kabul had knocked out the city's electricity.

"We are beginning another front in our war against terrorism," Fleischer announced eight minutes later from the West Wing press briefing room.

Publicly, Bush betrayed no hint of what was in store when he and First Lady Laura Bush left Camp David in the morning,

President Bush poses for a photo in the Treaty Room of the White House in Washington after announcing airstrikes on Afghanistan, Oct. 7, 2001.

skipping Sunday services at the chapel there and heading straight for the nearby firefighters memorial.

In his heavy overcoat, Bush gripped his wife's hand, lowered his head, squeezed his eyes shut. Rev. Bevon Smith gave the invocation:

"We pray for our president, George W. Bush. Grant him wise judgment, determined leadership and firm resolve as he guides our great country through these difficult days." ∎

ABOVE: **President Bush meets with CIA director George Tenet (far left), Vice President Dick Cheney and National Security Advisor Condoleezza Rice, Oct. 7, 2001, in the Oval Office of the White House, the day the president announced airstrikes on Afghanistan.**

LEFT: **A still of Osama bin Laden from a pre-taped statement. The videotape of bin Laden, in a cave-like space at an undisclosed location, was shown on TV news network Al Jazeera shortly after the beginning of the American-led attacks in Afghanistan, Oct. 7, 2001.**

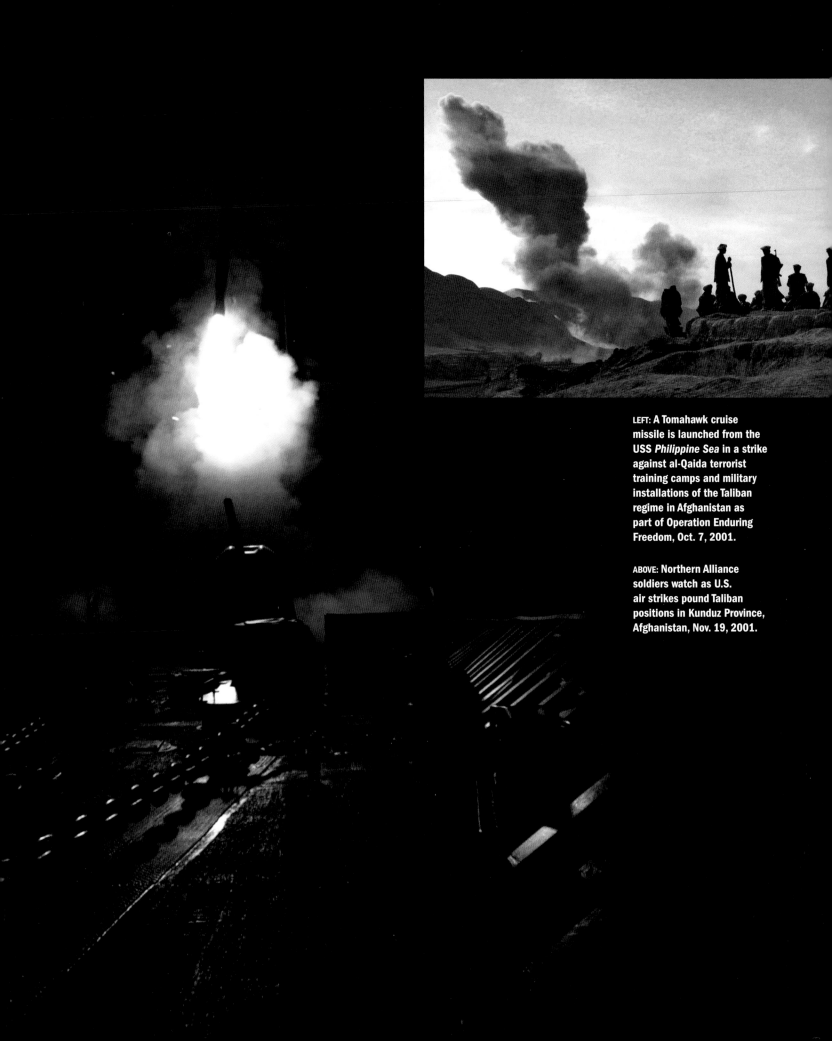

LEFT: A Tomahawk cruise missile is launched from the USS *Philippine Sea* in a strike against al-Qaida terrorist training camps and military installations of the Taliban regime in Afghanistan as part of Operation Enduring Freedom, Oct. 7, 2001.

ABOVE: Northern Alliance soldiers watch as U.S. air strikes pound Taliban positions in Kunduz Province, Afghanistan, Nov. 19, 2001.

EXPLOSIONS ROCK AFGHANISTAN AS U.S. AND BRITAIN LAUNCH MILITARY STRIKE; BIN LADEN REPORTEDLY ALIVE

By AMIR SHAH
The Associated Press

KABUL, Afghanistan (AP)—Thunderous explosions rocked the Afghan capital on Sunday night as the United States and Britain launched a military attack in Afghanistan. The country's ruling Taliban militia declared the assault a "terrorist attack" and said Osama bin Laden and the Taliban's leader had survived.

The strike began after nightfall Sunday in Kabul with five thunderous blasts followed by the sounds of anti-aircraft fire. Electricity was shut off throughout the city for more than two hours afterward.

The southern Afghan city of Kandahar, headquarters of the Taliban and home of Taliban leader Mullah Mohammed Omar, was also hit and the airport control tower was damaged, a Taliban source said by telephone. The source, speaking on condition of anonymity, said several explosions occurred in the eastern city of Jalalabad but he did not have further details.

Without citing sources, Qatar's Al-Jazeera television said the strikes destroyed the Taliban headquarters in Kandahar. Al-Jazeera is often one of the first sources of information on bin Laden.

In Pakistan, Taliban ambassador Abdul Salam Zaeef told reporters that bin Laden, the main suspect in the Sept. 11 attacks, and Mullah Omar survived. "By the grace of God, Mullah Omar and bin Laden are alive," Zaeef said. . . .

In Washington, Pentagon officials said the United States and Great Britain launched 50 cruise missiles against terrorist targets inside Afghanistan in an attack that also involved the most sophisticated U.S. warplanes. Defense Secretary Donald H. Rumsfeld said an initial goal of the strikes was to render air defenses ineffective and to wipe out the Taliban's military aircraft.

Gen. Richard Myers, chairman of the Joint Chiefs of Staff, said 15 bombers and 25 strike aircraft, both sea and land-based, launched the missiles at 12:30 p.m. EDT, or 9 p.m. Kabul time. Myers, sworn into office less than a week ago, said the attacks included B-1, B-2 and B-52 bombers as well as ships and submarines in the region.

President Bush gave a live televised address after the strikes began, saying U.S. and British forces are taking "targeted actions"

against Taliban military capabilities and bin Laden's al-Qaida network.

In the days following the strikes at the World Trade Center and Pentagon, the president had issued a series of demands for the Taliban to hand over bin Laden, a Saudi exile. The Taliban offered to negotiate but refused a handover. "Now the Taliban will pay a price," Bush vowed.

A senior Pentagon official, speaking on condition of anonymity, said targets included air defenses, military communication sites and terrorist training camps inside Afghanistan.

Power went off throughout Kabul almost immediately after the first of the thunderous blasts, which appeared to have been in the southwest of the city. The southwestern part of Kabul includes the Darulaman Palace, an ancient royal residence, and the Balahisar Fort, an old Mogul style installation. The firing tapered off for a few minutes but resumed after a jet aircraft could be heard passing over the city.

The private, Islamabad-based Afghan Islamic Press agency quoted the Taliban as saying American planes had bombed areas near the Kabul airport in the northern part of the city. The agency said there were no details of casualties and no reports of damage to the city itself. It added, however, that "huge smoke is rising near Kabul airport."

In a statement carried by Afghan Islamic Press, an unnamed Taliban spokesman in Kandahar said all provincial airports in the country appeared to have been targeted "but we have not suffered any major damage." He said U.S. forces attacked Osama bin Laden's former residence in Kandahar, located near the airport.

Electricity was restored in Kabul more than two hours after the attack and the city was quiet, with no sign of panic. Kabul's one million people are inured to war after more than two decades of relentless fighting that has destroyed most of the city.

In their first official reaction, the Taliban called the assault a terrorist attack and vowed that America "will never achieve its goal." The statement was issued by Zaeef, the ambassador to Pakistan. Later, Taliban Deputy Defense Minister Mullah Nour Ali said "the people of Afghanistan will resist. They will never accept the rule of infidels."

Also Sunday, Al-Jazeera carried a tape which showed bin Laden praising God for the Sept. 11 attacks and saying the United States "was hit by God in one of its softest spots."

The tape, released after the U.S. and British strikes began, showed bin Laden dressed in fatigues and an Afghan headdress. It appeared to be daylight, which would mean that the tape was made before the nighttime attack Sunday.

"America is full of fear from its north to its south, from its west to its east. Thank God for that," bin Laden said on the tape. . . . "I swear to God that America will never dream of security or see it before we live it and see it in Palestine, and not before the infidel's armies leave the land of Muhammad, peace be upon him."

The Pakistani government, which has thrown its support to the U.S.-led coalition against terrorism, said it regretted that diplomatic efforts did not succeed and called for the U.S. action to remain "clearly targeted."

Pakistan had been the Taliban's closest ally until the Sept. 11 attacks. But Pakistani government spokesman Rashid Qureshi confirmed that Pakistan's airspace was used by U.S. and British forces to launch attacks Sunday night, and in the town of Chaman vehicles carrying Pakistani soldiers could be seen heading for the Afghan border.

Not all in Pakistan were behind the strikes, however. The influential and Taliban-sympathetic Afghan Defense Council, based in the eastern Pakistani city of Lahore, issued a call for "jihad," or holy war. The council comprises more than 30 religious and militant groups.

"It is the duty of every Muslim to support their brothers in this critical hour," central leader Riaz Durana said.

Earlier Sunday, the Taliban had made an 11th-hour appeal to prevent U.S. attacks: They offered to detain bin Laden and try him under Islamic law if the United States made a formal request. The Bush administration quickly rejected the Taliban proposal, with White House spokesman Scott McClellan saying Bush's demands "are clear and nonnegotiable."

Washington has also rejected Afghanistan's attempt to use eight jailed foreign aid workers as bargaining chips to pressure the United States to halt its planned anti-terrorist offensive. The eight aid workers in Kabul—four Germans, two Americans and two Australians—were arrested in August on charges of trying to convert Muslims to Christianity.

In a statement before the U.S. attacks began, the Taliban said they had sent thousands of troops to the border with Uzbekistan whose president has allowed U.S. troops use of an air base for the anti-terrorism campaign. Those claims about sending troops to the Uzbekistan border could not be independently verified.

However, Russia's Interfax news agency reported Saturday that Taliban troops were moving long-range artillery and multiple rocket launchers toward the border. More than 10 guns and rocket launchers had moved within range of the Uzbek border town of Termez, Interfax said, quoting Afghan opposition sources.

The Taliban are estimated to have some 40,000 fighters—around a quarter of them from bin Laden's organization—and many of those are involved in fighting a coalition of opposition forces in northern Afghanistan. The Taliban's enemies had made little progress against the larger, better-armed Taliban, but their fortunes have been bolstered since the Sept. 11 attacks with a decision by Russia to step up weapons shipments.

AFTER ATTACK ON AFGHANISTAN, CONDEMNATION IN PAKISTAN

By MUNIR AHMAD
The Associated Press

ISLAMABAD, Pakistan, Oct. 7, 2001 (AP)—Some of Pakistan's most influential clerics swiftly denounced U.S.-led strikes on Afghanistan's capital Sunday, calling them an attack against Islam and grounds for holy war. . . . Pakistan's government, which has thrown its support behind the U.S.-led coalition against terrorism, said it regretted that diplomatic efforts had failed and called for the U.S. action to remain "clearly targeted." There were scattered anti-American protests in major cities and threats of more demonstrations, but no violence was reported. . . .

After Sunday's attacks, the influential Afghan Defense Council, based in the eastern Pakistani city of Lahore, issued a call for holy war. "It is the duty of every Muslim to support their brothers in this critical hour," council leader Riaz Durana said. "We will support the Taliban physically and morally against the aggression of America."

Munawar Hassan, deputy chief of Jamaat-e-Islami, Pakistan's most powerful religious political party, called the strikes "an attack against Islam." President Bush has emphasized that the United States has no quarrel with Islam, only with terrorists and those who harbor them.

Condemnation also came from the militant group Harakat ul-Mujahedeen, one of several organizations whose assets were frozen by the United States, Pakistan and other countries as part of a campaign against movements linked to Osama bin Laden, the suspected mastermind of the Sept. 11 terrorist attacks.

"Americans have used their might to kill innocent people in Afghanistan instead of targeting training camps," said Amar Mehdi, spokesman for the group, which advocates the independence of Indian-ruled Kashmir.

The Taliban said Monday civilians had been killed in the U.S.-British barrage, though they did not say how many or where. The Pentagon said it was too early to be sure of any deaths.

Rashid Quereshi, a Pakistan government spokesman, said U.S. and British forces used Pakistan's airspace to launch the attacks. In a statement, Pakistan's Foreign Ministry implored the United States to take "every care" to minimize harm to Afghans buffeted by years of war, expressing hopes the operations "will end soon."

Pakistan shares a 1,050-mile border with Afghanistan. Languages, ethnicities and even family ties overlap, and many Pakistanis, even those with no sympathy for the ruling Taliban militia, are reluctant to see Afghanistan attacked.

In downtown Peshawar, near the Afghan border, knots of men gathered shouting "Osama! Osama!" and "America is a terrorist." ∎

A U.S. Consulate–sponsored matchbook with a picture of al-Qaida leader Osama bin Laden accompanied by an Urdu-language message offering a reward for his capture, Feb. 16, 2000. The matchbooks were circulated in the frontier city of Peshawar, Pakistan, on the border with Afghanistan. The message promised confidentiality for any informer. It also carried a misprint in the reward, offering $500,000 instead of the $5 million announced by Washington.

The Only Western Correspondents in Taliban-Controlled Kabul

By KATHY GANNON

AP News Director, Afghanistan and Pakistan

In the early evening of Sept. 11, 2001, I received a phone call from New York, where it was morning. It was Sally Jacobsen, my boss and the AP's international editor. A plane had hit one of the World Trade Center towers, she told me. It might be an accident, but . . .

Before she could finish her thought, a second plane flew into the second tower. She hung up.

I was in Kabul, the Afghan capital, where six Christian aid workers, including two young American women, were in jail, arrested by the Taliban for proselytizing. Two days earlier, two suicide bombers had killed Ahmad Shah Masoud, who had been fighting the Taliban since they ousted his government in 1996.

In Taliban-run Afghanistan, there were no televisions. They had been outlawed along with music. Radios were the only source of news. Thirty minutes after that call from New York, my Afghan colleague Amir Shah came into our small office on the second floor of the AP house. Another plane had smashed into the Pentagon. What was going on? It had become clear that the first thoughts by AP editors in New York were correct: This was terrorism. And al-Qaida leader Osama bin Laden who had been living in Afghanistan since May 1996, even before the Taliban took power, was they thought, the mastermind.

It seemed just minutes later when Amir Shah said a fourth plane had, unbelievably, crashed into a field. Without a television, with only a crackly broadcast spitting out the most horrific of news, we didn't know what to think. Amir was worried. Was bin Laden behind the attacks? If he was, Amir was sure of one thing: "Afghanistan will be set on fire."

It wasn't until we stopped at the United Nations Guest House where the American parents of the two imprisoned Christian charity workers were staying that I saw the horrifying images of the planes slamming into the towers.

Within 24 hours, the parents would be forced to leave Afghanistan. Was an attack by the United States imminent, I wondered? We had no way to know it would be Oct. 7, nearly a month later, before the assault called Operation Enduring Freedom would begin.

It was nighttime in Kabul, then a city of about 1.5 million people, when the attacks in America happened. Electricity was scarce. The streets were mostly quiet. Small, single-bulb lights illuminated the few shops still open.

Inside, we talked to residents. They couldn't tell you where New York was or what the World Trade Center Towers were. But they understood war, fear and loss. They were sad for America but, like Amir Shah, they feared they would pay the price. They were afraid.

On Sept. 12, Taliban Foreign Minister Wakil Ahmad Muttawakil held a press conference in Kabul's Intercontinental Hotel overlooking the city. He didn't know where bin Laden was, he told reporters. "I just know he is not here," he said with a grin.

In Kabul's well-off Wazir Akbar Khan neighborhood, where the AP office was located, there were several houses with Arabic-speaking men from Middle Eastern and North African countries. The breakaway republic of Chechnya had a consulate office in the region; members of Pakistani militant groups like Jaish-e-Mohammed, which would be linked in March 2002 to the death of American journalist Daniel Pearl, lived close by.

By Sept. 15, the Taliban ordered all foreigners out of Afghanistan, even the Red Cross. From our office in Kabul, I had been booking hotel rooms for the army of AP reporters I knew would be descending on Pakistan, which was also about to close its border with Afghanistan.

I left.

The bombing began on Oct. 7, 2001. The U.S.-led coalition, along with its so-called Northern Alliance allies, a collection of warlords-turned-anti-Taliban fighters who would later be handed power in Kabul, launched an offensive to oust the Taliban.

In the mountains around Kabul, the Taliban had placed anti-aircraft weapons, their only defense against the world's most powerful air force and army. The lights were turned off at night because the Taliban believed that the Americans couldn't hit what they couldn't see, a notion they came to understand was dead wrong.

Amir Shah would call each night and whisper the latest news to me in Islamabad. He would cover the satellite phones—the only communication source—with a scarf so the neighbors, most of whom were Taliban leaders, would not see the light from the devices. We couldn't call him for fear the ringing would be heard. We feared the Taliban would interpret the communication from an American news agency as U.S. spies directing the aircraft fire.

It was Oct. 23 when Amir got permission for me and AP photographer Dimitri Messinis to enter Kabul. We were the only Western journalists allowed into Taliban-controlled areas. Hundreds of journalists were camped out in neighboring Pakistan or

AP Islamabad bureau chief Kathy Gannon reports from the basement of the AP house in Kabul, Afghanistan, during a night of heavy bombing, Oct. 26, 2001. For more than two weeks during the U.S. bombing campaign, she and AP photographer Dimitri Messinis were the only Western correspondents in Kabul. Gannon has reported on Afghanistan for nearly three decades, chronicling the Soviet occupation, the fall of the Taliban and the withdrawal of foreign troops. Kathy Gannon, Dimitri Messinis and Amir Shah are shown together in a photograph on page 1.

in Tajikistan waiting to move with the Northern Alliance, but no western journalist was in Taliban-controlled areas until we arrived.

Kabul had become a city of fear. During the day, there was less bombing and people would venture out. But as darkness settled and the bombing intensified, the streets were deserted but for the occasional Taliban patrol and the howling of what seemed like an army of stray dogs.

Then the B-52 bombers began to circle in low. We moved to the basement. The bombing had gotten closer and closer to the city. One night, the B-52s pounded the hills behind the AP house that were impervious to the anti-aircraft weapons but were home to some of Kabul's poorest citizens. The next morning, we discovered some of the bombs had hit civilian homes that jut out across the hills.

We went to one home where five children had died as they slept. They were still in their beds when we got there. Amir Shah held back the tears. Like him, the children were ethnic Hazaras, perhaps the least prosperous of Afghanistan's ethnic groups.

"They could have been my children," he said.

On Nov. 13, 2001, two months and two days after the 9/11 attacks, the Taliban finally fled Kabul. The night before, a 2,000-pound bomb had slammed into a home that sat kitty-corner to the AP house. It blew me across the room, destroying the window and doorframes.

We fled the house soon after and headed to the Intercontinental Hotel. It was a scary ride through darkened streets. The Taliban knew the city was all but lost. They were jittery, shouting commands. Arabs on motorcycles roared past. We worried because we knew U.S. drones were taking aim; one slammed into a pickup truck not far from us. Later, we learned four Arabs were killed.

Perched on the hilltop, the Intercontinental seemed the perfect vantage point to watch the city. It wasn't yet 5 a.m. when we ventured out on Nov. 13. The sun had just begun to rise over the Hindu Kush Mountains.

The Taliban were gone. ■

Behind the Scenes in Kabul during Operation Enduring Freedom

By AMIR SHAH
AP Kabul Correspondent (retired)

Amir Shah, the now-retired longtime Kabul correspondent for The Associated Press, was the agency's eyes and ears in Afghanistan after the 9/11 attacks, when all foreigners were ordered to leave. His assignment was dangerous, delicate and often terrifying. Here, he remembers some of what happened behind the scenes in those days after the attacks and the early hours of the U.S. bombardment a month later.

ON NAVIGATING KABUL IN THE HOURS AFTER THE 9/11 ATTACKS IN THE U.S.: The first night after the attacks, I didn't sleep for 48 hours. I was working, working, working. The information and culture minister of the Taliban, he says, "Come, I want to talk with you about a couple of things." I go to meet him, and he says, "Be careful, all the Taliban officers left, they went back to Kandahar. The city is controlled by the Arabs, Osama's people. When you take film and pictures before, if they arrested you, I would help you. But this time, nobody can help you. Please don't take pictures and film."

I went to my house to visit my mother and I explained the story to her. She said, "Amir Shah, you have no brother no father, there's no other branch of the family. Don't go out." I said, "I will do my job, my work."

ON THE FIRST NIGHT OF THE AIR WAR BY U.S.-LED FORCES AGAINST THE TALIBAN: My satellite telephone was on the second floor of our old AP compound, and the window was near to the street. I put a blanket on top of me to hide the sound of my talking and giving updates. I was passing all the information to Kathy Gannon in Pakistan.

When the bombarding started the first night, I was talking very quietly. It was so quiet outside. I was telling the story through the phone slowly, very slowly. I was afraid because three days before, the Arabs across the street had been looking at all the houses and seeing who was suspicious to them. I was working alone. I was so afraid. I gave Kathy all of the information from under the blanket, and all through the night I reported.

Several times the city was bombarded. The Kabul AP office was shaking. And we had a full window, one window toward the north and one toward the southeast. So sometimes I'd jump up and look through the north window, sometimes through the southeast window, and I just looked at the scene—what was going on outside. And I just reported that. Because we were under curfew, it was not possible to leave the office at night to find what was going on. So I covered the bombarding from a distance.

The first night, after I passed all the information to Kathy, New York headquarters called me. They said, "What do you see?" And I told them that it was quiet except for the barking of the dogs. Wazir Akbar Khan, the diplomatic area of the city, was completely empty.

Anti-aircraft fire was flying into the sky, and F-16s were flying over Kabul. All the night they dropped bombs, but the bombs were very professionally placed. I thought it would be like the civil war when the Afghan pilots dropped bombs on people's houses, on pharmacies. I remembered that, and I was so worried about my house. So as soon as daylight came at 5 a.m., I took my car and I went to my house. And I saw my house was OK. And when I checked the hospitals, there were no civilian casualties.

I left the AP office to go around the city take some picture and see what was going on. I worked all day and through the second night. I was so sleepy.

ON HOW HE GOT AROUND REPORTING RESTRICTIONS: We needed photos. I had bought a new Corolla, and I had written a letter to the Traffic Department and I got its registration changed from a private car to a taxi. Why? Because in Kabul, there were no new private cars unless you were Taliban. No one else had new cars. But a taxi is low profile. Nobody knew this taxi belonged to a journalist taking pictures. So I was inside the car, looking like a taxi driver, taking pictures when nobody was looking.

One day I was standing in the city and filming, and suddenly a Taliban—a very big man with a long beard—came up. And thought, "Oh, my God, he saw my camera." My camera was a little HandyCam, and when he got close, I put it up to my hair, to my head, and I talked like I was on the phone. I said into the phone, "These infidels destroyed Afghanistan." He looked at me and then he walked away. Afterward, I said to myself, "I cheated him." He never realized it was a camera. ∎

LEFT: Photograph by Amir Shah of residents of Kabul removing belongings from a house damaged from bombardment Sunday, Oct. 21, 2001. Eight civilians, including four children, were allegedly killed when a bomb hit the house.

BELOW: Shah's photograph of Aghan families waiting on a roadside with their belongings to leave Kabul, Sept. 20, 2001.

Friday, October 19, 2001

BUSH SOARS IN THE POLLS

President Bush signs the USA Patriot Act in the East Room of the White House, Oct. 26, 2001. Standing behind the president, from left are: Attorney General John Ashcroft; Sen. Orrin Hatch, R-Utah; Sen. Patrick Leahy, D-Vt; Sen. Harry Reid, D-Nev; Rep. James Sensenbrenner of Wisconsin and Sen. Bob Graham, D-Fla.

By WILL LESTER
The Associated Press

WASHINGTON (AP)—Thrust into the role of wartime leader, President Bush has soared in the polls to a 90 percent approval rating. The political muscle that comes with such a number gives him a strong hand to lead the campaign against terrorism and try to strengthen the economy.

Democrats caution the clout doesn't automatically transfer to partisan political positions on unrelated domestic issues. Leaders from both parties say they expect the administration to try to keep a bipartisan tone on most issues while carrying out the anti-terror battle in coming months.

"He's getting a lot of credit for not passing partisan stuff through the Congress," said Vermont Gov. Howard Dean, a Democrat. "He's done a fine job of knowing he should try to get along with Democrats. His approval would be 50 percent really fast if he were to use this for partisan political purposes—any of the extreme tax proposals, the agenda of the religious right."

Utah Gov. Mike Leavitt, a Republican, said: "The most profound thing that's happened is that he's become America's president instead of the American president. When it comes to matters related to war, the political clout is unending. There's no question on matters of domestic policy he's been strengthened, especially to the degree by which they are related to the anti-terror campaign."

After the terrorist attacks Sept. 11, Congress quickly passed a $15 billion relief package for the airline industry, a $40 billion package to repair the terrorism damage and bolster security and are wrapping up details on an anti-terror bill that would give law enforcement new powers to search out terrorists.

Other measures have stalled, including an aviation security bill with a proposal to make airport screeners federal employees and a foreign aid bill held up in the Senate in a dispute over judicial appointments. . . .

Leaders from both parties said the president's high approval ratings are closely linked to the bipartisan approach he's governed with in the weeks after the Sept. 11 terrorist attacks.

"He's doing now what he did in Texas," said Arizona Gov. Jane Hull, a Republican. "He's reaching the ability to sit down with Republicans and Democrats. It's a shame that it takes a tragedy to create that spirit, but I think he'll be able to continue doing that in the future. The American people have shown they like that bipartisanship." ■

AP Wire, October 27, 2001

BUSH SIGNS TERROR BILL; AGENCIES' POWERS GROW

By SONYA ROSS
The Associated Press

WASHINGTON (AP)—President Bush signed an anti-terrorism bill Friday that gives police unprecedented ability to search seize, detain or eavesdrop in the pursuit of possible terrorists.

"This government will enforce this law with all the urgency of a nation at war," he said.

Federal officials said they planned to use the new powers right away, prompting civil libertarians to voice anew their concerns that American freedoms would be sacrificed in the name of public safety. The American Civil Liberties Union pledged to monitor police actions closely and scheduled a meeting with FBI Director Robert Mueller.

"This bill goes light years beyond what is necessary to combat terrorism," said Laura Murphy, ACLU Washington director. "While we are ourselves concerned for the country's safety we are also concerned by the attorney general's apparent gusto to implement certain provisions in the bill that threaten liberty."

After Bush signed the bill, Attorney General John Ashcroft issued orders to 94 U.S. attorney's offices and 56 FBI field offices to use the new powers to track down terrorists by intercepting their Internet and telephone communications and their financial transactions.

"Law enforcement is now empowered with new tools and resources necessary to disrupt weaken and eliminate the infrastructure of terrorism organizations," said Ashcroft, who had pressed hard for the bill's passage.

Bush said the legislation "upholds and respects" personal freedoms protected by the Constitution. But given the magnitude of the Sept. 11 attacks, he said the nation had little choice but to update surveillance procedures "written in the era of rotary telephones" to better combat sophisticated terrorists.

"We may never know what horrors our country was spared by the diligent and determined work of our police forces under the most trying conditions," Bush said. "They deserve our full support and every means of help that we can provide."

Lawmakers concerned about possible abuses of power, put an expiration date on part of the law. Unless Congress renews the measure before Dec. 31, 2005, the eavesdropping sections expire.

The president, an American flag pin on his lapel, signed the bill in an East Room ceremony attended by Vice President Dick Cheney, Director of Homeland Security Tom Ridge, Mueller, CIA Director George Tenet and nine members of Congress. Bush signed his name with one pen, handed it to House Judiciary Chairman Jim Sensenbrenner, a Wisconsin Republican, and distributed souvenir pens to everyone else. Senate Judiciary Chairman Patrick Leahy, a Vermont Democrat, snapped photos from the stage.

Leahy told reporters afterward that it was up to Congress—specifically the judiciary committees—to make sure through "constant oversight" that federal authorities are not too heavy-handed with their new enforcement powers. Leahy addressed worries about abuses of power by saying, "We have got to stop thinking about the Dillinger . . . days of law enforcement and start thinking of the realities of 2001. No matter what terror attacks we face today we're going to face more next year and the year after. This is something that is going to exist long after all of us are no longer in office and we've got to make sure we do the things to protect our nation."

Under the law, the FBI now has greater wiretapping and electronic surveillance authority. The law allows nationwide jurisdiction for search warrants and electronic surveillance of e-mail and the Internet. Agents can, for example, use roving wiretaps to monitor any telephone used by a terrorism suspect rather than getting separate authorizations for each phone that the suspect uses.

The law sets strong penalties for those who harbor or finance terrorists, and establishes new punishments for possessing biological weapons. It makes it a federal crime to commit an act of terrorism against a mass transit system. It increases the overall number of crimes considered terrorist acts and toughens the punishment for committing them.

Also, police would have greater ability to secretly search people's homes and business records.

The House and Senate approved Bush's anti-terrorism package in less than two months, skipping much of the normal committee processes. Lawmakers say they came up with a good bill. ■

AP Wire, Monday, December 10, 2001

U.S. BOMBS POUND TORA BORA CAVES

By *CHRIS TOMLINSON*
The Associated Press

TORA BORA, Afghanistan (AP)—With the hunt for Osama bin Laden now the main focus of the conflict in Afghanistan, U.S. bombs rained down on al-Qaida's Tora Bora cave complex on Monday. A brief skirmish between tribal forces and al-Qaida defenders followed the bombardment.

In the south, U.S. Marines searching for vanquished Taliban and al-Qaida members are building a facility that will hold prisoners temporarily at their desert base for processing.

Just after dawn, U.S. airstrikes hit Tora Bora, a vast network of caverns and tunnels carved deep into the White Mountains in Afghanistan's east where some say bin Laden might be hiding. Later, Afghan tribal fighters drove several aging Soviet-built tanks closer toward enemy positions at Tora Bora. They were forced back when al-Qaida troops emerged from the caves and fired mortars ahead of the armored convoy. There was a brief exchange of fire, but no casualties were reported.

For days, constant bombing by high-flying B-52s and other U.S. warplanes has aimed to weaken al-Qaida defenses ahead on anticipated ground assault by as many as 2,500 Afghan tribesmen. It is unclear when the attack will be launched. Haji Zahir, a militia commander and the son of provincial governor Abdul Qadir, said tribal forces would launch smaller guerrilla raids in the meantime.

Thousands of Pakistani soldiers and paramilitary troops were deployed along the border near Tora Bora on Monday in an attempt

A pair of F/18C Hornets circle the USS *Theodore Roosevelt* in the Arabian Sea after flying a mission over Afghanistan, Dec. 11, 2001.

An Afghan anti-Taliban fighter pops up from his tank as he spots a U.S. warplane bombing al-Qaida fighters
in the White Mountains of Tora Bora in Afghanistan, Dec. 10, 2001.

to prevent fleeing al-Qaida forces from entering the country. Helicopters dropped personnel on mountain ridges to monitor the movement of the Islamic militants, witnesses said.

Citing intelligence reports, U.S. officials, including Vice President Dick Cheney, and some Afghan commanders think bin Laden may be hiding somewhere near Tora Bora with a large number of mainly Arab al-Qaida fighters. However, other Afghan officials say he has probably fled to mountains near the southern city of Kandahar, which had been the Taliban's last stronghold until a chaotic surrender on Friday. Another fugitive, Taliban supreme leader Mullah Mohammed Omar is also thought to be on the run in the south.

On Sunday, Cheney said a videotape of bin Laden obtained by U.S. officials in Afghanistan makes clear that the al-Qaida leader was behind the terrorist attacks in the United States. *The Washington Post*, quoting unidentified senior government officials, said the tape shows bin Laden praising Allah for the attacks, which he said were more successful than anticipated.

"He does in fact display significant knowledge of what happened, and there's no doubt about his responsibility for the attack on Sept. 11," Cheney said. Just outside the Marine Camp Rhino, in the desert near Kandahar, a temporary prisoner of war camp was under construction.

Spokesman Capt. David Romley said fighters captured by Marines would be fed, given medical care and allowed visits by the international Red Cross. John Walker, an American who fought with the Taliban, was recuperating at Camp Rhino as a "military detainee," said another spokesman, Capt. Stewart Upton.

ABOVE: Marines with full battle gear prepare to board transport helicopters at the U.S. military compound at Kandahar airport for a mission to an undisclosed location in Afghanistan, Dec. 31, 2001. BELOW: This image taken from television footage in Mazar-i-Sharif, Afghanistan, shows John Walker Lindh, right, Dec. 1, 2001. Lindh, the young Californian who became known as the American Taliban after he was captured by U.S. forces in late 2001, pled guilty to two charges—supplying services to the Taliban and carrying an explosive during the commission of a felony—and was sentenced to 20 years in prison. He was released on three-year probation on May 23, 2019.

Walker, 20, of Fairfax, Calif., was in good condition and was recovering from dehydration and a gunshot wound in the leg, Upton said. Air Force Gen. Richard Myers, chairman of the U.S. Joint Chiefs of Staff, said Walker had been providing useful Information and no final decision had been made on what to do with him. . . .

Interim prime minister Hamid Karzai, who helped negotiate the agreement, is now preparing for his U.N. and U.S.-backed national administration to assume power in the capital, Kabul. It is expected to govern for six months. Also looking to take part in Afghanistan's reconstruction is former king Mohammad Zaher Shah, 87. He has lived in exile in Rome since being ousted in a 1973 coup and was planning to return to his homeland by March 21, the monarch's grandson said. Shah will preside over a council of tribal elders that is to help determine the shape of a permanent system of government. ∎

7,000 TALIBAN, AL-QAIDA BEING HELD

By DEBORAH HASTINGS
The Associated Press

ISLAMABAD, Pakistan, December 21, 2001 (AP)—About 7,000 people suspected of having ties to the Taliban and Osama bin Laden's al-Qaida network are being held and interrogated in Afghanistan, a spokesman for the U.S.-led coalition against terrorism said Friday.

"The situation changes almost by the hour, but I believe the latest number of prisoners to be around 7,000 in total," Kenton Keith, a former U.S. ambassador to Qatar, told a news conference.

Secretary of Defense Donald H. Rumsfeld said Friday that several senior al-Qaida and Taliban leaders are among the incarcerated, but he refused to identify them. . . .

Work was under way to identify all those detained so U.S. officials can choose who they want to take into American custody for interrogation, Rumsfeld said. "We're trying to identify all these people . . . and get a mugshot on them and get some fingerprints," he said.

Pentagon officials said early this month there were 5,000 to 6,000 in Afghan custody. But that was before a major al-Qaida stronghold was routed in the mountainous Tora Bora region earlier this week, when hundreds more were taken and hundreds fled. Many were later captured in Pakistan. . . .

The prisoners include more than 20 held by U.S. Marines at their base in Kandahar's airport in southern Afghanistan, where a detention camp has been hastily constructed.

Marine officials have said those prisoners are blindfolded, bound and hemmed in by razor wire. ■

A view of the al-Qaida–Taliban detainment facility build by U.S. Marines as seen from the air control tower at the Kandahar International Airport, the main coalition base in southern Afghanistan, Jan. 6, 2002.

AP Wire, Monday, January 7, 2002

U.S. WAR COMMANDER SAYS SEARCH OF TORA BORA CAVES ENDING WITH NO BIN LADEN

By ROBERT BURNS
The Associated Press

MACDILL AIR FORCE BASE, Fla. (AP)—The weeks-long search of caves in Afghanistan's Tora Bora region failed to find terrorist mastermind Osama bin Laden but yielded evidence that he was once holed up there with Taliban supporters, the U.S. war commander said Monday.

In an Associated Press interview at Central Command head-quarters, Gen. Tommy Franks said the search at Tora Bora, once thought a promising path to bin Laden's capture, was ending with no clue to bin Laden's whereabouts.

"We'll have that pretty well cleared and be out of there in the next day or so," Franks said.

Some U.S. special forces soldiers will remain in the mountain-ous Tora Bora area to "sweep" villages for potential intelligence and to act as liaisons with local tribal elders, he said.

Franks said that if the United States acquired information that bin Laden or other top suspects had fled into Pakistan he could either ask the Pakistanis to pursue them or U.S. forces could do it themselves.

"We could contact them and say, all right, we are observing people and we are going to follow them into Pakistan," he said, adding that the U.S. military has had a one-star general in Islam-abad, the Pakistani capital, since early October to develop that kind of cooperation. He said U.S. special forces soldiers are on the Pakistani side of the border to coordinate on this. . . .

Franks said the Tora Bora search focused on eight main cave complexes. It provided evidence that bin Laden and high-level officials of the Taliban militia that supported him for five years had been in the area "at one point or another," he said.

Indeed, Franks indicated they had been there relatively recently, but he said he could not confirm reports that bin Laden had slipped away just before Afghan tribal forces and U.S. special operations troops arrived in early December to rout al-Qaida fighters from their final stronghold.

The Army four-star general said he was convinced that he took the right approach in searching the Tora Bora area—choosing not to send in large numbers of U.S. ground forces—even though the effort is ending with no clear clues to where bin Laden may be hiding.

Franks said he would not rule out sending larger numbers of ground troops into Afghanistan at some point but intended to stick to his approach of coordinating with local Afghan tribal forces to provide intelligence on the whereabouts of bin Laden and his top lieutenants.

"I'm not interested in acceleration; I'm interested in continu-ation—focus, to get us where we want to go," Franks said in an hour-long interview.

Gen. Tommy Franks, the commander of U.S. forces in Afghanistan, talks to reporters at the International Security Assistance Force (ISAF) headquarters in Kabul, Aug. 25, 2002.

ABOVE: U.S. Marines scan the northwest perimeter of the American military compound at Afghanistan's Kandahar airport using sophisticated thermal imagery equipment, Jan. 14, 2002. BELOW: Senators Joseph Lieberman (D-Conn.), right, and John McCain (R-A.Z.), left, arrive at Bagram Air Base in Afghanistan, Jan. 7, 2002. They, and several other senators, were there to visit with U.S. troops stationed at the base and gather information about operations there.

Continuing with the current approach also means keeping U.S. bombers and attack aircraft in the skies over Afghanistan daily so that timely intelligence on the ground can be acted upon, he said. . . .

Franks said he remained confident that the U.S. military eventually will get bin Laden and other top terrorist targets in Afghanistan, as well as Taliban leader Mullah Mohammed Omar and his top deputies. In the meantime he reserved judgment on whether bin Laden remains in hiding inside Afghanistan or—as some members of Congress have speculated—has fled to Pakistan.

"At this point I've not been persuaded that we know that to be a fact," he said, referring to comments on Sunday by Sen. John Edwards, D-N.C., and others who took a fact-finding trip to Central Asia. The senators said intelligence indicates that bin Laden has fled Afghanistan.

"Our intelligence people, from a national perspective, look at literally hundreds of reports every day," Franks said. "And what we try to do, before we characterize them as believable, is have something that sort of substantiates what we think." ∎

With New Experiences, a Reporter Evolves

By TED ANTHONY
Director of Newsroom Innovation

Two decades later, it's almost impossible to recapture the feeling of being a correspondent in Pakistan and Afghanistan in the months after 9/11, watching a society reemerge and begin to rebuild from a generation of war. For me, as a journalist, it was the very front-row seat to history that had drawn me to the profession. And the access: The new, U.S.-backed government was full of ministers whom we could interview simply by walking into their offices. They'd put out a tray of raisins and almonds and just chat. For someone like me—based at the time in China, where access to any sort of senior official was absurdly difficult if not nonexistent—it felt like an endless journalism buffet.

When I was growing up, my father would tell me stories about his time teaching in Kabul, the Afghan capital, in 1951, and how much of an impression it made on him. Afghan items he'd brought home were strewn about our suburban Pittsburgh house when I was growing up in the 1970s, and he had many old photos of the landscapes he'd seen. So I felt Afghanistan through his memories even before I encountered it myself a half century later. And when I did, it was as much of a revelation and a sensory overload as I'd ever imagined.

I wrote the following in June 2002 when I returned to Kabul to cover the *loya jirga*, the colossal meeting of ethnic groups that would end up electing Afghanistan's first post-Taliban leader, Hamid Karzai.

◆ ◆ ◆

In the months after September 11, I was sent to Pakistan and to Afghanistan from my home in Beijing, where I am based as a correspondent. I am here again in Kabul as I write this in early June.

Because of those hijackers, because of their anger and violent acts. I have met kind people and seem new places that have changed my view of the Earth. The terrorists would hate it, but their acts have helped me produce new experiences, new friendships, new mindsets, even new optimism.

I have given the Afghan Consular Officer at Bagram Air Base my passport to stamp, and watched him dutifully record my name and data in his official ledger—a 101 Dalmatians notebook. I have had Russian- and American-made automatic weapons pointed at me.

I have seen the Islamabad Best Western, and noted the irony. I have asked questions of the Taliban ambassador to Pakistan, and been surprised when he told a joke.

I have traveled rutted highways dotted with hand-painted signs that warn: "Beware of mines at the side of the road."

I have reported on an Afghan refugee in Pakistan who was injured, then arrested when a grenade he had been trying to throw at Western journalists exploded in his hand. He had just learned a relative had died in a U.S. bombing, and so decided to take out his fury on the next passing reporter. He went to a corner frequented by journalists to throw the grenade he had bought for the equivalent of $3. He had lost someone important to him, and spent probably most of the money that he had to lash out in the best way that he could.

I have seen women entirely covered in powder-blue burqas, with only a netting over the eyes to let them see the world, move like ghosts through Kabul's streets. I have seen, slowly, women begin to emerge from them. I saw a woman veiled up to her eyes sitting with her husband. And just as I was thinking how our worlds were so utterly different, she reached into her bag, pulled out a canister of Pringles, shoved a few under her veil and began to crunch.

Burqa-clad women walk along a shopping street in front of a giant portrait of Afghan president Hamid Karzai in Kabul, Oct. 1, 2003.

I have contemplated what a strange world it is when my can of tuna—packed in Thailand, exported to America, reshipped to China and carried with me into Afghanistan—has traveled more than some of my high school classmates.

I have kept a promise to a young waiter at the Sharenow restaurant in Kabul. In January, I photographed him with my digital camera. He asked for a print, and I promised him that, if I ever came back, I would bring one. I printed it out in Beijing and, two weeks ago, I showed up unannounced and handed it to him. He stopped, put down his tray, put his hand over his heart and—"*Tash-a-cour*, sir"—thanked me in Dari.

I have seen a crowded field of stars at night over Kabul, one of the only world capitals with so little electricity that the night sky shines exuberantly even in the middle of the city.

I have made an Afghan friend who tells me, "I never saw the face of my father. He died when I was 2 and we were too poor to afford photographs." And another who tells me, "When the Taliban came, I had only Western pants, no *shalwar kameez*. So I had to buy them. And when the Taliban left, I had only *shalwar kameez*, no Western pants. So I had to buy them again."

I have met a gentleman named Munir, a Pakistani who's one of the best human beings I've ever come across in my travels. Through him, and through my experiences, I—part Christian by religion, part Jewish by birth, wary of any organized faith—have come to respect Islam, while not understanding it yet.

Brave new world, that has such people in it. ∎

ABOVE LEFT: Afghan refugee children ready to leave to their country from a UN transit camp near Peshawar, Pakistan, Sept. 30, 2002.

ABOVE RIGHT: A mine sweeper searches for mines in Ghazni province, 125 miles west of Kabul, Afghanistan, Sept. 18, 2002.

LEFT: An Afghan vendor sells eggs by lantern light in Kabul's crowded main market, March 5, 2005. Three years after the fall of the Taliban regime, Afghanistan still struggled with its destroyed public works.

CHAPTER 4
JUSTICE

Among Americans' many and justifiable fears related to Sept. 11 was the unfathomable notion that the enemy who had perpetrated the bloody carnage would go unpunished. Therefore, a bullseye was drawn on Osama bin Laden and al-Qaida.

Within several days of the attack, the FBI received over 36,000 leads and issued hundreds of subpoenas. By the 14th of the month they had arrested the first suspect, but released little information about the capture. The federal government moves quickly to stamp its efforts with official code names and monikers, and accordingly on Sept. 20 the FBI launched "PENTTBOM," an odd-sounding and little-used acronym for its investigation. Also named was the military response: "Operation Infinite Justice."

The first breakthrough was officially announced by FBI director Robert Mueller, when the bureau released the photos and names of the 19 suspected suicide hijackers. He asserted some had been linked to Osama bin Laden's network. Preliminary information reported that as many of as eight of them were thought to be Saudi nationals.

With the hijackers dead, hope was placed on extracting information from captured enemy fighters from the Afghan war in progress. The detainees were housed at what would become one of the most infamous military prisons in the world, Guantanamo Bay, where the United States maintains a naval station on the southeastern coast of Cuba. In January 2002, U.S. troops built a hastily constructed

high-security detention center at the base's "Camp X-Ray," where intense and often controversial interrogations of 158 detainees would take place.

The U.S. brushed aside criticism of the harsh conditions and interrogations, maintaining that the detainees were not technically prisoners of war and therefore not subject to guarantees under the Geneva Conventions. In addition to the initial 158 prisoners, small batches of captured fighters were shipped to Guantanamo later, possibly making a case to al-Qaida and Taliban fighters that surrender was not a tenable option. At home, questions were raised about the quality of information that prisoners might surrender under duress and torture, such as feigned drowning or suffocation and sleep deprivation. The term "enhanced interrogation techniques"—which did not come into common usage until several years later—became a divisive practice that some said was a black eye for America, though a case was made by the military for its efficacy.

By early 2003, a major suspect was arrested in Rawalpindi, near the Pakistani capital of Islamabad: Khalid Sheikh Mohammed, a suspected architect of the Sept. 11 attacks. He was among three arrested in the Pakistani raid for the murder of more than 3,000 people allegedly killed in the onslaught. Mohammed, 37, had not yet been charged for the Sept. 11 events, but had been charged in a bizarre 1995 terror plot to assassinate Pope John Paul II, hijack and blow up 11 airliners in order to stop travel between Asia and the U.S., and crash a plane into CIA headquarters in Virginia. Mohammed remains at Guantanamo as of this writing, still awaiting trial.

The elusive bin Laden evaded capture until May 2, 2011. His demise on that day came during a dramatic raid by the Navy's SEAL Team Six monitored, live, by President Barack Obama and his national security team in the Situation Room at the White House.

Intelligence reports placed the 9/11 mastermind at a compound about 60 miles from Islamabad, the Pakistani capital. Donning night goggles and assault gear, two dozen U.S. Navy SEALs shinnied down ropes from Chinook helicopters into the hideout and raided bin Laden's home. It was later revealed that he was shot in the head and died on the spot. His body was carried onto the helicopters and photographed as evidence the master terrorist was in fact dead, although it was decided by the administration not to release any photographs of the body.

Bin Laden's body was transferred to the USS *Carl Vinson* on the Arabian Sea. His corpse was washed and placed in a white sheet according to Muslim religious rites, given final prayers in Arabic, then buried at sea.

The section of the Pentagon that was hit by hijacked American Airlines Flight 77 on Sept. 11, 2001 is lit up by artificial light as round-the-clock recovery efforts continue the day after the attack. A large American flag hangs from the roof on the far right.

AP Wire, Friday, September 14, 2001

FEDERAL AUTHORITIES MAKE FIRST ARREST IN ATTACKS PROBE

By JOHN SOLOMON and KAREN GULLO
The Associated Press

WASHINGTON (AP)—Federal authorities made the first arrest Friday in the worldwide investigation of this week's terrorist attacks, apprehending a suspect in New York they believe may have relevant information, government officials said.

The suspect was arrested on a material witness warrant, the Justice Department said. It was issued after authorities determined the individual had information highly relevant to the investigation and was likely to flee, one official said, speaking on condition of anonymity. Officials declined to identify the suspect or say what information they were seeking.

It was the first break in the investigation that has spanned the globe. The FBI has received over 36,000 leads and has issued hundreds of subpoenas. It released the identities Friday of the 19 hijackers.

Authorities said they were still investigating whether more terrorists might be at large. They were searching for 100 people they want to question in connection with Tuesday's devastating attacks on the World Trade Center and the Pentagon.

Sen. Richard Shelby, R-Ala., the top Republican on the Senate Intelligence Committee, declined to discuss what he had learned from intelligence briefings but said he feared cities may still remain in danger. "You've got to assume there was probably more planned, maybe for the aftershock," Shelby said.

On that front, the FBI provided warnings to two Southeast cities—Richmond, Va., and Atlanta—that information developed since Tuesday's attacks suggested terrorists may have had plans for attacks in those cities, law enforcement officials said. But late Friday, further investigation left officials doubtful of the threat.

"I'm not discounting it totally, but there's nothing specific about it," said Gary McConnell, director of the Georgia Emergency Management Agency. "I'm not getting any more alarmed since I knew about it last night than prior to knowing about it."

The information came from an acquaintance of one of the hijackers, law enforcement officials said, speaking only on condition of anonymity. The information was shared with the cities, but the witness failed a lie-detector test Friday evening, suggesting his account was not credible, the officials said.

The investigation, named PENTTBOM, involved one of the worst acts of terrorism ever on U.S. soil.

A list of more than 100 people has been distributed to thousands of local police departments, the Federal Aviation Administration, border patrols and FBI field offices, said Attorney General John Ashcroft.

"We believe they may have information that could be helpful to the investigation," said Ashcroft.

Federal officials wouldn't say whether the 100 names include suspects in the plot to hijack and crash four jetliners Tuesday.

The FBI on Friday released the names of 19 hijackers who commandeered and brought down the planes. Many lived in Florida and several had gone to pilot training school in Venice, Fla. Some of the 19 have been linked to Osama bin Laden or his organizations, according to current and former U.S. officials. The officials said

On Oct. 12, 2000, al-Qaida terrorists exploded a small boat alongside the USS *Cole* as it was refueling in the Yemeni port of Aden. The blast ripped a 40-foot-wide hole near the ship's waterline, killing 17 American sailors and injuring many more. Khalid al-Mihdhar of Saudi Arabia, one of the hijackers on American Airlines Flight 77, was linked to the *Cole* attack. This picture shows the *Cole* at Ingalls Shipbuilding in Pascagoula, Miss., where it had been brought by the FBI to examine for additional evidence.

President George W. Bush looks over a panel displaying the newly created list of Most Wanted Terrorists with
FBI Director Robert Mueller, Oct. 10, 2001, at the agency's headquarters in Washington, D.C.

four of the dead hijackers had been linked to bin Laden's al-Qaida network: Waleed al-Shehri, Ahmed al-Ghamdi, Hamza al-Ghamdi and Saeed al-Ghamdi.

In addition, U.S. intelligence were checking the background of suspected hijacker Khalid al-Mihdhar, to see if he is connected to Zein al-Abidine al-Mihdhar, the former head of the Islamic Army of Aden in Yemen who was executed a few years ago in connection with a kidnapping. The group was one of three to claim credit for last fall's bombing of the USS *Cole*.

Among the 19 was Mohamed Atta, 33, of Hollywood and Coral Springs, Fla., identified by German authorities as being tied to an Islamic fundamentalist group that planned attacks on American targets. The Justice Department said Atta was aboard American Airlines Flight 11 that took off from Boston's Logan Airport and crashed into the north tower of the World Trade Center.

All the hijackers had Middle Eastern names. FBI Director Bob Mueller would not comment on whether any of the hijackers were associated with bin Laden, a wealthy Saudi who administration official believe is behind the attacks.

Investigators are focused on several locations within the U.S., including Florida, where several of the hijackers lived and attended flight training school. Seven of the 19 hijackers lived in Delray Beach, Fla.

Federal authorities have launched a massive search for people who assisted the hijackers, believing that there may have been a vast network of people who plotted and carried out Tuesday's attacks. FBI Deputy Director Tom Pickard is leading the investigation.

Hundreds of subpoenas have been issued, more than 30 search warrants have been searched and investigators have seized computers and other documents.

ABOVE: Edward Felt, 41—a computer engineer and technology director of BEA Systems from Matawan, N.J., and devoted husband and father to two daughters—was on United Flight 93 for a last-minute business trip to San Francisco on Sept. 11.

RIGHT AND OPPOSITE: A declassified transcript of a call between a 911 operator and Edward Felt, a passenger on United Flight 93. Five minutes before the plane crashed, Felt was able to call 911 from his cellphone to alert them of the hijacking in progress.

FD-302a (Rev. 10-6-95)

265D-NY-280350

Continuation of FD-302 of ___911 Call___ , On 9/11/2001 , Page 2

Caller:	"Highjacking in pro--"
911:	"Excuse me? Hey somebody's reporting a--"
Caller:	"Highjacking in progress."
911:	"Sir I'm losing you, where are you at?"
Caller:	"United flight 93."
911:	"Wait a minute, wait, United--night flight--United flight. United flight 93."
Caller:	"Highjacking in progress!"
911:	"Okay, where you at up? Where are you at up?"
Caller:	"I'm in the bathroom, United flight 93."
911:	"Okay, where are you at?"
Caller:	"I don't know."
911:	"Where are you at?"
Caller:	"I don't know where the plane is."
911:	"Where did you take off at?"
Caller:	"Newark to San Francisco."
911:	"Newark to San Francisco."
Caller:	"United flight 93."
911:	"I got it, okay stay on the phone with me sir."
Caller:	"I'm trying to...(UI) at the bathroom. I don't know what's going on."
911:	"Hey somebody get the FAA, Newark to San Francisco and they got a highjacking in progress. Okay, yeah. Dude, get somebody

REQ. #35-13   000000221

FD-302a (Rev. 10-6-95)

265D-NY-280350

Continuation of FD-302 of _____911 Call_____ , On 9/11/2001 ___ , Page __3__

	from the airport on the line. This is a highjacking in progress. Are you still there sir?"
Caller:	"Yes I am."
911:	"What's your name sir?"
Caller:	"EDWARD FELT."
911:	"EDWARD FELT? What's your phone number sir?"
Caller:	"Seven, three, two (732)."
911:	"Go ahead."
Caller:	"Two, four, one (241)."
911:	"Go ahead."
Caller:	"Six, nine, seven, four (6974)."
911:	"How big of a plane sir?"
Caller:	"It's like a seven-fifty-seven (757)."
911:	"This is a seven-fifty-seven (757). Hey we need. It's a seven-fifty-seven (757). Sir, sir?"
Caller:	"Yes."
911:	"Okay, how many peoples on the plane?"
Caller:	"It was--it was pretty empty, maybe (UI)."
911:	"Can you still hear me sir, sir, sir can you still hear me? It's over (UI). There's a plane...said the plane's going down. It's over Mt. Pleasant Township somewhere. Sir? It's going down. You better make an announcement on (UI). It's over Mt. Pleasant somewhere. Hello? (Call terminated.)

RIGHT: **An FBI special agent (left) speaks to two FBI chaplains at ground zero, Sept. 18, 2001.**

BELOW: **Members of the FBI Evidence Team meet outside the Pentagon Building hours after the Sept. 11 attacks.**

Investigators also recovered voice and data recorders from the plane that smashed into the Pentagon and the data recorder from the flight that crashed near Pittsburgh. Mueller said the data recorders for the Pentagon flight had yielded some information, but the voice recordings for the flight had yielded nothing so far.

The FBI has a transcript of communications between the pilots and air traffic controllers for a portion of the flight that crashed in Pennsylvania, officials said.

Ashcroft appealed to the public for information about the 19 persons identified as hijackers on the four planes by calling 1-866-483-5137. The Justice Department had originally said there were 18 hijackers, but then ascertained that five hijackers, not four, were on American Airlines Flight 77, which hit the Pentagon.

Besides Atta, the hijackers who were believed included Hani Hanjour, who was on the flight that crashed into the Pentagon; Wail al-Shehri and Abdulaziz al-Omari, who were on one of the Boston flights; Marwan al-Shehhi, hijacking on United Flight 175 out of Boston and Ziad Jarrah, who flew on United Flight 93 out of Newark, N.J., which crashed in a field 80 miles from Pittsburgh.

The FBI dispatched teams of agents to airports, where authorities are supposed to be checking passenger lists against the list of 100 people wanted for questioning. ∎

MISSING FLIGHT RECORDERS (BLACK BOXES)

ATTENTION: If above units or components, including loose circuit boards or 3.5" magnetic tape reels, are found, document location, secure immediately and provide to the FBI. Items may be blackened, charred or rusted in appearance with no discernable lettering.

LEFT: An FBI poster on a construction wall at ground zero—photographed a week after the 9/11 attacks—asking for information on missing flight recorders from the two planes that crashed into the World Trade Center.

BELOW: A FEMA worker stands on a portion of the fuselage of United Airlines Flight 175 on the roof of the destroyed 5 World Trade Center, Oct. 25, 2001.

GOVERNMENT REACHES FOR "PENTTBOM" AND "OPERATION INFINITE JUSTICE" TO NAME ITS TERRORISM RESPONSE

By JENNIFER LOVEN
The Associated Press

WASHINGTON, Sept. 20, 2001 (AP)—When Washington gets serious, it moves quickly to stamp its efforts with official monikers.

"PENTTBOM" is the code name for the government's FBI-led investigation into who was behind last week's terror attacks. And "Operation Infinite Justice" was announced as the designator for the anti-terrorist military action being planned in retaliation.

Defense Secretary Donald H. Rumsfeld said Thursday the administration is reconsidering, because in the Islamic faith such finality is considered something provided only by Allah, the Arabic word for God.

The soldiers at the Pentagon typically reach for loftier images for their operations than the crime-busters at the FBI and Justice Department.

The derivation of PENTTBOM is simple. "Pen" is short for Pentagon and the two "T's" stand for the twin towers of the World Trade Center. "Bom" is for bomb, even though both buildings were struck by jetliners flown by suicidal hijackers.

One of law enforcement's most famous code names is UNABOM, the 18-year investigation that eventually captured Theodore Kaczynski and was so named because the mail bomber's early targets involved people connected to universities and airlines. . . .

At the Defense Department, the job of giving any military campaign a two-word nickname falls to the commander of the armed forces in the region it targets.

The words are generated with the help of a computer database that spits out the first word and establishes parameters for the second, to prevent duplication.

In high-profile operations, such as the planned war on terrorism, the choice is given final approval by the defense secretary and the chairman of the Joint Chiefs of Staff.

Secretary of State Colin Powell—who led the Joint Chiefs during the 1991 Persian Gulf War—described in his 1995 autobiography how his staff and that of Gen. Norman Schwarzkopf named the military buildup.

"The image of a shield popped up early. . . . We settled on a name we all thought had just the right ring, and the mobilization in the Saudi sands to defend the kingdom thus became 'Desert Shield,'" Powell wrote in *My American Journey*.

But once the American military operation turned offensive, the Pentagon needed a new name. "Norm suggested Desert Storm. Stormin' Norman's storm," Powell wrote. "It was a natural, and we all went for it." ■

President George W. Bush meets with his cabinet and advisers, Sept. 15, 2001, at Camp David, Md. Looking on are Vice President Dick Cheney, left, and Secretary of State Colin Powell.

AP Wire, Friday, September 28, 2001

PHOTOS OF SUSPECTED HIJACKERS RELEASED

By KAREN GULLO
The Associated Press

WASHINGTON (AP)—The FBI released photos Thursday of the 19 suspected suicide hijackers with a plea for citizens to help with identities of some that are still in doubt. Director Robert Mueller said some attackers had been linked to Osama bin Laden's network.

Separately, more arrests were made of Middle Eastern men who obtained bogus licenses to haul hazardous materials. The FBI said those men were not connected to the hijackers, who crashed planes into the World Trade Center and the Pentagon. The FBI isn't certain about the identities of all the hijackers.

"It is our hope that the release of these photos will prompt others who may have seen the hijackers to contact the FBI with any information they may have that would be helpful to the investigation," said Attorney General John Ashcroft.

The release of the photos, which come from passports, driver's licenses and other documents identified with the hijackers, marked a change for authorities, who until now have kept them under wraps so that potential witnesses and others shown the photos get a fresh look at the men.

Mueller said the FBI believes the names and photographs match those on the manifests of the hijacked planes. But questions remain about whether those are the true names of the hijackers.

"What we are currently doing is determining whether, when these individuals came to the United States, these were their real names or they changed their names for use with false identification in the United States," said Mueller. He said there was evidence that one or more of the hijackers had had contacts with al-Qaida, the network associated bin Laden. He declined to be more specific. . . .

Regarding the FBI's list of 19 hijackers, some of the names have slightly different spellings and others have additional names added, compared with the list released by the FBI on Sept. 14. At least four of the identities released Sept. 14 have been challenged by people with the same or similar names.

Saudi Arabia Embassy officials, for example, have said that a Saudi electrical engineer named Abdulaziz al-Omari—the same name as one of the alleged hijackers on the plane that crashed into the Pentagon—had his passport and other papers stolen in 1996 in Denver when he was a student, and reported the theft to police there at the time.

The FBI director said there was some evidence that "one or more" of the hijackers was related. ∎

FBI Director Robert Mueller, right, answers a reporter's question as U.S. Attorney General John Ashcroft looks on, during a press conference at the FBI building in Washington, Sept. 27, 2001. Panels with photos of the 19 suspected suicide hijackers are shown behind them.

AP Wire, Wednesday, January 9, 2002

PRISON CAMP FOR WAR PRISONERS FROM AFGHANISTAN GOES UP IN GUANTANAMO BAY AMID MASSIVE SECURITY

Watchtower security teams man their positions during a rehearsal for handling incoming detainees at Camp X-Ray, a detention camp within the Guantanamo Bay Naval Base in Cuba, Jan. 10, 2002.

By TONY WINTON
The Associated Press

GUANTANAMO BAY NAVAL BASE, Cuba (AP)—U.S. troops were hurriedly building makeshift cells out of chain-link fences for the first Afghan inmates expected this week at this remote U.S. Navy base in Cuba.

"I have 100 cells prepared," said Brig. Gen. Mike Lehnert, who is leading a joint task force of 660 service men and women deployed to build the new prison camp at Guantanamo Bay Naval Base.

The military led a group of reporters Wednesday on a tour of the temporary cells that will hold the first suspected Taliban and al-Qaida members, due here by week's end.

"Our job is to take these terrorists out of the fight by locking them up," Lehnert said.

He said treatment of the detainees—in temporary, outdoor cells with metal roofs—would be "humane but not comfortable." Officials hope to build 220 such cells, and eventually 2,000 permanent ones to hold war detainees.

In Washington, White House spokesman Ari Fleischer said the government would decide the detainees' legal status case by case.

Two U.S. Army military policemen escort one of Camp X-Ray's first 20 first detainees to his cell, Jan. 11, 2002.

"They will be provided with food and appropriate medical care," he said. "And I think it's safe to say that no matter where they are, Guantanamo or anywhere else, their conditions will be much better than the conditions under which they existed when they lived in Afghanistan."

The military is building the high-security detention facility at the base's Camp X-Ray, used in the past decade to hold migrants from Haiti and Cuba intending to enter the United States illegally. The camp is surrounded by guard towers and several rings of fences topped with coils of barbed wire.

The prisoners and those assigned to guard them will add to the 2,700 people normally on the 45-square-mile base, the oldest U.S. overseas outpost.

The U.S. military first seized Guantanamo Bay in 1898 during the Spanish-American War. President Theodore Roosevelt leased the land from Cuba in 1903, and President Franklin Roosevelt ordered the base expanded in 1939.

Ever since Fidel Castro's communist revolution, in 1959, the U.S. military presence on Cuban soil has been a source of irritation to the communist government. Under the first lease, the United States agreed to pay Cuba 2,000 gold coins a year, now valued at $4,085. Washington continues to pay that amount every year, but Castro's government refuses to cash the checks. Cuban soldiers patrol the area around the base, where they have planted thousands of land mines. After Castro ordered the base's water supply cut in 1964, the U.S. military built a desalination plant, making the base self-sufficient.

While Cuba has opposed U.S. military action in Afghanistan, it condemned the Sept. 11 terror attacks on the United States and said it supports efforts to eliminate international terrorism. The Cuban government has said it has no opinion of U.S. plans to hold Afghan war detainees at the base.

In all, U.S. forces report holding 364 suspected Taliban or al-Qaida members, Gen. Richard Myers, chairman of the U.S. Joint Chiefs of Staff, said in Washington. It was unclear how many would initially be brought to Guantanamo.

Until they arrive, U.S. forces in Afghanistan guarding the suspects are being extremely careful, aware that the fighters are willing to die to attack Americans.

"Obviously, any time you have detainees who will sacrifice their life to kill you or what you stand for . . . that's the most dangerous type of individual you can have in your control," Myers said. ■

AP Wire, Wednesday, January 23, 2002

GUANTANAMO INTERROGATIONS BEGIN

By PAISLEY DODDS
The Associated Press

GUANTANAMO BAY NAVAL BASE, Cuba (AP)—U.S. investigators started interrogating 158 detainees of the Afghan war at this remote U.S. outpost Wednesday, postponing the arrivals of others to concentrate on the questioning and expand jail space.

In Washington, President Bush brushed aside an international outcry over treatment of the detainees, telling legislators that they "should be proud" of the U.S. treatment of terrorist suspects.

But some legislators plan a one-day visit Friday to see for themselves, according to the aides of Florida Rep. Ileana Ros-Lehtinen and Rep. Steve Buyer of Indiana, both Republicans who are part of the delegation.

White House spokesman Ari Fleischer cast the detainees as suicidal fanatics who would "engage in murder once again" if set free.

Military officials in Guantanamo said the detainees were not allowed lawyers as officers from several U.S. civilian and military agencies questioned them on a variety of subjects including the training of terrorists. The interrogations are taking place in a tent set up at Camp X-Ray, the hastily built detention center fortified by three rows of fences topped by coils of razor wire and watch-towers and patrolled by attack dogs.

Members of the International Committee of the Red Cross plan to monitor the interrogations, representative Darcy Christen said from Geneva, but he was not sure how that would be done.

"We have a large enough population to begin interviews," said Brig. Gen. Mike Lehnert, the Marine in charge of the detention camp at the U.S. Naval base on Cuba's eastern tip. Given the current size of the prison, the number of detainees now held allows the military to separate those who have been interviewed from the others, Lehnert said. "It wouldn't do to have them comparing notes."

Lehnert said also said that an increase in prisoners now could interfere with the interrogations. The last flight, on Tuesday, raised the population to 158. All are suspected terrorists who fought for al-Qaida or the ousted Afghan Taliban regime that sheltered that network.

Because Guantanamo officials won't identify inmates by nationality, they have refused to say whether a flight last week carried six Algerian terrorist suspects arrested by Bosnian authorities and turned over to the United States, as U.S. military

U.S. Secretary of Defense Donald H. Rumsfeld, center right, exits the detention facility at Camp X-Ray after touring the facilities, Jan. 27, 2002.

in Kandahar had reported. However, Britain, Sweden, Yemen, Saudi Arabia and Australia have said citizens of their country are among detainees in Guantanamo.

Several European government and human rights activists have complained about treatment of prisoners, after newspapers published photographs of newly arrived detainees with their eyes blinded by blacked-out goggles, their hearing impaired by ear muffs and their noses covered by surgical masks. U.S.

military say the precautions are necessary during the daylong flights from Kandahar.

Germany's foreign ministry said Wednesday it called in the U.S. ambassador to discuss the treatment of the terrorism suspects, including the conditions of their detention.

In London, a delegation of British Muslims told a U.S. official the United States had humiliated and degraded the prisoners.

Amnesty International also has said the 8-by-8 foot cells made of chain-link fences are smaller than international standards demand.

Military officials have stressed that the cells are temporary. By Wednesday, workers had built 220 such cells with walls of chain-link fence under a corrugated metal roof, and more were being built by the day, said Army Lt. Col. Bill Costello. The military is awaiting approval to build a more permanent prison that would meet U.S. prison requirements.

The Red Cross and several European countries demanded this week that the detainees be recognized as prisoners of war. Under the Geneva Conventions, POWs must be tried under the same procedures as U.S. soldiers, by court-martial or civilian court, not through military commissions as the Bush administration has proposed.

Lehnert said no decision had been made on the prisoners' status. "Once it is determined . . . I will be told whether they will be given legal counsel," he said.

The military was "being guided" by the Geneva Conventions, but "to say we're following every aspect of the Geneva Convention would be inaccurate," Lehnert said. He said the interrogations would help authorities determine whether detainees should be sent elsewhere.

A petition by U.S. human rights activists was put on hold Tuesday in Los Angeles as a federal judge said he had doubts about his court's jurisdiction. The petitioners want the detainees' identities disclosed and more details on why they're being held.

On Wednesday, 400 copies of the Quran Muslim holy book, with passages in Arabic and English, were delivered to the camp for distribution to prisoners.

A Bangladeshi-born Muslim Navy cleric, one of 12 in the U.S. military, was to arrive later Wednesday. Among other things, camp officials want to discuss whether detainees should be allowed to grow back the long hair and beards that devout Muslim men wear and that were shaved off in detention.

Lehnert said there have only been minor incidents with detainees: One bit a guard on the arm last week, another spat on a guard on Tuesday. The prisoner was separated from the rest and taken to another cell until he calmed down, officials said.

About 230 detainees remain at a U.S. base at Kandahar airport, in southern Afghanistan. ■

RIGHT: **Rear Admiral Jan C. Gaudio, Commander, Navy Region Southeast, 2005.**

ADMIRAL DEFENDS TREATMENT OF PRISONERS

PALM BEACH, Fla., Jan. 23, 2002 (AP)—A U.S. Navy admiral defended Wednesday the military's treatment of the al-Qaida and Taliban prisoners being held at Guantanamo Bay, Cuba, saying they are getting medical care and plenty of food.

"These people are being treated better than where they came from," said Rear Admiral Jan C. Gaudio, commander of Navy's southeast region, which includes Cuba. "They're getting the best medical care the Navy can provide."

The 158 prisoners have been receiving three meals a day and many are gaining weight while being held at the temporary prison constructed on the U.S. military base at Guantanamo, he said.

"The average prisoner's weight when they came in was just 110 pounds," Gaudio said in a speech to the Navy League's Palm Beach branch. "They'd been eating rats and horses up in those caves."

Gaudio also defended the use of masks, although none of the prisoners has tested positive for tuberculosis. "They have attempted to bite and spit at their guards and we want to prevent any possibility of body fluids being transmitted," he said. He added that the blacked-out goggles the prisoners are forced to wear are also necessary to prevent escape. "We don't want them to be able to orient their surroundings," Gaudio said. ■

RED CROSS JOINS CRITICS OF GUANTANAMO DETAINMENTS

WASHINGTON, Oct. 11, 2003 (AP)—The International Committee of the Red Cross joined the rising criticism of the makeshift prison for terror suspects at Guantanamo Bay, Cuba, on Friday, citing "worrying deterioration" in prisoners' mental health. The prison has drawn protests from a dozen international and U.S. groups as some prisoners approach two years there without charges or access to lawyers.

The complaint from the International Red Cross was the third this week about the prison system the Bush administration has devised for holding and trying suspects in the war on terror. Seven legal briefs, filed by former diplomats, former military judges and others, asked the Supreme Court on Thursday to hear the cases of some of the 660 prisoners in Cuba as well as American Yaser Hamdi, who is being held in a Navy brig in South Carolina.

On Monday, the American Civil Liberties Union joined four other U.S. rights groups in filing a request under the Freedom of Information Act for records relating to allegations of torture and abuse in Guantanamo and other U.S. detention facilities. ■

LEFT: An inmate of Camp X-Ray is escorted by two guards while other inmates are seen in their chain-link fence cells, March 15, 2002

ABOVE: Demonstrators dressed in orange prison-like jumpsuits and hoods take part in a demonstration outside the Supreme Court in Washington, Dec. 5, 2007, as the court heard arguments about the rights of prisoners being detained at Guantanamo Bay.

AP Wire, Monday, November 25, 2002

PRESIDENT SIGNS MEASURE TO CREATE GIANT NEW DOMESTIC SECURITY DEPARTMENT

By SCOTT LINDLAW
The Associated Press

WASHINGTON (AP)—President Bush signed legislation Monday creating a new Department of Homeland Security devoted to preventing domestic terror attacks. He promised it "will focus the full resources of the American government on the safety of the American people."

The president picked Tom Ridge as the department's first secretary.

"Today we are taking historic action to defend the United States and protect our citizens against the dangers of a new era," Bush said.

His signature launched the most sweeping federal reorganization since the Defense Department's birth in 1947, a process that his spokesman said could take up to two years to complete.

Internal documents set a more ambitious goal of Sept. 30, 2003, administration officials said. The first wave of agencies are scheduled to join March 1, and include the Secret Service, Coast Guard, Customs Service, Immigration and Naturalization Service, Transportation Safety Administration and the General Service Administration's federal protective services, officials said on condition of anonymity.

The changes will continue in phases according to a plan developed by a multi-agency transition team housed near the White House for months.

The FBI loses its National Infrastructure Protection Center on April 1. The Pentagon's national communication system moves to the new department May 1. The Agriculture Department's Plum Island Animal Disease Center shifts June 1.

Bush said he will nominate Navy Secretary Gordon England to be Ridge's deputy, and Asa Hutchinson, the head of the Drug Enforcement Administration, to be undersecretary of border and transportation security.

"With a vast nation to defend, we can neither predict nor prevent every conceivable attack in a free and open society," Bush said in an East Room event. "No department of government can completely guarantee our safety against ruthless killers who move

New York City Police Detective Edward Bogdanowicz stands guard outside the New York Stock Exchange with other members of the NYPD's Hercules squad, Dec. 22, 2003. Several days before, Homeland Security had announced it was raising the national terror alert from "Code Yellow" to "Code Orange," or high risk. New York City maintained a Code Orange status from the introduction of the color-coded system in March 2002.

and plot in shadows, yet our government will take every possible measure to safeguard . . . our people."

Bush also reported progress in the war on terror. Democrats have questioned whether progress is being made, with Osama bin Laden apparently alive. "Many terrorists are now being interrogated. Many terrorists have been killed. We've liberated a country," Bush said. "This act takes the next critical steps in defending our country against the continuing threat of terrorism. The threat of mass murder on our own soil will be met with a united, effective response."

The bill became snarled in partisan disputes on Capitol Hill, with Democrats refusing to grant the president the broad powers he sought to hire, fire and move workers in the new department. Bush would not yield, and made the disagreement a political issue, railing against Democrats as he campaigned for Republican candidates through the fall. Democrats reversed course after their Election Day loss of Senate control was attributed partly to the homeland security fight.

Bush invited union leaders to the signing ceremony and told them, "we look forward to working with you to make sure your people are treated fairly in this new department."

The new Cabinet department—an idea Bush initially opposed—will swallow 22 existing agencies with combined budgets of about $40 billion and employ 170,000 workers, the most sweeping federal reorganization since the Defense Department's birth in 1947.

White House spokesman Fleischer said the department will come together piece by piece but will not be fully functional for at least a year, and perhaps two. "Just like any entity there are going to be growing pains . . . and that must be anticipated in the creation of this department," he said. . . .

Earlier Monday, Bush signed port security legislation, which he says will protect the nation's coasts and harbors by adding security agents, restricting access to sensitive areas and requiring ships to provide more information about the cargo, crew and passengers they carry. ■

Homeland Security Director Tom Ridge unveils a color-coded terrorism warning system—the Homeland Security Advisory System—in Washington, March 12, 2002. The system was replaced in 2011 with a new non-colorized system called the National Terrorism Advisory System that provides alerts "specific to the threat" with "a specified end date."

AP Wire, Sunday, March 2, 2003

9/11 ARREST A BLOW TO AL-QAIDA

WASHINGTON (AP)—Leaders of the congressional intelligence committees said Sunday the capture of a top al-Qaida operative is a major blow to the terror group and will give U.S. officials the chance to learn about attacks that may have been planned.

Khalid Sheikh Mohammed, suspected mastermind of the Sept. 11 attacks, is "really a big fish," said Sen. Pat Roberts, chairman of the Senate committee. "If there was one person that we wanted to get, it was this man."

Roberts, R-Kan., portrayed Mohammed's arrest Saturday in Pakistan as "a giant step backward for the al-Qaida. This must send a message—will send a message to the al-Qaida, who is mounting a spring offensive for use in Afghanistan. Now their operations commander is simply out of operations."

The House chairman, Rep. Porter Goss, predicted that Mohammed's capture "is going to lead to other successful activities very shortly, I'm sure."

"This is a success on the war on terror and the organization of it, the unraveling of it. This is what we've promised to do—to win the war on terror," Goss, R-Fla., told ABC's *This Week*.

U.S. authorities have taken Mohammed out of Pakistan to an undisclosed location after capturing him in a joint raid by CIA and Pakistani agents, a senior government official in Pakistan

Members of the U.S. Army 4th Psychological Operations Group (POG) watch a news brief in an unidentified location announcing the arrest of Khalid Sheikh Mohammed, suspected mastermind of the Sept. 11 attacks, March 3, 2003.

said Sunday. Mohammed, 37, is perhaps the most senior al-Qaida member after bin Laden and his deputy, Ayman al-Zawahri.

"We got the operations manager; more coming. Look out, al-Qaida," Roberts told *Fox News Sunday*.

A naturalized Pakistani who was born in Kuwait, Mohammed is on the FBI's most-wanted list and allegedly had a hand in many of al-Qaida's most notorious attacks. The U.S. government had offered a reward of up to $25 million for information leading to his capture. Roberts and Goss said Mohammed could provide invaluable information to U.S. investigators if he talks.

"We can learn from him, I hope," about what operations "are out there that we can defend against and forestall," Goss said. "This gives us obviously more focus and more clarity on exactly where to go and what to look at."

U.S. officials say Mohammed organized the Sept. 11, 2001, terror mission that sent hijacked passenger jets crashing into the World Trade Center, the Pentagon and a field in Pennsylvania, killing more than 3,000 people.

There also has been suspicion that Mohammed was involved in last year's kidnapping and murder of *Wall Street Journal* reporter Daniel Pearl, and may have even carried out his execution. But even before then, Mohammed was wanted in connection with plots in the Philippines to bomb trans-Pacific airliners and crash a plane into CIA headquarters. Those were broken up in 1995. He also has been linked to April's bombing of a synagogue in Tunisia. At least 19 tourists, mostly Germans, were killed then. ■

INTERROGATION TACTICS HALTED, PAPER REPORTS

WASHINGTON, June 28, 2004 (AP)—The CIA has suspended use of some White House–approved aggressive interrogation tactics employed to extract information from reluctant al-Qaida prisoners, *The Washington Post* said.

Citing unnamed intelligence officials, the newspaper reported in Sunday's editions that what the CIA calls "enhanced interrogation techniques" were put on hold pending a review by Justice Department and other lawyers. The techniques include such things as feigned drowning and refusal of pain medication for injuries.

The paper quoted current and former CIA officers aware of the recent decision as saying the suspension reflects the agency's concern about being accused of unsanctioned and illegal activities, as it was in the 1970s.

The decision applies to CIA facilities around the world, but not to military prisons at Guantanamo Bay, Cuba, and elsewhere, *The Post* said. A CIA spokesman declined to comment on the issue, it said.

It said CIA interrogations will continue, but without the suspended techniques, which also include feigning suffocation, "stress positions," light and noise bombardment and sleep deprivation. The newspaper said the interrogation methods were approved by Justice Department, and National Security Council lawyers in 2002, outlined to congressional leaders and required the authorization of CIA Director George J. Tenet for use. ■

Osama bin Laden and his deputy, Ayman al-Zawahiri, in Kabul during an interview with Pakistani journalist Hamid Mir, November 2001. After bin Laden's death in 2011, al-Zawahiri became the leader of al-Qaida.

AP Wire, Thursday, July 22, 2004

SEPT. 11 PANEL RECOMMENDS BROAD INTELLIGENCE OVERHAUL IN FINAL REPORT

By HOPE YEN
The Associated Press

WASHINGTON (AP)—The United States government could not protect its citizens from the Sept. 11 terrorist attacks because it failed to appreciate the threat posed by al-Qaida operatives who exploited those lapses to carry out the deadliest assault ever on American soil, the chairman of the Sept. 11 commission said Thursday.

In issuing the panel's 567-page final report, commission chairman Tom Kean said none of the government's efforts to thwart a known threat from al-Qaida had "disturbed or even delayed" Osama bin Laden's plot. "[They] penetrated the defenses of the most powerful nation in the world," Kean said. "They inflicted unbearable trauma on our people, and at the same time they turned international order upside down."

While faulting institutional shortcomings, the report does not blame President George W. Bush or former President Bill Clinton for mistakes contributing to the 2001 attack. Kean and commission vice chairman Lee Hamilton presented Bush with a copy of the report Thursday morning. Bush thanked them for a "really good job" and said the panel makes "very solid, sound recommendations about how to move forward."

"I assured them that where the government needs to act we will," Bush said.

The commission recommended the creation of a new intelligence center and high-level intelligence director to improve the nation's ability to disrupt future terrorist attacks. An intelligence-gathering center would bring a unified command to the more

A Barnes & Noble bookstore in Springfield, Ill., displays *The 9/11 Commission Report*, July 22, 2004. The report, which was a best-selling book, comprised 576 pages that offered a complete account of the circumstances surrounding the 9/11 attacks, as well as provided recommendations for guarding against future attacks.

than dozen agencies that now collect intelligence overseas and at home.

Overseeing the center would be a new Senate-confirmed national intelligence director, reporting directly to the president at just below full cabinet rank, who "would be able to influence the budget and leadership" of the CIA, FBI, Homeland Security Department and Defense Department.

The panel also determined the "most important failure" leading to the Sept. 11 attacks "was one of imagination. We do not believe leaders understood the gravity of the threat."

Hamilton, a former Democratic congressman, appealed for political unity at the heights of America's power. A "shift in mindset and organization" within the U.S. intelligence apparatus and a smoother transition between presidencies are also necessary, he said, to ensure "that this nation does not lower its guard every four or eight years."

"The U.S. government has access to vast amounts of information but it has a weak process, a weak system of processing and using that information," Hamilton said. "Need to share must replace need to know."

Kean, the former Republican governor of New Jersey, said the 9/11 attacks "were a shock, but should not have come as a surprise. By September 2001, the executive branch of the U.S. government, the Congress, the news media, and the American public had received clear warning that Islamist terrorists meant to kill Americans in high numbers." Hamilton added that after the Sept. 11 attacks, the government's efforts "rightly included military action to topple the Taliban and pursue al-Qaida."

"But long-term success demands the use of all elements of national power: diplomacy, intelligence, covert action, law enforcement, economic policy, foreign aid, public diplomacy and homeland defense," said Hamilton, a former Democratic congressman from Indiana. "If we favor one tool while neglecting others, we leave ourselves vulnerable."

The report, which is the culmination of a 20-month investigation into the plot that killed nearly 3,000 people in New York, Washington and Pennsylvania, describes the meticulous planning and determination of hijackers who sought to exploit weaknesses in airline and border procedures by taking test flights.

A surveillance video that surfaced Wednesday shows four of the hijackers passing through security gates at Washington Dulles International Airport shortly before boarding the plane they would crash into the Pentagon. In the video, the hijackers can be seen undergoing additional scrutiny after setting off metal detectors, then being permitted to continue to their gate.

The commission did not recommend creation of a new domestic intelligence agency similar to Britain's MI5, as proposed by some in Congress. Instead, the report endorsed steps already being taken by FBI Director Robert Mueller to create a specialized intelligence service within the FBI.

Beyond government reorganization, the report also says that the United States and its allies must embark on a global strategy of

Family members of the victims of the Sept. 11 terrorist attacks sit in on a public hearing held by the 9/11 Commission (the National Commission on Terrorist Attacks Upon the United States) in Washington, June 16, 2004.

diplomacy and public relations to dismantle the terror network led by Osama bin Laden and defeat the militant Islamic ideology that feeds such terror groups.

"To Muslim parents, terrorists like bin Laden have nothing to offer their children but visions of violence and death. America and its friends have the advantage—our vision can offer a better future," the report said.

The commission also says the U.S. government must do more at home to guard against future terror attacks, including such things as setting national standards for issuance of drivers' licenses and other identification, improving "no-fly" and other terrorist watch lists and using more biometric identifiers to screen travelers at ports and borders. ■

AP Wire, Friday, May 5, 2006

"YOU WILL DIE WITH A WHIMPER"

By MATTHEW BARAKAT and MICHAEL J. SNIFFEN
The Associated Press

ALEXANDRIA, Va. (AP)—U.S. Judge Leonie Brinkema sent Zacarias Moussaoui to prison for life Thursday, to "die with a whimper," for his role in the Sept. 11, 2001, terrorist attacks.

The convicted terrorist declared: "God save Osama bin Laden—you will never get him."

Brinkema and the unrepentant Moussaoui capped the two-month trial with an intense exchange that will mark the defendant's last public words before his incarceration in a maximum-security prison, possibly in Colorado.

A day earlier, a jury rejected the government's case to have Moussaoui executed, deciding instead he should spend life in prison with no chance of parole. Not all jurors were convinced that Moussaoui, who was in jail on immigration charges prior to Sept. 11, had a significant part in the attacks, despite his boastful claims that he did.

Brinkema firmly refused to be interrupted by the 37-year-old defendant as she disputed his declaration from a day earlier: "America, you lost. . . . I won."

"Mr. Moussaoui, when this proceeding is over, everyone else in this room will leave to see the sun . . . hear the birds . . . and they can associate with whomever they want," she said. She went on: "You will spend the rest of your life in a supermax prison. It's absolutely clear who won."

And she said it was proper he will be kept away from outsiders, unable to speak publicly again.

"Mr. Moussaoui, you came here to be a martyr in a great big bang of glory," she said, "but to paraphrase the poet T. S. Eliot, instead you will die with a whimper."

At that point, Moussaoui tried again to interrupt her, but she raised her voice and spoke over him. "You will never get a chance to speak again, and that's an appropriate ending."

Brinkema sentenced Moussaoui to six life terms without the chance of parole, with two terms to be served consecutively. She informed him of his right to appeal the sentence and said she would ask his court-appointed lawyers to file the required notice as a precaution before relieving them from the case.

"I believe it would be an act of futility," she said of an appeal, "but you do have a right."

Moussaoui walked into the courtroom flashing a victory sign. He spoke for less than five minutes; the judge told him he could not use his sentencing to make a political speech.

"You have branded me as a terrorist or a criminal or whatever," he said. "Look at yourselves. I fight for my belief."

He concluded: "God save Osama bin Laden—you will never get him." ■

A courtroom sketch depicting Zacarias Moussaoui walking into the courtroom flashing a victory symbol, before his sentencing by Judge Brinkema, May 4, 2006. He was sent to the United States Penitentiary, Administrative Maximum Facility (USP Florence ADMAX) near Florence, Colo.

ABOVE: A courtroom sketch artist's rendering showing Rosemary Dillard (center at podium), who lost her husband Eddie on 9/11, speaking to al-Qaida conspirator Zacarias Moussaoui, left, as family members of 9/11 victims—Lisa Beilke, right, Abraham Scott, second from right, and Lisa Dolan, second from left—listen in U.S. District Court, Alexandria, Va., during the sentencing of the convicted al-Qaida conspirator, May 4, 2006. U.S. District Judge Leonie Brinkema, center, sentenced Moussaoui to six consecutive life terms in prison without parole.

LEFT: Rosemary Dillard, center, whose husband, Eddie Dillard, died on Flight 77 after it hit the Pentagon on 9/11, hugs an unidentified U.S. Marshal after speaking to the press after Moussaoui's sentencing, May 4, 2006. Lisa Dolan, whose husband, Bob Dolan, died in the Pentagon, is at left.

135

AP Wire, Saturday, November 14, 2009

NEW YORKERS WORRY ABOUT TRIAL FOR 9/11 MASTERMIND

By *DAVID B. CARUSO*
The Associated Press

NEW YORK (AP)—The move to put the self-proclaimed Sept. 11 mastermind on trial just blocks from ground zero raises a host of legal, political and security questions, chief among them: Can a fair-minded jury be found in a city still nursing deep wounds from the attack on the World Trade Center?

Some also worry that the trial of Khalid Sheikh Mohammed will make New York an even bigger terrorist target, and that he will use the proceedings to incite more violence against Americans.

The loudest protests Friday came from relatives of the victims, many of whom oppose any civilian trial for terror suspects especially at the federal courthouse 1,000 yards from the spot where nearly 3,000 people died. "If we have to bring them to the United States, New York City is not the place to have it, let alone in a courthouse that is in the shadows of the twin towers," said Lee Ielpi, whose firefighter son died in the 9/11 attacks. The city's wounds, he said, are simply still too raw. "Ripping that scab open will create a tremendous hardship," he said.

Some city leaders seemed to relish the chance to hold the evildoers accountable at the scene of the crime. "It is fitting that 9/11 suspects face justice near the World Trade Center site where so many New Yorkers were murdered," Mayor Michael Bloomberg said.

Police Commissioner Raymond W. Kelly also said that holding the trial in the city most devastated by the 2001 attack is appropriate, and he pronounced the police department prepared to meet any security challenge.

It may be years before Mohammed is brought to trial, and there is no guarantee the proceedings will actually be held in the city. A defense attorney is almost certain to ask the judge to move the proceedings to someplace less likely to produce a jury tainted by extreme hatred of the defendant, said James Benjamin, a New York City lawyer who has studied terrorism prosecutions. Still, he added, the city has handled big terrorism cases before. . . . "The courts have handled many sensational cases fairly and effectively over the years," Benjamin said.

Civil rights groups, including the American Civil Liberties Union and Human Rights Watch, said Mohammed is likely to be treated more fairly in New York, despite the hatred for him here, than he would before a military tribunal.

In announcing that Mohammed and four other Guantanamo Bay detainees will be brought to trial in New York, Attorney General Eric Holder expressed confidence that a "searching, complete" selection process would produce a fair-minded jury. "We can come up with a process that ensures the defendants can get a fair trial in New York," he said.

Still, others with close personal ties to the case predicted chaos. "It will be a travesty!" said Debra Burlingame, sister of Charles Burlingame, one of the pilots of the airliners hijacked on Sept. 11. She said Mohammed's court appearances will be a "three-ring circus," with the defendant using every opportunity to spout anti-American views as he did in front of 9/11 family members who traveled to Guantanamo to face him in court. . . .

Rep. Peter King, a Republican who favors trials before a military tribunal, said that providing security for the Mohammed case would further stretch the police department's resources. "They already have 1,000 cops working on counterterrorism," he said. . . . As for Mohammed, the congressman warned: "I think this is the moment he's been waiting for." ∎

Jean Gerena holds a photo of her brother-in-law, Emeric Harvey, who was killed in the 9/11 attacks, during the protest outside the federal courthouse in downtown New York Dec. 5, 2009.

ABOVE: **Several hundred people joined a rally in the rain near Manhattan's federal courthouse complex to protest the plan to put major terrorism suspects on trial in New York City, Dec. 5, 2009. One protestor, draped in an American flag bearing the names of all the victims of the 9/11 attacks, watches Attorney General Eric Holder on a big screen during the rally.**

LEFT: **Protestors shout during the rally.**

AP Wire, Tuesday, April 5, 2011

IN A CHANGE OF PLANS, AG SAYS 9/11 SUSPECTS TO FACE TRIBUNALS

By EILEEN SULLIVAN and PETE YOST
The Associated Press

WASHINGTON (AP)—Yielding to political opposition, Attorney General Eric Holder announced Monday that 9/11 mastermind Khalid Sheikh Mohammed and four alleged henchmen will be referred to military commissions for trial rather than to a civilian federal court in New York.

The families of those killed in the Sept. 11, 2001, attacks have waited almost a decade for justice, and "it must not be delayed any longer," Holder told a news conference. Holder had announced the earlier plan for trial in New York City in November 2009, but that foundered amid widespread opposition to a civilian court trial from Republicans and even some Democrats, particularly in New York. Congress passed legislation that prohibits bringing any detainees from the prison at Guantanamo Bay, Cuba, to the United States.

Monday, Holder called the congressional restrictions unwise and unwarranted and said a legislative body cannot make prosecutorial decisions. Most Republicans applauded the turnabout, but Holder said he still is convinced that his earlier decision was the right one. The Justice Department had been prepared to bring "a powerful case" in civilian court, he said.

In New York on Monday, the government unsealed and got a judge to dismiss an indictment in the case that charged Mohammed and the others with 10 counts relating to the Sept. 11, 2001, terrorist attacks. The dismissal was because the defendants will not be tried in civilian court. The indictment said that in late August 2001, as the terrorists in the United States made final preparations, Mohammed was notified about the date of the attack and relayed that to Osama bin Laden.

Some 9/11 family members supported the switch to military commissions. "We're delighted," said Alexander Santora, 74, father of deceased firefighter Christopher A. Santora. The father called the accused terrorists "demonic human beings; they've already said that they would kill us if they could, if they got the chance they would do it again."

Nancy Nee, whose firefighter brother George Cain died at the World Trade Center, said that the five men are "war criminals as far as I'm concerned, and I think that a military trial is the right thing to do."

However, a top Democrat, Senate Judiciary Committee Chairman Patrick Leahy, of Vermont, said he is disappointed with the decision not to prosecute in federal court. "I believe that our justice system, which is the envy of the world, is more than capable of trying high-profile terrorism and national security cases," Leahy said.

Republican lawmakers welcomed the shift. "It's unfortunate that it took the Obama administration more than two years to figure out what the majority of Americans already know: that 9/11 conspirator Khalid Sheikh Mohammed is not a common criminal, he's a war criminal," said House Judiciary Committee Chairman Lamar Smith, of Texas.

Senate Judiciary Chairman Jeff Sessions, of Alabama, said he was "pleased that the Obama administration has finally heeded those who rebuked their decision and the trial is being held where it belongs."

The American Civil Liberties Union criticized the administration's decision. Cases prosecuted in military commissions now "are sure to be subject to continuous legal challenges and delays, and their outcomes will not be seen as legitimate. That is not justice," ACLU Executive Director Anthony D. Romero said.

Holder said it is unclear whether the five men could receive the death penalty if they plead guilty in military court. . . .

During a military hearing at Guantanamo Bay in 2007, Mohammed confessed to planning the 9/11 attacks and a chilling string of other terrorist plots. Many of the schemes, including a previously undisclosed plan to kill several former U.S. presidents, were never carried out or were foiled by counterterrorism authorities.

Mohammed made clear that al-Qaida wanted to down a second trans-Atlantic aircraft during would-be shoe bomber Richard Reid's failed operation later in 2001. The other four alleged co-conspirators are Walid bin Attash, a Yemeni who allegedly ran an al-Qaida training camp in Afghanistan; Ramzi bin al-Shibh, a Yemeni who allegedly helped find flight schools for the hijackers; Ali Abd al-Aziz Ali, accused of helping nine of the hijackers travel to the United States and sending them $120,000 for expenses and flight training; and Mustafa Ahmed al-Hawsawi, a Saudi accused of helping the hijackers with money, Western clothing, traveler's checks and credit cards. ■

ABOVE: In this depiction by courtroom sketch artist Janet Hamlin, alleged Sept. 11 co-conspirators, left, sit with their legal teams in the courtroom during a hearing at the Camp Justice compound for the U.S. war crimes commission on Guantanamo Bay, July 16, 2009. From left to right are Walid bin Attash, Ali Abd al-Aziz Ali and Mustafa Ahmed al-Hawsawi. Three of the five defendants in the case attended the hearing.

Attorney General Eric Holder pauses during a news conference at the Justice Department in Washington, April 4, 2011, where he announced plans to try 9/11 mastermind Khalid Sheikh Mohammed and four alleged henchmen before a military commission in Guantanamo Bay instead of in New York City.

AP Wire, Monday, May 2, 2011

BIN LADEN WENT DOWN FIRING

By KIMBERLY DOZIER and DAVID ESPO
The Associated Press

WASHINGTON (AP)—A U.S. official says Osama bin Laden went down firing at the Navy SEALs who stormed his compound.

An official familiar with the operation says bin Laden was hit by a barrage of carefully aimed return fire. The official spoke on condition of anonymity because aspects of the operation remain classified. The official says two dozen SEALs in night-vision goggles dropped into the high-walled compound in Pakistan by sliding down ropes from Chinook helicopters in the overnight raid.

In the White House Situation Room, Vice President Joe Biden and President Barack Obama, left, and members of the National Security team tensely follow live updates on the mission against Osama bin Laden, May 1, 2011. Next to the president, seated, from left, are: Brigadier General Marshall B. "Brad" Webb; Deputy National Security Advisor Denis McDonough; Secretary of State Hillary Rodham Clinton; and Secretary of Defense Robert Gates. Standing, from left, are: Admiral Mike Mullen, Chairman of the Joint Chiefs of Staff; National Security Advisor Tom Donilon; Chief of Staff Bill Daley; Tony Blinken, National Security Advisor to the Vice President; Audrey Tomason, Director for Counterterrorism; John Brennan, Assistant to the President for Homeland Security and Counterterrorism; and Director of National Intelligence James Clapper.

U.S. officials say bin Laden was killed near the end of the 40-minute raid. The SEALs retrieved bin Laden's body and turned the remaining detainees over to Pakistani authorities.

THIS IS A BREAKING NEWS UPDATE. Check back soon for further information. AP's earlier story is below.

Declaring the killing of Osama bin Laden "a good day for America," President Barack Obama said Monday the world was safer without the al-Qaida terrorist and mastermind of the Sept. 11, 2001 attacks. His administration used DNA testing to help confirm that American forces in Pakistan had in fact killed bin Laden, as U.S. officials sought to erase all doubt about the stunning news.

"Today we are reminded that as a nation there is nothing we can't do," Obama said of the news bound to lift his political standing and help define his presidency. He hailed the pride of those who broke out in overnight celebrations as word spread around the globe.

An elite crew of American forces killed bin Laden during a daring raid on Monday, capping the world's most intense manhunt. Bin Laden was shot in the head during a firefight and then quickly buried at sea. White House officials were mulling the merits and appropriateness of releasing a photo.

As spontaneous celebrations and expressions of relief gave way to questions about precisely what happened and what comes

ABOVE: President Obama reads his statement to photographers after making a televised statement on the death of Osama bin Laden from the East Room of the White House, Sunday night, May 1, 2011. Bin Laden was killed by an elite crew of Navy SEALs during a daring raid in Pakistan, capping the world's most intense manhunt.

RIGHT: A large, jubilant crowd reacts to the news of Osama bin Laden's death at the corner of Church and Vesey Streets, adjacent to ground zero, during the early morning hours of May 2, 2011 in New York.

News vendor Wilbur Hathaway sells a newspaper to a customer at First & Pike News, where *The Seattle Times* was selling at about three times the normal rate, May 2, 2011. The newspaper featured a banner headline about the death of Osama bin Laden.

next, U.S. officials warned that the campaign against terrorism is not nearly over and that the threat of deadly retaliation against the United States and its allies was real.

Senior administration officials said the DNA testing alone offered near 100 percent certainty that bin Laden was among those shot dead. Photo analysis by the CIA, confirmation by a woman believed to be bin Laden's wife on site, and matching physical features like bin Laden's height all helped confirmed the identification.

"We can all agree this is a good day for America," a subdued Obama said during a Medal of Honor ceremony in the glimmering White House East Room.

Still, it was unclear if the world would ever get visual proof.

Senior U.S. officials said bin Laden was killed toward the end of the firefight, which took place in a building at a compound north of Islamabad, the Pakistani capital. His body was put aboard the USS *Carl Vinson* and placed into the North Arabian Sea. Traditional Islamic procedures for handling the remains were followed, the officials said, including washing the corpse, placing it in a white sheet.

Across the government, Obama's security team used the occasion to warn that the campaign against terrorists was hardly over.

"The fight continues and we will never waver," Secretary of State Hillary Rodham Clinton said Monday. Her comments had echoes of former President George W. Bush's declaration nearly a decade ago, when al-Qaida attacks against America led to war in Afghanistan and changed the way Americans viewed their own safety.

Turning to deliver a direct message to bin Laden's followers, she vowed: "You cannot wait us out." . . .

Obama himself had delivered the news of bin Laden's killing in a dramatic White House statement late Sunday. "Justice has been done," he said.

Officials say CIA interrogators in secret overseas prisons developed the first strands of information that ultimately led to the killing of Osama bin Laden.

The military operation that ended bin Laden's life took mere minutes, and there were no U.S. casualties.

U.S. Blackhawk helicopters ferried about two dozen troops from Navy SEAL Team Six, a top military counter-terrorism unit, into the compound identified by the CIA as bin Laden's hideout and back out again in less than 40 minutes. Bin Laden was shot after he and his bodyguards resisted the assault, officials said.

Three adult males were also killed in the raid, including one of bin Laden's sons, whom officials did not name. One of bin Laden's sons, Hamza, is a senior member of al-Qaida. U.S. officials also said one woman was killed when she was used as a shield by a male combatant, and two other women were injured.

The compound is about a half-mile from a Pakistani military academy, in a city that is home to three army regiments and thousands of military personnel. Abbottabad is surrounded by hills and with mountains in the distance.

Critics have long accused elements of Pakistan's security establishment of protecting bin Laden, though Islamabad has always denied it, and in a statement the foreign ministry said his death showed the country's resolve in the battle against terrorism.

Bin Laden's death came 15 years after he declared war on the United States. Al-Qaida was also blamed for the 1998 bombings of two U.S. embassies in Africa that killed 224 people and the 2000 attack on the USS *Cole* that killed 17 American sailors in Yemen, as well as countless other plots, some successful and some foiled.

"We have rid the world of the most infamous terrorist of our time," CIA director Leon Panetta declared to employees of the agency in a memo Monday morning. He warned that "terrorists almost certainly will attempt to avenge" the killing of a man deemed uncatchable. "Bin Laden is dead. Al-Qaida is not," Panetta said.

Retaliatory attacks against the U.S. and Western targets could come from members of al-Qaida's core branch in the tribal areas

Crowds gathers outside the White House in Washington early in the morning of May 2, 2011, to celebrate after President Obama's announcement of the death of Osama bin Laden.

This heart dedicated to the Navy SEALS who carried out the bin Laden mission was hung on the fence overlooking the crash site at the temporary memorial to United Flight 93 in Shanksville, Pa., on May 2, 2011.

of Pakistan, al-Qaida franchises in other countries, and radicalized individuals in the U.S. with al-Qaida sympathies, according to a Homeland Security Department intelligence alert issued Sunday and obtained by The Associated Press.

While the intelligence community does not have insight into current al-Qaida plotting, the department believes symbolic, economic and transportation targets could be at risk, and small arms attacks against other targets can't be ruled out.

In all, nearly 3,000 were killed in the Sept. 11 attacks.

As news of bin Laden's death spread, hundreds of people cheered and waved American flags at ground zero in New York, the site where al-Qaida hijacked jets toppled the twin towers of the World Trade Center. Thousands celebrated all night outside the White House gates. Many people said they were surprised that bin Laden had finally been found and killed. John Gocio, a doctor from Arkansas who was gathering what details he could from TV screens at O'Hare Airport in Chicago, marveled: "After such a long time, you kind of give up and say, 'Well, that's never going to happen.'" . . .

A couple of people posed for photographs in front of the White House while holding up front pages of Monday's newspapers announcing bin Laden's death. The development seems certain to give Obama a political lift. Even fierce critics such as former Vice President Dick Cheney praised him. . . .

The few fiery minutes in Abbottabad followed years in which U.S. officials struggled to piece together clues that ultimately led to bin Laden, according to an account provided by senior adminis-

tration officials who spoke on condition of anonymity because of the sensitivity of the operation. Based on statements given by U.S. detainees since the 9/11 attacks, they said, intelligence officials have long known that bin Laden trusted one al-Qaida courier in particular, and they believed he might be living with him in hiding.

Four years ago, the United States learned the man's identity, which officials did not disclose, and then about two years later, they identified areas of Pakistan where he operated. Last August, the man's residence was found, officials said.

"Intelligence analysis concluded that this compound was custom built in 2005 to hide someone of significance," with walls as high as 18 feet and topped by barbed wire, according to one official. Despite the compound's estimated $1 million cost and two security gates, it had no phone or Internet running into the house.

By mid-February, intelligence from multiple sources was clear enough that Obama wanted to "pursue an aggressive course of action," a senior administration official said. Over the next two and a half months, the president led five meetings of the National Security Council focused solely on whether bin Laden was in that compound and, if so, how to get him, the official said.

Obama made a decision to launch the operation on Friday, shortly before flying to Alabama to inspect tornado damage, and aides set to work on the details.

Administration aides said the operation was so secretive that no foreign officials were informed in advance, and only a small circle inside the U.S. government was aware of what was unfolding half a world away. ■

TAKING CREDIT FOR KILLING BIN LADEN SPARKS DEBATE

By KEN DILANIAN
The Associated Press

WASHINGTON, Nov. 7, 2014 (AP)—Some special operations service members and veterans are unhappy that one of their own has taken credit publicly for killing Osama bin Laden. Others say they have gotten used to the idea that their brethren might break the code of silence and seek to profit from their deeds. That internal debate gained intensity this week when retired Navy SEAL Robert O'Neill acknowledged that he had fired two rounds into the forehead of the al-Qaida leader during the 2011 raid on his secret compound in Pakistan. O'Neill says more and more people were becoming aware of his role and that his name was bound to become public anyway.

O'Neill had recounted his version of the bin Laden raid in February 2013 to *Esquire* magazine, which identified him only as "the shooter." In a story Thursday, *The Washington Post* identified him by name as he described shooting the leader of the terrorist group behind the attacks of Sept. 11, 2001.

One current and one former SEAL confirmed to The Associated Press that O'Neill was long known to have killed bin Laden. Defense Department officials confirmed that O'Neill was a member of SEAL Team Six and was part of the raid, but they said they could not confirm who fired the fatal shot, noting that other SEALs on the mission also fired at bin Laden.

If O'Neill discloses classified information during the interviews he could be subject to an investigation or action by the Justice Department, the Defense Department officials said. They spoke on condition of anonymity because they were not authorized to discuss the matter by name.

O'Neill told *The Post* that shots also were fired by two other SEAL team members, including Matt Bissonnette, who described the raid somewhat differently in his book *No Easy Day*. His lawyer said Bissonnette is under federal criminal investigation over whether he disclosed classified information in the book, which he did not vet with the military. In the *Esquire* piece, O'Neill makes no mention of Bissonnette shooting bin Laden. . . . . .

In the *Esquire* piece, O'Neill said he was one of two SEALs who went up to the third floor of the building where bin Laden was hiding. The first man fired two shots at bin Laden as he peeked out of the bedroom, but O'Neill says those shots missed. The man then tackled two women in the hallway outside of bin Laden's bedroom.

O'Neill went into the bedroom, he recounts. "There was bin Laden standing there. He had his hands on a woman's shoulders, pushing her ahead, not exactly toward me but by me, in the direction of the hallway commotion. It was his youngest wife, Amal."

O'Neill added: "In that second, I shot him two times in the forehead. Bap! Bap! The second time as he's going down. He crumpled onto the floor in front of his bed and I hit him again. Bap! Same place. . . . He was dead." ■

Retired Navy SEAL Robert O'Neill, who says he shot and killed Osama bin Laden, poses for a portrait before an interview in Washington, Nov. 14, 2014.

AP Wire, Monday, May 2, 2011

BIN LADEN'S DEATH SPARKS RELIEF, OUTRAGE

By DEB RIECHMANN and KARL RITTER
The Associated Press

KABUL, Afghanistan (AP)—News of Osama bin Laden's death has stirred strong emotions, from a profound sense of relief across much of the globe to outrage among sympathizers who vowed to avenge the al-Qaida leader.

Most world leaders on Monday welcomed President Barack Obama's announcement of the helicopter raid on a compound in Pakistan, congratulating the U.S. for killing bin Laden or expressing satisfaction that the search for the world's most wanted terrorist was over.

"This is the fate that evil killers deserve," said outgoing Lebanese Prime Minister Saad Hariri, deploring the harm that bin Laden did to "the image of Islam and Arab causes."

French President Nicolas Sarkozy hailed "the tenacity of the United States" in its hunt for the mastermind of the Sept. 11 attacks. Italian Premier Silvio Berlusconi called his death a "great result in the fight against evil."

Spontaneous, celebratory rallies broke out in New York City at ground zero, where the World Trade Center towers fell nearly 10 years ago, and outside the White House where Obama announced bin Laden's death.

"Here in New York, it is impossible not to be reminded of the murderous legacy of Osama bin Laden," EU foreign policy chief Catherine Ashton said while on a visit to the city. "He and the al-Qaida network have been responsible for the deaths of thousands of innocent people across the world, including the Arab world." Ashton said "we need to remain vigilant in our efforts to completely disable the al-Qaida network, as the threat of retaliatory action remains serious."

In Afghanistan, where bin Laden was given refuge by the country's previous Taliban rulers, local officials erupted in applause when President Hamid Karzai told them the news.

"[His hands] were dipped in the blood of thousands and thousands of children, youths and elders of Afghanistan," Karzai told reporters, and repeated his claim that the fight against terrorism should not be fought in Afghan villages, but across the border in hideouts in Pakistan where bin Laden was killed.

But others in the war-torn nation disagreed about bin Laden's legacy. "He was like a hero in the Muslim world," said Sayed Jalal, a rickshaw driver in the eastern Afghan city of Jalalabad. "His struggle was always against non-Muslims and infidels, and against superpowers."

At the site of the 1998 bombing of the U.S. Embassy in Kenya, a man who lost his eyesight in the attack prayed in front of a wall commemorating those killed.

"This is a day of great honor to the survivors and victims of terrorism in the world," Douglas Sidialo told AP Television News. "A day to remember those whose lives were changed forever. A day of great relief to us victims and survivors, to see that bin Laden has been killed." . . .

Afghan president Hamid Karzai addresses media representatives at the presidential palace in Kabul, May 2, 2011. President Karzai said that the killing of Osama bin Laden in neighboring Pakistan proved his administration's long-standing position that the war on terror was not rooted in Afghanistan.

Outside the iconic Taj Mahal hotel in Mumbai, India, one of the sites of the 2008 terror siege that killed 166, some people didn't believe bin Laden was dead. Others said killing him had made the world a little safer. "It's a good feeling there is one terrorist less," said Sufyan Khan, a 20-year-old Muslim student.

Elsewhere, those who followed or sympathized with bin Laden expressed shock and dismay, or vowed revenge. "My heart is broken," Mohebullah, a Taliban fighter-turned-farmer in eastern Afghanistan, told The Associated Press in a telephone interview. "In the past, we heard a lot of rumors about his death, but if he did die, it is a disaster and a black day."

Salah Anani, a Palestinian-Jordan militant leader accused of links to al-Qaida, said, "There will soon be another leader."

Bin Laden's former sister-in-law, Swiss-born Carmen Binladin, told the AP that he would have wanted to die "rather than face justice in an American court." She said his family in Saudi Arabia will have received the news of his death with "a great sense of sadness."

U.S. embassies and Americans across the globe were on alert for possible reprisals. German Foreign Minister Guido Westerwelle said a "backlash" from al-Qaida sympathizers could not be ruled out. . . .

In Israel, Prime Minister Benjamin Netanyahu called bin Laden's death "a resounding victory for justice, for freedom and for the shared values of all democratic countries that fight shoulder to shoulder against terror."

The leader of the Palestinian militant Hamas government in Gaza, Ismail Haniyeh, condemned the killing, saying the operation marked "the continuation of the American oppression and shedding of blood of Muslims and Arabs."

Venezuela, which often criticizes U.S. policy, also offered a voice of dissent. Vice President Elias Jaua told state-run television it was "questionable from a human point of view to celebrate killing as an instrument for resolving problems." . . .

Kenyan President Mwai Kibaki called the strike against bin Laden "an act of justice to those Kenyans who lost their lives and the many more who suffered injuries" in the 1998 embassy bombings in Kenya and Tanzania. The attacks blamed on al-Qaida killed 224 people and injured thousands.

In Iraq, the former epicenter for al-Qaida's war against the U.S., both Shiite and Sunni civilians celebrated bin Laden's death. "The crimes committed by al-Qaida against the Iraqi people as well as other people all over the world, shows that this terrorist group poses a clear danger to the world's security," Iraqi government spokesman Ali al-Dabbagh said.

Al-Qaida linked groups like the Islamic State of Iraq were responsible for some of the most heinous crimes committed in the country. As recently as last fall, the Islamic State of Iraq, using at least some fighters from abroad, raided a Baghdad church, killing 68 people.

"We are very happy to hear about the killing of the boss of terrorism in the world," said Mardin Yalda, 45, who survived the horrific

AL-QAIDA CONFIRMS BIN LADEN'S DEATH

CAIRO, May 6, 2011 (AP)—Al-Qaida has issued its first confirmation of Osama bin Laden's death in an Internet statement posted on militant websites. Today's statement by the terror network says bin Laden's blood "will not be wasted" and it will continue attacking Americans and their allies. ■

Supporters of Pakistani religious party Jamiat Ulema-e-Islam (Assembly of Islamic Clerics) rally to condemn the killing of Osama bin Laden in Quetta, Pakistan, May 2, 2011.

siege. "During his life, bin Laden was the source of suffering and agony for many innocent people, whether Christians or Muslims."

Several Muslims said bin Laden's death will help restore the image of Islam as a religion of peace, not violence and radicalism.

"Bin Laden's acts robbed us of freedom to talk and move around," said Mohammad al-Mansouri, a prominent lawyer and human rights activist in the United Arab Emirates. "He turned us into targets at home and suspects in every foreign country we traveled to."

Others said the al-Qaida leader should have been brought to justice instead of killed.

"Osama bin Laden has been responsible for preaching hatred and using terrorism to kill innocent people around the world and it would have been more suitable for him to be captured alive and put on trial in an international court," said Mohammed Shafiq, head of the Ramadhan Foundation, a Muslim organization in Britain.

NATO called bin Laden's death a "significant success" and said the alliance, with 150,000 troops in Afghanistan, would make sure the country "never again becomes a safe haven for extremism."

But Russia's ambassador to NATO downplayed bin Laden's significance, saying the al-Qaida leader "was only a symbol" who had long since retired and been replaced by younger commanders.

Security analysts questioned whether the fact that bin Laden was found in a compound about 60 miles (100 kilometers) from the Pakistani capital could complicate relations between the U.S. and Pakistan.

"He's the world's most wanted man but he didn't seem to be Pakistan's most wanted man," said Gareth Price, a researcher at Chatham House in London. "Why had Pakistan not spotted he is living in a nice tourist resort just outside Islamabad?"

Pakistan's High Commissioner to Britain, Wajid Shamsul Hasan, insisted that his nation was not aware of bin Laden's presence in Abbottabad. "Had we known it we would have done it ourselves," Hasan told the BBC. ∎

An Iraqi man in Baghdad reads a newspaper with front page headlines reporting the killing of Osama bin Laden, May 3, 2011. The news headline, in Arabic, translates as "The Killer Is Killed."

PRESIDENT MEETS RAID PARTICIPANTS A DAY AFTER VISIT TO GROUND ZERO

WASHINGTON, May 6, 2011 (AP)—President Barack Obama's carefully calibrated response to the killing of Osama bin Laden is shifting from remembrance to appreciation.

One day after laying a wreath at the site of the World Trade Center in New York City, the president was to go to Fort Campbell, Ky., to thank participants in the daring raid on bin Laden's compound in Pakistan five days ago. . . . White House officials say at Fort Campbell Obama will express his gratitude to the raid participants privately. But the president, joined by Vice President Joe Biden, also will address soldiers who have returned recently from Afghanistan, a public forum where the military triumph will be hard to mask.

Obama so far has tried to avoid rejoicing publicly over bin Laden's death. But he has maintained a steady stream of events and activities that have kept the success of the remarkable commando operation at the forefront.

On Thursday, he visited New York fire and police stations that responded to the Sept. 11, 2001, attack that was carried out by bin Laden's al-Qaida operatives, and he met privately with victims' families. He also has given an interview about the operation to CBS that will air Sunday on *60 Minutes*.

In New York, Obama did not mention bin Laden by name. He didn't have to. "When we say we will never forget, we mean what we say," Obama told firefighters.

At the same time, the White House is wary of overplaying its hand. Obama has decided not to release photographs of bin Laden's corpse, saying, "We don't need to spike the football." ■

President Obama and firefighters toast during a lunch at the Engine 54, Ladder 4, Battalion 9 firehouse in New York, May 5, 2011. The firehouse, known as the "Pride of Midtown," lost 15 firefighters on 9/11—an entire shift and more than any other New York firehouse.

AP Wire, Wednesday, February 4, 2015

LAWYERS: EVIDENCE SHOWS SAUDI ARABIA AIDED 9/11 HIJACKERS

By LARRY NEUMEISTER
The Associated Press

NEW YORK (AP)—Lawyers for victims of the Sept. 11 attacks say they have new evidence that agents of Saudi Arabia "directly and knowingly" helped the hijackers, including sworn testimony from the so-called 20th hijacker and from three principals of the U.S. government's two primary probes of the attacks.

The Embassy of Saudi Arabia in Washington said in a statement Wednesday that Zacarias Moussaoui's claims come from a "deranged criminal" and that there is no evidence to support them. It said Saudi Arabia had nothing to do with the deadly 2001 attacks.

The lawyers filed documents in Manhattan federal court to buttress claims Saudi Arabia supported al-Qaida and its leader at the time, Osama bin Laden, prior to the attacks. They have always said "the Saudi government directly and knowingly assisted the 9/11 hijackers," but now say facts and evidence supporting the assertion "are compelling."

They said an "expansive volume" of new evidence—including U.S. and foreign intelligence reports, government reports and testimony from al-Qaida members—support lawsuits seeking billions of dollars from countries, companies and organizations that aided al-Qaida and other terrorist groups.

They said evidence likely to be released soon includes a congressional report detailing evidence of Saudi 9/11 involvement

Portraits of the 19 al-Qaida hijackers are displayed at the National September 11 Memorial Museum, May 14, 2014, in New York.

and nearly 80,000 pages of material relating to an FBI probe of Saudis who supported 9/11 hijackers in Florida.

They also cited their own research, including last year's Moussaoui interview at the maximum-security prison in Florence, Colo. Moussaoui repeated some assertions made previously, including that a 1990s plot by al-Qaida to shoot down Air Force One and assassinate President Bill Clinton was assisted by a top Saudi Embassy employee, along with claims there were direct dealings between senior Saudi officials and bin Laden.

The lawyers also said their case is boosted by sworn statements by 9/11 commissioners John Lehman and Bob Kerrey, as well as Bob Graham, co-chairman of the Joint Congressional Inquiry into 9/11. Graham says he believes "there was a direct line" between some Sept. 11 terrorists and the government of Saudi Arabia while Lehman, a former Navy secretary, explained close historical ties between the kingdom's government clerics and al-Qaida, the lawyers noted.

The court filing, coming less than two weeks after the death of Saudi King Abdullah, was made to meet a deadline set by Judge George B. Daniels.

In a website statement, the Saudi embassy noted the Sept. 11 attack had been the "most intensely investigated crime in history and the findings show no involvement by the Saudi government or Saudi officials."

As for Moussaoui, the statement said: "His words have no credibility. His goal in making these statements only serves to get attention for himself and try to do what he could not do through acts of terrorism—to undermine Saudi-U.S. relations."

Moussaoui was arrested on immigration charges in August 2001 after employees of a Minnesota flight school became alarmed he wanted to learn to fly a Boeing 747 with no pilot's license. He was in custody on Sept. 11 and pleaded guilty in April 2005 to conspiring with the hijackers to kill Americans. A psychologist testified for the defense at death penalty proceedings that Moussaoui had paranoid schizophrenia. Jurors spared his life. ■

U.S. JUDGE: SAUDI ROYALS MUST ANSWER QUESTIONS IN 9/11 LAWSUIT

NEW YORK, Sept. 11, 2020 (AP)—Two members of Saudi Arabia's royal family will have to answer questions about the Sept. 11 attacks in what lawyers for victims call a turning point in a long-running lawsuit, a federal judge ruled.

U.S. Magistrate Judge Sarah Netburn in a written ruling unsealed late Thursday ordered Saudi Arabia to make the royals—and other Saudi witnesses, including current and former government official—available for depositions. It was unclear how and when the witnesses will be deposed, but the decision means "we can start uncovering what they know," plaintiff's attorney Jim Kreindler said Friday.

The members of the royal family include Prince Bandar bin Sultan, who is a former intelligence chief in Saudi Arabia and was the kingdom's U.S. ambassador from 1983 to 2005, court papers said.

Some relatives of Sept. 11 victims claim that agents of Saudi Arabia knowingly supported al-Qaida and its leader at the time, Osama bin Laden, before hijackers crashed planes into New York's World Trade Center, the Pentagon and a Pennsylvania field. The nearly 3,000 deaths were commemorated Friday on the 19th anniversary of the attacks. The families are seeking billions of dollars in damages.

Michael Kellogg, an attorney for Saudi Arabia, declined to comment on Friday. The Saudi government has long denied involvement in the attacks. ∎

RIGHT TOP: Saudi prince Bandar bin Sultan seen at his palace in Riyadh, June 4, 2008. In a written ruling unsealed on Sept. 10, 2020, a federal judge in New York stated that the prince is among two members of Saudi Arabia's royal family who will have to answer questions about the Sept. 11 attacks, in what lawyers for victims call a turning point in a long-running lawsuit.

RIGHT BOTTOM: Rosaleen Tallon, center, who lost her brother Sean Tallon of FDNY Ladder 10 during the 9/11 attacks, speaks to reporters in Brooklyn in regard to news of President Donald Trump's canceled plan for secret talks with Afghanistan's Taliban insurgents, May 29, 2007. Tallon says she wants U.S. troops home and wants the country to focus on getting answers from Saudi Arabia about 9/11.

ANOTHER JUDGE QUITS LONG-STALLED 9/11 TRIAL

OFF LIMITS

TRESPASSERS WILL BE PROSECUTED

The sun sets behind the closed Camp X-Ray detention facility in Guantanamo Bay, April 17, 2019.

By BEN FOX
The Associated Press

WASHINGTON (AP)—Another military judge has stepped down from the Sept. 11 war crimes tribunal at the U.S. Navy base at Guantanamo Bay, Cuba, a further blow to an already long-stalled case.

Marine Col. Stephen F. Keane said in an order issued Friday that he must recuse himself from the case because of his past work for the government and personal connections to victims of the Sept. 11, 2001, terrorist attacks. He was appointed last month.

Keane is the fifth judge to preside over the trial by military commission for five men held at Guantanamo who are charged with planning and assisting the hijacking plot that killed nearly 3,000 people in New York, Virginia and Pennsylvania.

Keane said he believes he could serve as an impartial judge in the death penalty case. But the Marine colonel said he did not want to cause further delays or grounds for appeal in a case that has been bogged down in pretrial proceedings since the May 2012 arraignment.

"My continued presence as the military judge in this case arguably creates an appearance of bias," Keane wrote.

Keane, describing his possible conflicts, noted that he grew up in the New York City area and had a close relative who worked for the Fire Department but retired before the Sept. 11 attacks. He also served in a Defense Department counter-terrorism task force, in which he conducted legal reviews concerning the transfer of detainees from Afghanistan to Guantanamo, where the U.S. now holds 40 prisoners.

He also served as a Marine Corps fellow at the Justice Department, working on counter-terrorism issues dealing with al-Qaida, though not on any work directly involving the five defendants in the Guantanamo war crimes case.

In addition, Keane said has a "significant personal connection" to people who were "directly affected by the events of 9/11," though he did not provide any details.

The five defendants face charges that include terrorism and nearly 3,000 counts of murder in violation of the laws of war. The men include Khalid Sheikh Mohammad, who has portrayed himself as the architect of the Sept. 11 attacks and other plots. ■

CHAPTER 5

IN MEMORIAM

"How can we forget Sept. 11?" is a rhetorical question expressed by many over the course of two decades. For countless others, it is "How shall we remember?"

The day itself was full of terror, chaos and grief, as well as haunting images indelibly captured by photographers and news cameras, but perhaps no presentation was as gripping as the September 11 Photo Project, a compilation edited by Michael Feldschuh, a Wall Street executive, and James Austin Murray, a New York City firefighter and 9/11 first responder.

Though one of many photo collections of the day's events, the September 11 Photo Project was unique and organic. It debuted at a SoHo gallery a month after the attack, beginning with 200 submissions and growing to more than 3,500 within a month. As its fame grew, amateur and professional photographers continued contributing their images. Eventually, the number grew to over 5,000 stunning images. The exhibit toured seven cities over two years and was viewed by 300,000 visitors.

In late October, the Concert for New York City at Madison Square Garden brought together Paul McCartney, David Bowie, Elton John, Billy Joel, Bon Jovi, Adam Sandler, the Who and other performers. It was one of a series of concerts held in the country to honor first responders, their families and those lost in the attacks and raise money for disaster relief.

On the six-month anniversary of the attack, as "America the Beautiful" spilled melodiously into the night air over New York's ground zero, two pillars of light soared toward the heavens as if filling a hole torn from the skyline and the hole in so many hearts. (The Tribute in Light art installation became a tradition that has continued every year on Sept. 11.) In Washington, the 189 that died at the Pentagon were memorialized by Defense Secretary Donald H. Rumsfeld and top military officers. Church bells chimed in Shanksville, Pa., at 10:06 a.m. in memory of the 44 passengers who perished on United Flight 93.

On the first anniversary of the attack, the nation turned its eyes to the crash sites once more. At ground zero in New York, Mayor Michael Bloomberg began with a moment of silence at precisely 8:46 a.m., when the first plane struck. Soon after, in a vigil that took 2 1/2 hours, 197 survivors and family members of loved ones lost read the names of the 2,801 that perished here in alphabetical order, starting with Gordon Aamoth Jr., 32, and ending with Igor Zukelman, 29. At the Pentagon, where 189 perished, President Bush, with wistful cello music in the background, declared, "Though they died in tragedy, they did not die in vain." Soon after the ceremony, the President flew to Shanksville, to commemorate the deaths of the 44 killed when a passenger revolt quashed the plan to crash into the White House. Around the nation and the world there were thousands of other solemn remembrances.

Grand permanent monuments to the fallen were on the drawing board for ground zero in New York, the Pentagon and at Shanksville. While they were under construction, a 15-city tour of memorabilia traveled to major U.S. cities featuring survivors' stories and artifacts from the Port Authority of New York and New Jersey, which owned the World Trade Center. First to open, on Sept. 11, 2008, was the National 9/11 Pentagon Memorial, a two-acre park built on an angle parallel to Flight 77's path before it crashed. Here, cantilevered benches, each bearing a victim's name, provide solace for the site's visitors. On Sept. 10, 2011, at the 10-year anniversary, a permanent Flight 93 National Memorial was dedicated in Shanksville.

The National September 11 Memorial at ground zero in New York officially opened on Sept. 11, 2011. It honors the 2,977 killed at the three crash sights and the six killed in the World Trade Center bombing of Feb. 26, 1993. On May 21, 2014, the 9/11 Memorial Museum was dedicated at the site. With 110,000 square feet of subterranean space, the museum's mission is to remember "the story of 9/11 through artifacts, imagery, personal stories and interactive technology." The memorial, comprising two one-acre pools with the largest man-made waterfalls in the U.S., drowns out the sounds of the city, providing visitors with a solemn, contemplative sanctuary.

On Sept. 11, 2007, an enormous memorial flag hanging from the Pentagon roof is illuminated near the spot where American Airlines Flight 77 crashed into the Department of Defense headquarters six years earlier.

Monday, October 22, 2001

SUPERSTARS OFFER RELIEF AT NYC CONCERT

By NEKESA MUMBI MOODY
The Associated Press

NEW YORK (AP)—Paul McCartney, David Bowie, Elton John, Billy Joel joined other performers Saturday in a "Concert for New York," which served as a benefit for the city while celebrating its resiliency in a time of crisis.

David Bowie kicked off the mammoth concert with a poignant rendition of Paul Simon's "America," then rocked a crowd that included thousands of firefighters, police officers and rescue workers with the appropriately titled "Heroes."

"It's an absolute pleasure to play for you tonight," Bowie told the crowd at "Concert for New York," which was broadcast from Madison Square Garden live on VH1.

Despite the tragic circumstances that led to the concert, the star-studded event was anything but somber—instead, it was a raucous celebration. One of the biggest ovations was reserved for the 6,000 firefighters, police officers and rescue workers honored for their efforts in the Sept. 11 attack on the World Trade Center.

"I met children who lost their daddies and I met a lot of people who survived," former President Clinton said backstage. "This is the first time they've had a chance to clap their hands and shout and dance. This is a great gift to them." Firefighters and police officers laughed and danced in the aisles.

Saturday Night Live cast member Will Ferrell got laughs with his impersonation of President Bush, and Adam Sandler used his Operaman character in a risqué segment that mocked Osama bin Laden. There's not a day that goes by that people don't want to laugh," Sandler said backstage. "People are in great pain and you want to just laugh and feel good for a minute and that's what comedy is trying to do right now."

Paul McCartney was the night's final act. Wearing an American flag pin and T-shirt with "FDNY" printed on the back, the former Beatle sang five songs, including "Lover to a Friend," a new single he said would raise money for the Sept. 11 Fund, "Yesterday," and "Freedom," which he wrote in the aftermath of the World Trade Center attack.

Its lyrics included the line, "I will fight for the right to live in freedom.

"This is one of the greatest nights for me," he told the crowd. "I want to thank you guys for everything you've done, on behalf of the British, on behalf of America, on behalf of the world." ■

Paul McCartney is surrounded on stage by New York City rescue workers at the end of the "Concert for New York" at New York's Madison Square Garden, Oct. 20, 2001.

NYC NEARS FINAL COUNT OF VICTIMS OF TRADE CENTER ATTACK

NEW YORK, Jan. 10, 2002 (AP)—City officials are close to determining a final count of the people who were killed in the attack on the World Trade Center, police said Wednesday.

The city's total has stood at 2,893 for three days, decreasing from near 7,000 in the immediate aftermath of Sept 11 attacks. Officials eliminated mistakes and duplicated entries in missing-person reports, and the tally could still be reduced further, said police department Chief Charles Campisi, who heads the effort. "We're very, very close," Campisi said. "I would say we're 99 percent there."

Included within that total are 309 missing, for whom no remains have been found. Campisi said that number will drop as the medical examiner's office identifies the more than 12,000 body parts collected among the ruins of the collapsed towers. That process will not affect the total, because as the number of missing drops, the number of confirmed dead will increase.

Throughout the 17 weeks since the Sept 11 attack, the numbers have fluctuated, sometimes drastically. The official city count peaked at 6,729 on Sept 24, but it dropped by more than 1,000 six days later when then-Mayor Rudolph Giuliani announced that cross-checks of names had eliminated duplications.

Chasing the errors has been "labor intensive," Campisi said. "It was a very monumental task," he said. "We worked diligently on it, knowing that this would be a permanent part of history." The errors were due in part to the flooding of the police database with missing-person reports from multiple sources, including family members, the American Red Cross, airlines, employers and law enforcement agencies.

Campisi said some victims may remain missing. . . . "With the explosion and intense heat and crushing of the buildings, there will be people unaccounted for."

An ongoing Associated Press tally of people confirmed dead and those reported dead or missing stood at 3,018 on Wednesday. That number also includes 189 people who died in the attack on the Pentagon and 44 who died when a hijacked jet crashed in Pennsylvania. ∎

TOP: **A New York Police Department detective in a decontamination lab at Fresh Kills landfill in Staten Island inspects a police service pistol recovered from the World Trade Center debris, Jan. 14, 2002. Approximately 5,000 pieces of personal property found in the debris had been screened at the lab from Sept. 11, 2001 to Jan. 14, 2002.**

BOTTOM: **Identification cards found in the tons of debris removed from the site of the World Trade Center attacks sit in colored bins in a trailer at Fresh Kills Jan. 14, 2002. Detectives worked to sort through the personal belongings recovered from the debris in the hopes of returning the items to families.**

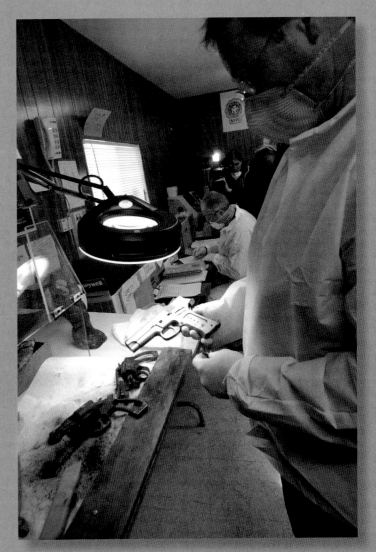

The Tribute in Light shines over the Manhattan skyline and the Statue of Liberty in New York, on the anniversary of the terrorist attacks on the World Trade Center, Sept. 11, 2004. The memorial was first presented on March 11, 2002, the six-month anniversary of the attacks, and has been presented by the Municipal Art Society every year since.

AP Wire, Monday, March 11, 2002

TRIBUTE IN LIGHT UNVEILED IN NYC

By SARA KUGLER
The Associated Press

NEW YORK (AP)—To the strains of "America the Beautiful," two pillars of light soared skyward from beside ground zero Monday night, filling a hole torn in the nation's most revered skyline when terrorists brought down the World Trade Center six months ago.

As relatives of some of the thousands killed stood and watched, 12-year-old Valerie Webb activated 88 powerful searchlights arranged to simulate the twin towers. Her father, Port Authority police officer Nathaniel Webb, still hasn't been found in the ruins nearby.

"The lights will reach up to the skies and into heaven, near where the heroes are now," said Arthur Leahy, holding a picture of his brother James Leahy, a New York police officer who died on Sept. 11. The ethereal "Tribute in Light" memorial was designed to help lessen the aching loss felt across the country since that day. It will shine each night until April 13.

The lighting capped a day of tributes from Boston, New York and rural Pennsylvania to the nation's capital, where President Bush offered words of resolve at a White House ceremony attended by more than 100 ambassadors as well as victims' relatives and members of Congress. "History will know that day not only as a day of tragedy, but as a day of decision when the civilized world was stirred to anger and to action," Bush said, calling on nations to press the fight against terrorism.

At the Pentagon, where 189 people died on Sept. 11, Defense Secretary Donald H. Rumsfeld met with military leaders from nations in the anti-terrorism coalition. And in Shanksville, Pa., church bells tolled at 10:06 a.m. in memory of the 44 victims aboard United Flight 93, the fourth hijacked jet to crash that day. It went down in the countryside, apparently after some of the passengers fought back.

As the memorial of light slowly gained power, soprano Jessye Norman sang "America the Beautiful" and Mayor Michael Bloomberg said the tribute "reminds us there is still much in this world to be hopeful about and that the human spirit will always prevail."

In nearby Battery Park, a pile of flowers and pictures of the dead and missing grew at the base of *The Sphere*, a damaged steel and bronze sculpture that once stood in the trade center plaza and has been dedicated as a temporary memorial.

People cheered from their Brooklyn rooftops as the searchlights beamed skyward. In New York Harbor, more than 100 relatives of those killed watched from a boat. Many said the new memorial is comforting, but a permanent tribute remains an important goal.

"We expect there to be a more significant memorial when it's all done," said Jack Lynch, whose son, firefighter Michael Lynch, died in the attack.

The tributes began hours earlier. Several hundred people gathered at Battery Park for moments of silence at 8:46 a.m. and 9:03 a.m., the precise times that two planes hit the towers and caused the catastrophe that killed 2,830 people.

"At that hour we saw the worst of mankind," Gov. George Pataki said. "We saw the face of evil."

Former Mayor Rudolph Giuliani told the crowd to look to the victims "for our inspiration and our sense of purpose. They would want us to lift up our heads very, very high."

Greek Orthodox Archbishop Demetrios asked God to "remember those who six months ago were taken from us, from this very place, in a most cruel and exceedingly painful way."

Church bells rang across the city, and the names of the 23 police officers killed were read aloud at police precincts. "They were called on to act and did so with the highest valor," said Capt. David Barrere outside the 76th Precinct in Brooklyn.

The 343 firefighters killed in the trade center were honored, too, with a bell-ringing at the morning service. Guests, including many victims' relatives, were given yellow daffodils.

The Sphere was gashed and partially crushed by falling debris. The sculpture was created in 1971 by artist Fritz Koenig and dedicated as a monument to world peace through international trade.

"It survived the collapse of the twin towers, as did the idea that catalyzed its creation: a peaceful world based on trade and the free movement of people and ideas," Bloomberg said. "This is just a temporary memorial. . . . The real memorial will be in our hearts."

The names of the victims from the trade center, the Pentagon and the plane crash in Pennsylvania were read aloud at St. Paul's Chapel in lower Manhattan. The church was a relief center after the attack, and still serves breakfast to recovery workers. . . .

Across the city, at a Queens church, hundreds of firefighters attended the funeral of Richard D. Allen. The Fire Department has held 148 funerals in the six months since the attack.

On Sunday, search crews found a battered fire engine in the rubble at ground zero, nearly six months to the day after its final run. Engine 55 firefighters managed to pry a crumpled door off the rig and add it to a memorial near the front of their firehouse in Manhattan's Little Italy. Five of their own died Sept. 11. "That was the rig the guys went there in," firefighter John Olivero said. "That was their last ride." ∎

AP Wire, Wednesday, May 29, 2002

LAST BEAM COMES DOWN

By SARA KUGLER
The Associated Press

NEW YORK (AP)—Hundreds of construction workers at ground zero watched last night as the last steel beam left standing at the demolished World Trade Center was cut down, marking the end of the recovery effort after the Sept. 11 terrorist attacks.

The 30-foot girder survived when the twin towers collapsed into a mountain of 1.8 million tons of rubble. For months, it was covered by debris, but as the pile shrank, the column was revealed, still standing where it was planted when the south tower was built more than 30 years ago.

During the last few months, workers topped the beam with a flag and covered the sides with spray-painted messages and photographs of victims.

"It means a lot to people—it's like a flag, which is a piece of cloth, but it represents our country and an idea," said Richard Streeter, who has operated an excavator at the site since Sept. 12. "The idea of the beam is our strength, our resilience."

Construction workers who have labored at the site watched as the column was severed with a torch, draped with a flag and a wreath, and placed onto a flatbed truck. Some workers wrote messages on the girder, while others touched it as if it were a coffin.

"The construction workers who have dedicated themselves to this effort are on the verge of completing an enormous job, and in many ways, this is their night to reflect and remember," Mayor Michael Bloomberg said. . . . The ceremony was the first of three planned for construction workers, rescue workers and families in a gradual farewell to the round-the-clock recovery operation. Tomorrow, the beam will be removed from the site in a procession past an honor guard of police officers and firefighters. It will be put into storage and might be used someday in a memorial.

The ceremony, organized by the city, will begin at 10:29 a.m., the moment the second of the towers crumbled. A Fire Department bell will ring the signal for a fallen firefighter, after which a stretcher with a folded flag will be carried out of the site, honoring the victims whose remains have not been found. . . .

Port Authority Police Lt. Mark Winslow said yesterday at the site: "Everybody's pretty somber, because we've been doing this for almost nine months and we don't want to leave. But we did all we could here." ∎

RIGHT: **Iron workers remove the flag from the top of the last remaining steel beam of the World Trade Center from ground zero, May 28, 2002.**

OPPOSITE TOP: **Construction and recovery workers watch as an ironworker cuts down the last remaining steel beam from the site of the Sept. 11 terrorist attacks in New York. The beam was removed from ground zero in the first of a series of ceremonies marking the end of the sorrowful cleanup, May 28, 2002.**

TRIBUTES TO SEPT. 11 ATTACKS ABOUND

By STEPHANIE GASKELL
The Associated Press

May 13, 2002 (AP)—The images are powerful. Workers hanging from the windows of the World Trade Center as the massive towers burn. People gathered in the streets of New York, staring up at the sky. Helicopters flying over the burning Pentagon. A lone firefighter digging through the rubble. A child placing flowers at a makeshift memorial. These images, and thousands more, have been captured in several books recording the events surrounding the terrorist attacks of Sept. 11. Accompanied by emotional tales of survival and loss, hope and heroism, they are historical records bound together as a reminder of how the world changed that day.

The September 11 Photo Project . . . edited by Michael Feldschuh, is a compilation of work featured at a gallery in New York's SoHo district during the months following the attacks. The exhibit opened on Oct. 13, 2001, with 200 submissions and grew to more than 3,500 photos. The book features many pictures and notes displayed as they were on the walls of the gallery. . . .

Portraits 9-11-01: The Collected "Portraits of Grief" from The New York Times . . . is a compilation of obituaries written by the staff of *The New York Times* for each victim of the World Trade Center attacks. For months, they appeared daily in a special section of *The Times*, "A Nation Challenged." They offer a glimpse into the lives that were lost that day—"the names and faces behind the unimaginable statistics." . . . .

All or part of the proceeds from each book will be donated to one of several Sept. 11 charities. ∎

Iron workers place the last remaining steel beam of the World Trade Center— draped with a wreath and an American flag—onto a flatbed truck after it was cut down, May 28, 2002.

AP Wire, Thursday, September 11, 2003

BELLS TOLL, CHILDREN READ NAMES OF THE LOST AT SEPT. 11 ANNIVERSARY SERVICE

By ERIN MCCLAM
The Associated Press

NEW YORK (AP)—The voices of children marked the profound horror and grief of Sept. 11 on Thursday, joining in song at ground zero and reading the names of 2,792 loved ones who died there exactly two years ago. Two hundred children and young adults, each of whom lost a relative in the most devastating terrorist assault in U.S. history, approached the microphones in pairs and began reading the names.

Many included personal messages. Christina Marie Aceto, 12, said: "I love you, Daddy. I miss you a lot. Richard Anthony Aceto."

Two bagpipers and a drummer opened the ceremony, marching onto the site of the World Trade Center with an American flag that once flew over its ruins. A children's choir sang "The Star-Spangled Banner."

"We come here to honor those that we lost, and to remember this day with sorrow," said Mayor Michael Bloomberg.

Minutes later, the anniversary ceremony at ground zero paused for a moment of silence—the first of four commemorating the times when each jetliner crashed into a tower and when each skyscraper collapsed. Across the nation, bells tolled, firefighters stood at attention, and in many places, moments with no words at all were held for the second anniversary of the terrorist assault that killed more than 3,000 people.

On the White House lawn, President Bush bowed his head in silence at 8:46 a.m., the moment that the first terrorist-hijacked plane struck the World Trade Center. He left the lawn without speaking, but earlier, he described his thoughts after a morning church service.

"We remember the lives lost," Bush said. "We remember the heroic deeds. We remember the compassion, the decency of our fellow citizens on that terrible day.

"We pray for the husbands and wives, the moms and dads and the sons and daughters and loved ones. . . . We pray for strength and wisdom."

Secretary of Defense Donald H. Rumsfeld presided over a somber ceremony at the Pentagon and attended a wreath-laying ceremony at nearby Arlington National Cemetery. Solicitor General Ted Olson, whose wife, Barbara, died in the attack, told Justice Department employees that an unrelenting fight against terrorism is the best way to honor the memory of those who perished. "Their suffering and deaths must fuel our dedication to stamp out this cancer," Olson said.

Anthony Taccetta, 10, right, holds a photo of his uncle, New York firefighter Lenny Ragaglia, as he joins mourners gathering to remember those lost during the terrorist attacks on the World Trade Center, Sept. 11, 2003. Ragaglia, who died in the attack, was with Engine 54.

Mayor Michael Bloomberg watches a young boy walk away from the podium during ceremonies marking the second anniversary of the terrorist attacks on the World Trade Center, Sept. 11, 2003.

DEADLINE NEARS FOR 9/11 FAMILIES TO SEEK SPECIAL AID

WASHINGTON, Dec. 15, 2003 (AP)—The unprecedented program to compensate victims of the Sept. 11, 2001, attacks may cost far less than its original $6 billion estimate, the fund's administrator said. The total payout could run as low as "$2 (billion) to $3 billion—well under what had been estimated," Kenneth Feinberg, the fund's special master, said in an interview just days before the Dec. 22. . . .

Feinberg said the disparity stems from the fund's creation in late 2001, when the death toll was in flux. Hundreds of names of people feared killed in the attack were eventually removed from the list. Others have suggested that so-called "offsets"—individual life insurance and other death benefits that are deducted from the government's awards—are holding down the overall cost.

Dozens of applications are still being received every day from the families of those killed and wounded in the terrorist attacks. Participation from the families of those killed was at nearly 75 percent as of Friday. . . .

Analysts say some still-distraught families are procrastinating about applying, while other families are determined to forsake the fund to file negligence lawsuits. The fund was created by Congress soon after the attacks to provide financial aid to the families of those killed or injured, and to protect the commercial aviation industry from crippling litigation. Families agree not to sue the airlines or other U.S. entities in exchange for compensation. Awards are based on the victim's projected lifetime income plus such variables as the number of children in the family and the amount of money available from such other sources as life insurance. . . .

Bill Doyle, whose son Joey died on the 101st floor of the trade center's north tower, said he struggled over whether to join the fund or sue but is now so confident in the fund that he's working long hours to encourage other families to apply. "Even two years later, some people still just don't want to deal with it," said Doyle. ■

In rural Pennsylvania, church bells began tolling solemnly shortly after 10 a.m., marking the moment hijacked Flight 93 crashed in a field just outside Shanksville as passengers tried to fight off their hijackers.

In New York, families began arriving at the World Trade Center site well before the ceremony, many wearing ribbons of white or black, symbolizing mourning, or yellow, for hope. Many carried flowers—daisies, petunias and roses to leave at the site during the ceremony. The footprint of the trade center's north tower was outlined by a 4-foot fence draped with banners bearing drawings and messages painted by children of the victims.

One of them was a simple red heart, outlined in black, with the inscription: "To my Dad, Steve Chucknick. You're in my heart forever. Love always, your son Steven."

Children whose relatives were among the victims began the solemn, careful task of reading the names of the victims in a morning ceremony. In breaks, Bloomberg and other dignitaries read poems and inspirational quotations.

"I know I'm very proud of my children," said Lynn Morris, whose husband, Seth Allan Morris, died Sept. 11, 2001, and whose two children, 11-year-old Madilynn and 9-year-old Kyle, were reading names. "It's amazing the strength that they have developed over the years."

A silent vigil began Wednesday night in New York at St. Paul's Chapel, once in the shadow of the trade center.

"There's no getting over it; there's just getting through it," said the Rev. Julie Taylor, 33. . . .

Lynn Morris looked up articles so that Madilynn and Kyle could match faces to the names. Madilynn was reading 14 names, finishing with that of her father, who was 35 and worked at Cantor Fitzgerald in the trade center. "I thought it would be a good way to honor my dad," Madilynn said, "and to honor the other people." ■

Family members gather to pay their respects to victims of the attacks during a memorial service at ground zero, Sept. 11, 2003.

AP Wire, Thursday, September 12, 2002

GROUP BURIAL HONORS 184 VICTIMS OF ATTACK ON PENTAGON

By CONNIE CASS
The Associated Press

ARLINGTON, Va. (AP)—In a single casket, remains that symbolically represent all 184 victims of the attack on the Pentagon were buried with full military honors Thursday at Arlington National Cemetery, the resting place of the nation's unknown soldiers.

In a quiet postscript to the nation's Sept. 11 observances, Defense Secretary Donald H. Rumsfeld eulogized the dead as patriots who died "here at home, not on a faraway battlefield."

He offered special condolences to the families of five victims whose remains were never identified, including 3-year-old Dana Falkenberg, who died aboard American Airlines Flight 77.

"Today, these five join the unknown of past wars even as we pursue the war that is still unfolding," Rumsfeld said, standing next to the flag-draped casket.

A granite monument with five sides, like the Pentagon, will be placed over the grave next week. It will stand on a hill with a tree-dappled view of the spot where the hijacked jet smashed into the Pentagon. Names of all 184 victims are inscribed on the 4-foot-5-inch-tall marker.

A year after the memorial to the victims of the 9/11 terrorist attack on the Pentagon opened in Arlington National Cemetery, Secretary of Defense Donald H. Rumsfeld again visited the site. He and Gen. Richard B. Myers, U. S. Air Force, chairman of the Joint Chiefs of Staff, place a memorial wreath on the monument, Sept. 11, 2003.

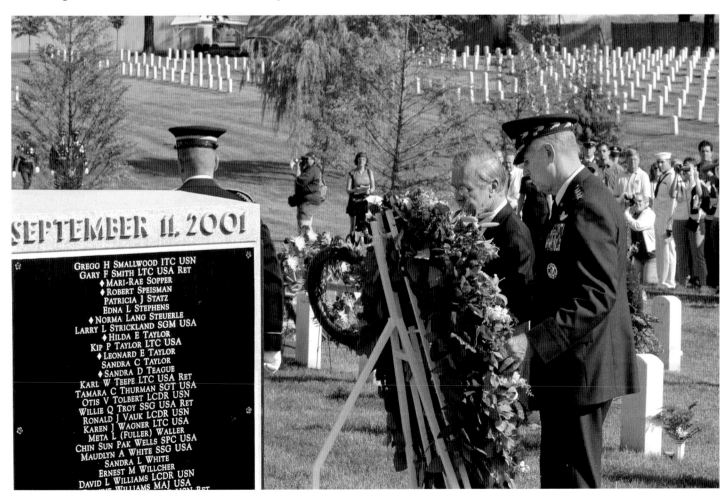

BUSH FINALIZES PATRIOT DAY, DAY OF PRAYER FOR SEPT. 11

By TERENCE HUNT
The Associated Press

ABOARD AIR FORCE ONE (Sept. 4, 2003)—President Bush will attend a prayer service of remembrance and observe a moment of silence to mark the second anniversary of the terrorist attack of Sept. 11, 2001.

While Bush will be in Washington, Vice President Dick Cheney will attend a memorial service at ground zero in New York City and Secretary of Defense Donald H. Rumsfeld will take part in a wreath laying ceremony at Arlington National Cemetery.

Interior Secretary Gale Norton will attend a ceremony at Shanksville, Pa., the site where one of the four terrorist-hijacked planes crashed.

"September 11 is a somber day for remembrance, reflection and prayer," said presidential spokesman Scott McClellan. He said it also was an occasion for the nation to reaffirm its commitment and resolve in the war against terrorism. . . .

Next Wednesday, on the eve of the anniversary, Bush will have a dinner at the White House and a screening of *Twin Towers*, an Academy Award-winning documentary of the attacks on the World Trade Center towers. The following day he will attend a prayer service at St. John's Episcopal Church at Lafayette Square, which is frequently attended by presidents. He will be accompanied by the First Lady.

Then the president, his wife, Laura, and members of his staff will gather on the South Lawn to observe a moment of silence at 8:46 a.m., the moment when the first plane hit the World Trade Center. . . .

Bush signed two proclamations Thursday, one of which designated Sept. 11 as a national day of prayer and remembrance. The second designated the day as Patriot Day.

They call on Americans to hold candlelight vigils and prayer services to mark the day and direct governors to fly the flag at half-staff in honor of the victims of the terrorist attack. ■

President George W. Bush, with First Lady Laura Bush, comments on the anniversary of the attacks on America two years ago after a memorial service at St. John's Episcopal Church in Washington, Sept. 11, 2003.

"It cries out, do not forget. Do not forget, Americans," Brig. Gen. James T. Spivey Jr. said in his funeral address.

Some 1,000 relatives of victims sat solemnly, some hugging and weeping, many holding pictures of their loved ones, as the crowd sang "Amazing Grace" on Thursday. After the funeral, a caisson drawn by six horses carried the casket behind the U.S. Army Band and two platoons of service members from the Army, Navy, Air Force and Marines.

The service marked the end of a year of Sept. 11 burials at Arlington. Individual funerals from the Pentagon attack began here on Sept. 25; the last was April 9. In all, 64 of the dead had already been buried at Arlington, most of them next to the site of the new monument. Many other victims, including some who were working inside the Pentagon on Sept. 11, did not qualify for an individual burial site at the nation's most prestigious cemetery, which is limited to active duty personnel and certain former service members.

All the cremated remains buried Thursday were determined to have come from victims, because they did not have a genetic trait shared by the terrorists, said Chris Kelly, spokesman for the Armed Forces Institute of Pathology. Some of the remains buried could not be linked to an individual victim. Others were identified after a victim had been buried, and were included in the shared grave at the family's request. . . .

Donna Teepe buried her husband, retired Lt. Col. Karl W. Teepe, in a similar Arlington service on Oct. 15, when she was still too dazed to note the bugler playing taps and other ceremonial flourishes. "I missed a lot of it," she said, watching hundreds of other family members line up to file by the shared casket. "It's good to see it now." ■

168

AP Wire, Monday, March 13, 2006

WORLD TRADE CENTER MEMORIAL CONSTRUCTION BEGINS

By AMY WESTFELDT
The Associated Press

NEW YORK (AP)—Without shovels in the ground or political ceremony, construction began Monday on the World Trade Center memorial, drawing protests from dozens of relatives of Sept. 11 victims, a coalition of whom are preparing for a court battle over plans to build over the twin towers' historic footprints.

Trucks rolled down a ramp into the site with lumber and other equipment at about 8 a.m. Construction workers began cleaning the memorial area of debris, checking the towers' footprints for damage and installing protective wooden coverings over parts of the original foundation. Front-end loaders removed gravel fill that has been covering the north tower footprint, while workers dug into the gravel with pickaxes. After six to eight weeks of preliminary work, concrete will be poured to create footings to support the "Reflecting Absence" design.

About 100 family members of trade center victims protested Monday, saying the memorial's underground design disrespects the dead and would destroy the historic footprint.

Rebuilding officials "have now officially dishonored the memory of the 9/11 dead, and they have violated the public trust," said Anthony Gardner of the Coalition of 9/11 Families, which last week filed a lawsuit to halt the building. The coalition's lawyer,

ABOVE: Following a press conference, John Whitehead, center, president of the World Trade Center Memorial Foundation, prepares to tour the construction for the 9/11 Memorial at ground zero in New York, March 13, 2006.

LEFT: Rosaleen Tallon, second from left, leads a group of 9/11 family members in protest against the construction underway of a 9/11 memorial at ground zero because of its underground design, March 13, 2006. Tallon's brother Sean Tallon, 26, a firefighter from Ladder 10, died in the 9/11 attacks.

TUNNEL TO TOWERS RUN HONORS SEPT. 11 FIREFIGHTER

NEW YORK, Sept. 25, 2006 (AP)—Thousands of people participated Sunday in a race named for the heroics of a firefighter who was killed on Sept. 11 after he ran through a tunnel to get to the World Trade Center on his day off.

The Tunnel to Towers Run honored Stephen Siller, a father of five who heard about the 2001 terror attack while he was going to play golf with his brothers in Brooklyn.

The annual 3.1-mile run follows the path he took, running through the Brooklyn–Battery Tunnel with 75 pounds of gear on his back to save lives at the twin towers. The tunnel, the longest continuous underwater vehicular tunnel in North America, connects south Brooklyn and Manhattan's Wall Street area, near the trade center complex.

Photos of the 343 firefighters killed on Sept. 11 were displayed Sunday along the race route. Firefighters from every state showed up, many running in full gear. Family members of Sept. 11 victims also participated.

"When you go through the tunnel and you see the pictures of all the guys," said runner LuAnne Campanella, whose firefighter brother-in-law was killed on Sept. 11, "it's very emotional."

Former Mayor Rudolph Giuliani, who was in office on the day of the terrorist attack, witnessed the run, which raised money for a children's foundation named for the 34-year-old Siller. "This is a beautiful thing," Giuliani said, "because they get to recreate what he did and remember how brave he was running here." ■

Alan Fuchsberg, said a hearing is scheduled for Wednesday to present their arguments.

Dozens of family members held up renderings providing by rebuilding officials of the memorial next to pictures of their loved ones. Some chanted "no underground memorial."

Gov. George Pataki last week called the start of construction "a very important milestone," but no groundbreaking ceremony was planned for the next several weeks. Officials said they wanted to meet a schedule to build the memorial by 2009.

The Coalition of 9/11 Families' argument that the memorial would damage the historic footprints has been echoed by preservation groups who have sent letters to rebuilding officials.

The "Reflecting Absence" design, by architect Michael Arad, was chosen two years ago out of more than 5,200 competition entries. It marks the fallen towers near their footprints with two stone reflecting pools at street level, surrounded by trees. The pools go 70 feet below ground, where visitors find surrounding each pool the names of the nearly 3,000 people killed in the 2001 attacks and the 1993 trade center bombing.

Families have said the memorial would dishonor the dead by placing their names below street level and might be difficult to evacuate quickly.

Rosaleen Tallon, the sister of a firefighter killed in the 2001 attacks, said Monday's activity wouldn't stop the overnight vigil she has held outside her brother's firehouse, across from ground zero, since last week. "There is always opportunity until concrete is poured" to halt construction, she said.

Stefan Pryor, president of the Lower Manhattan Development Corp., the agency in charge of ground zero rebuilding, said the design would "fulfill the highest standards of both safety and beauty." He said the agency would continue to hear family members' concerns. . . .

The World Trade Center Memorial Foundation has raised just over $100 million of a $500 million goal; it still has not calculated the costs of operating the facility. Foundation president Gretchen Dykstra said the beginning of construction should jump-start fundraising and should quiet skeptics who thought no plans would be realized at the site. . . .

Dykstra called it "a momentous day," but stressed that "it's not a day of celebration."

The 13 construction workers included Thomas Bilotti, who lost friends at the trade center and said he was "sad and proud" to be part of the effort.

"It's about time that somebody's working here," said Bilotti. "It's been long enough." ■

LEFT: Firefighters and runners enter the Brooklyn–Battery (Hugh L. Carey) Tunnel at the start of the annual Stephen Siller Tunnel to Towers memorial event, Sept. 28, 2014, in Brooklyn.

OPPOSITE: An aerial view of the 9/11 Memorial construction site, 2010.

AP Wire, Thursday, September 11, 2008

PENTAGON MEMORIAL STANDS ON "HALLOWED GROUND"

By MATTHEW BARAKAT
The Associated Press

ARLINGTON, Va. (AP)—For tourists, the new memorial to 184 people who died at the Pentagon in the Sept. 11, 2001, terrorist attacks is not especially convenient. Nor is it ideal from a security perspective to have 24-hour public access right outside the U.S. military's nerve center. But there is little dispute the new memorial, which opens to the public today, was built right where it should have been: at the spot where American Airlines Flight 77 plowed into the west wall of the Pentagon.

"This is hallowed ground," said James Laychak, whose brother, David Laychak, was killed in the attack.

Defense Secretary Robert Gates will speak at a ceremony dedicating the memorial this morning. It opens to the public this evening.

The memorial, built on an angle parallel to the plane's path just before if crashed, consists primarily of 184 cantilevered benches, each bearing a victim's name. The two-acre park will be open 24 hours a day, seven days a week, and will be patrolled by the Pentagon Police Department. While it is just a short walk from a Metro subway station, it is on a patch of land previously trafficked almost exclusively by Pentagon workers.

William R. Stout, deputy chief of operations for the Pentagon Police Department, acknowledged some ambivalence about the location. "If you're asking me as deputy chief of operations if I'm happy with the location, I'd have to say 'no,'" Stout said. "But

A moment of silence is observed during the dedication of the National 9/11 Pentagon Memorial in Arlington, Va., Sept. 11, 2008, on the seventh anniversary of the Sept. 11 attack.

Attendees at the dedication ceremony walk through the 184 memorial benches, Sept. 11, 2008. Each bench bears a victim's name.

overall, it seems logical to me to have it here. . . . We'll have eyes on it all the time."

It was not a given that the memorial would be located at the site of the crash. The Pentagon suggested about 10 different options. But family members were adamant that the memorial be built where the plane hit, Laychak said.

Memorials are also planned in New York and western Pennsylvania at the sites where other hijacked planes hit Sept. 11, but the Pentagon Memorial is the first to be completed. It has avoided some of the controversies that have plagued other sites.

Some family members of those who died when United Flight 93 went down in a field in Shanksville, Pa., say a grove of trees planned there mimics the Muslim crescent. Proponents say it represents a "broken circle," not a crescent. In New York, work on the memorial stopped for a time as officials sought to cut costs from a project approaching the $1 billion mark. Construction of the memorial is entwined with overall redevelopment efforts at the World Trade Center site, and has been delayed. Project managers have already given up on a 2009 completion date and have recently warned that it might not be completed by the current goal of Sept. 11, 2011.

Laychak said he is curious to see how the public will react to and interact with the Pentagon Memorial. He believes its design puts visitors in a reflective state of mind. "I look forward to seeing some of the customs and traditions that will develop," he said. . . .

The Pentagon Memorial emphasizes the diversity of those who died there. The benches are arranged by the victims' ages, so the first one visitors see as they enter is dedicated to Dana Falkenberg, a 3-year-old passenger on Flight 77, and the last to retired Navy Capt. John D. Tamnicky Sr., another passenger who was 71.

Paper bark maple trees have been planted throughout the memorial, selected because they retain their leaves late into fall and turn a deep red when the colors change, said Lea Hutchins, a spokeswoman for the Pentagon Renovation Program. From the memorial, the rebuilt section of the Pentagon remains clearly visible, the new limestone a slightly lighter shade than the old.

Planes coming in to nearby Reagan National Airport fly low and loud along the Potomac River. Laychak, for all the time he has spent at the memorial, has not yet visited the bench engraved with his brother's name. He is waiting for memorial's dedication so he can see it for the first time together with his family. "I wanted to save that moment," he said. ∎

AP Wire, Sunday, September 11, 2011

SEPT. 11 MARKED WITH NEW MEMORIAL TO THE DEAD

By SAMANTHA GROSS and LARRY NEUMEISTER
The Associated Press

NEW YORK (AP)—The names of the Sept. 11 dead, some recited by children barely old enough to remember their fallen mothers and fathers, echoed across ground zero Sunday in a haunting but hopeful tribute on the 10th anniversary of the terror attack. "Hope can grow from tragedy," Vice President Joe Biden said at the Pentagon.

Weeping relatives of the victims streamed into a newly opened memorial at the spot where the World Trade Center stood. They placed pictures and flowers beside names etched in bronze, and traced them with pencil and paper. President Barack Obama and his predecessor, George W. Bush, bowed their heads and touched the inscriptions.

Obama, standing behind bulletproof glass and in front of the white oak trees of the memorial, read a Bible passage after a moment of silence at 8:46 a.m., when the first jetliner slammed into the north tower 10 years ago.

The president, quoting Psalm 46, invoked the presence of God as an inspiration to endure: "Therefore, we will not fear, even though the earth be removed, and though the mountains be carried into the midst of the sea."

The New York ceremony was the centerpiece of a day of remembrance across the country. It was a chance to reflect on a decade that changed American life, including two wars and an overhaul of everyday security at airports and in big cities.

In a commemoration at the Pentagon, Biden paid tribute to "the 9/11 generation of warriors."

"Never before in our history has America asked so much over such a sustained period of an all-volunteer force," he said. "So I can say without fear of contradiction or being accused of exaggeration, the 9/11 generation ranks among the greatest our nation has ever produced, and it was born, it was born, it was born right here on 9/11."

Defense Secretary Leon Panetta observed a moment of silence at 9:37 a.m., marking the time a jet struck the headquarters of the nation's military. He paid tribute to 6,200 members of the U.S. military who have died in the Iraq and Afghan wars.

In Shanksville, Pa., a choir sang at the Flight 93 National Memorial, and a crowd of 5,000 listened to a reading of the names of 40 passengers and crew killed aboard the fourth jetliner hijacked that day a decade ago. Obama and his wife traveled to the Pennsylvania town after their visit to New York and placed a wreath at the memorial.

During the president's visit, members of the crowd chanted, "USA! USA!" One man called out: "Thanks for getting bin Laden!" This is the first anniversary observance since Osama bin Laden was killed by U.S. forces in Pakistan. . . .

In New York, family members read aloud the names of 2,983 victims—2,977 killed in New York, Washington and Pennsylvania on Sept. 11, 2001, and six killed in the first terror attack on the trade center, a truck bomb in 1993.

"You will always be my hero," Patricia Smith, 12, said of her mother.

Nicholas Gorki remembered his father, "who I never met because I was in my mother's belly. I love you, Father. You gave me the gift of life, and I wish you could be here to enjoy it with me."

Alex Zangrilli said: "Dad, I wish you were here with me to give me advice, to be on the sidelines when I play sports like all the other dads. . . . I wish we had more time together."

President Barack Obama and First Lady Michelle Obama, along with former President George W. Bush and former First Lady Laura Bush, pause at the North Memorial Pool of the National September 11 Memorial in New York, at a dedication ceremony on the tenth anniversary of the 9/11 attacks against the United States, Sunday, Sept. 11, 2011. The pool sits in the footprint of the north tower, formerly 1 World Trade Center.

OPPOSITE: Friends and relatives of the victims of 9/11 gather for the ceremony at the National September 11 Memorial at the World Trade Center site, Sunday, Sept. 11, 2011.

LEFT: The World Trade Center Flag is presented during the ceremony, Sept. 11, 2011.

RIGHT: Robert Peraza, who lost his son Robert David Peraza in the attacks at the World Trade Center, pauses at his son's name at the North Pool of the 9/11 Memorial, Sept. 11, 2011.

BELOW: Friends and relatives of the victims of 9/11 gather for the ceremony at the National September 11 Memorial at the World Trade Center site, Sunday, Sept. 11, 2011.

OPPOSITE: Elle Jackman, 6, helps her mother, Iris Jackman, do a rubbing of her aunt's name, Brook Alexander Jackman, on the wall of the North Pool, Sept. 11, 2011.

Peter Negron, 21, whose father worked on the 88th floor of the north tower, said that in the decade since the attack, he had tried to teach his younger brother lessons he had learned from their father.

"I decided to become a forensic scientist," Negron said. "I hope that I can make my father proud of the young men my brother and I have become. I miss you so much, Dad."

Cellist Yo-Yo Ma played a mournful Bach composition. James Taylor sang the melancholy "Close Your Eyes," and Paul Simon strummed a raw version of "The Sound of Silence." . . .

Obama and Bush were joined by their wives as they walked up to one of the two reflecting pools built over the towers' footprints, part of the Sept. 11 memorial that was opened to relatives of the victims.

Some family members held children on their backs who were not yet born when the towers were attacked.

As the sun rose, an American flag fluttered over six stories of the rising 1 World Trade Center. The sky was clear blue with scattered white clouds and a light breeze, not unlike that Tuesday morning 10 years ago. But by the time a moment of silence was observed at 9:59 a.m. to mark the moment when the first tower fell, thick clouds had moved over the sun, and it remained overcast well into the afternoon.

The site looked utterly different than it had for any other Sept. 11 anniversary: Along with the names in bronze, there were two manmade waterfalls directly on the footprints of the towers, surrounded by dozens of white oak trees.

Many of the victims' loved ones left flowers at the memorial. Some stuck small flags in the recesses created by each letter. Some just stood and wept.

Mary Dwyer, 36, of Brooklyn, said it was moving to finally be able to stand in the place where her sister, Lucy Fishman, died. "It's the closest I'll ever get to her again," she said. ■

MYSTERY SURROUNDS LOSS OF RECORDS, ART, ON 9/11

By CRISTIAN SALAZAR and RANDY HERSCHAFT
The Associated Press

NEW YORK, Aug. 31, 2011 (AP)—Letters written by Helen Keller. Forty-thousand photographic negatives of John F. Kennedy taken by the president's personal cameraman. Sculptures by Alexander Calder and Auguste Rodin. The 1921 agreement that created the agency that built the World Trade Center. Besides ending nearly 3,000 lives, destroying planes and reducing buildings to tons of rubble and ash, the Sept. 11, 2001, attacks destroyed tens of thousands of records, irreplaceable historical documents and art.

In some cases, the inventories were destroyed along with the records. And the loss of human life at the time overshadowed the search for lost paper. A decade later, dozens of agencies and archivists say they're still not completely sure what they lost or found, leaving them without much of a guide to piece together missing history. . . .

The trade center was home to more than 430 companies, including law firms, manufacturers and financial institutions. Twenty-one libraries were destroyed, including that of *The Journal of Commerce*. Dozens of federal, state and local government agencies were at the site, including the Equal Employment Opportunity Commission and the Securities and Exchange Commission. The Central Intelligence Agency had a clandestine office on the 25th floor of 7 World Trade Center, which also housed the city's emergency command center and an outpost of the U.S. Secret Service.

The first tangible losses beyond death were obvious, and massive. The Cantor Fitzgerald brokerage, where more than 650 employees were killed, owned a trove of drawings and sculptures that included a cast of Rodin's *The Thinker*, which resurfaced briefly after the attacks before mysteriously disappearing again. Fragments of other sculptures also were recovered.

The Ferdinand Gallozzi Library of U.S. Customs Service in 6 World Trade Center held a collection of documents related to U.S. trade dating back to at least the 1840s. And in the same building were nearly 900,000 objects excavated from the Five Points neighborhood of lower Manhattan. . . .

Jan Ramirez, the curator of the National September 11 Memorial & Museum, said there was no historical consciousness surrounding the site before it was destroyed. "It was modern, it was dynamic. It was not in peril. It was not something that needed to be preserved," she said. "Now we know better." ■

Designing for a Constituency of Thousands

By KAREN MATTHEWS
AP New York City Bureau Reporter

I heard the first plane hit the World Trade Center as I was getting my 3 1/2-year-old ready for preschool. I grabbed my daughter and went outside, where I saw but could not comprehend the gaping wound in the north tower. A massive fireball erupted as the second plane hit the south tower.

In the days following Sept. 11, 2001, all of us in the New York City bureau of The Associated Press covered different aspects of the attacks. Living just a few blocks from the smoking ruins, I wrote about the aftermath of the attacks in the neighborhood, where police barricades kept businesses closed and phone service was spotty for months.

The process of rebuilding the lower Manhattan site dubbed ground zero proved to be contentious and drawn out; it has not yet been completed 20 years later. Trade center developer Larry Silverstein wanted to rebuild all of the 10 million square feet of office space that had been destroyed as quickly as possible. Many family members of the nearly 3,000 terror victims wanted to ban office buildings and dedicate all of the trade center acreage to the memory to their loved ones.

Officials ended up approving architect Daniel Libeskind's master plan, which set aside half the site for a memorial. A worldwide competition for a memorial design was announced in April 2003.

More than 5,000 designs were submitted. A neighbor in my building submitted one; I remember poring over her plan with interest.

The winning design, announced Jan. 6, 2004, was from Michael Arad, then an unknown 34-year-old architect working for the New York City Housing Authority. Called *Reflecting Absence*, Arad's design featured waterfalls cascading into twin reflecting pools where the towers had stood. Landscape architect Peter Walker added a grove of swamp white oak trees surrounding the pools.

The memorial opened to the public on the tenth anniversary of the attacks in September 2011. When I interviewed Arad a few days before the dedication, he said he had been deeply affected by the September 2001 terrorist attacks and had started working on a memorial design even before the competition was announced.

"When I entered the competition it was a very private act," Arad said. "It was something that I did by myself, sketching in my study, imagining the kind of memorial that I might want to visit someday. But when the design was selected all of a sudden it went from a constituency of one to a constituency of thousands." ∎

A swamp white oak is lowered into position at the National September 11 Memorial in New York, Aug. 28, 2010. It was one of 16 oaks installed in the new grove that day, and the first of nearly 400 trees eventually planted around the eight-acre memorial.

LEFT: Michael Arad, who designed the Reflecting Absence memorial, poses in front of the ongoing construction at ground zero.

BELOW: One World Trade Center and surrounding buildings are reflected in one of the pools designed by Michael Arad at the National September 11 Memorial, Sept. 11, 2013.

OBAMA AT 9/11 MUSEUM: "NOTHING CAN BREAK US"

By JONATHAN LEMIRE and JENNIFER PELTZ
The Associated Press

NEW YORK (AP)—President Barack Obama praised the new Sept. 11 museum on Thursday as "a sacred place of healing and of hope" that captures the story and the spirit of heroism and helping others that followed the attacks.

"It's an honor to join in your memories, to recall and to reflect, but above all to reaffirm the true spirit of love, compassion, sacrifice and to enshrine it forever in the heart of our nation," he told an audience of victims' relatives, survivors and rescuers at the ground zero museum's dedication ceremony. "Like the great wall and bedrock that embrace us today, nothing can ever break us. Nothing can change who we are as Americans."

After viewing some of the exhibits, including a mangled fire truck and a memorial wall with photos of victims, the president recounted the story of Welles Crowther, a 24-year-old World Trade Center worker and former volunteer firefighter who became known as "the man in the red bandanna" after he led other workers to safety from the trade center's stricken south tower. He died in the tower's collapse.

One of the red bandannas he made a habit of carrying is in the museum, and Crowther's mother, Alison, told the audience she hoped it would remind visitors "how people helped each other that day, and that they will be inspired to do the same in ways both big and small. This is the true legacy of Sept. 11."

By her side was Ling Young, one of the people Welles Crowther rescued.

"It was very hard for me to come here today, but I wanted to do so, so I could say thank you to his parents," she said.

Before the ceremony, Obama walked quietly through an expansive hall with former New York Mayor Michael Bloomberg. First Lady Michelle Obama, former President Bill Clinton and former Secretary of State Hillary Rodham Clinton followed behind them.

The museum, which commemorates the 2001 terrorist attack, as well as the 1993 World Trade Center bombing, opens to the public on May 21.

New York Gov. Andrew Cuomo, New Jersey Gov. Chris Christie, current New York Mayor Bill de Blasio, former Mayor Rudy Giuliani and former New York Gov. George Pataki were among those attending, as was actor Robert De Niro, a museum board member. ∎

Quote by the Roman poet Virgil, forged from pieces of recovered World Trade Center steel by artist Tom Joyce. The quote sits within the artwork *Trying to Remember the Color of the Sky on That September Morning* by artist Spencer Finch on display in the National 9/11 Memorial Museum. Each of the colored tiles is its own shade of blue, one tile for each of the deceased.

President Barack Obama speaks at the dedication ceremony for the National September 11 Memorial Museum on May 15, 2014, in New York.

LIFETIME AID URGED FOR 9/11 RESCUERS

By GLYNN A. HILL
The Associated Press

WASHINGTON, June 11, 2015 (AP)—Advocates for ailing Sept. 11 first responders urged Congress on Thursday to permanently extend a law providing medical monitoring and treatment for the rescue workers, saying they need reassurance that their health care will not be cut off.

Dr. John Howard, the administrator of the World Trade Center Health Program, told members of the House Energy and Commerce Committee that extending the law would help clinicians treat victims, and allow administrators to better plan patient care. He pointed out that there are affected individuals in 429 of the 435 congressional districts.

"It's stressful to be told on a year-to-year basis that your care might be taken away," Howard said. "From the administrative perspective, it's stressful because we have to constantly prepare for when this may end."

Proponents of the law are seeking its permanent extension in part because some illnesses may not manifest until years later, after the statute of limitations for worker's compensation or certain state laws may have run out. The law, which is set to expire in October 2015, established the World Trade Center Health Program to provide medical monitoring and treatment for first responders affected by Sept. 11-related illnesses. It also reactivated the September 11th Victim Compensation Fund, which is set to expire in October 2016. . . .

The law, called the James Zadroga 9/11 Health and Compensation Reauthorization Act, is named after a New York police officer who participated in rescue and recovery efforts at the World Trade Center after the terrorist attack of Sept. 11, 2001. He died in 2006 from respiratory failure that was said to be related to his Sept. 11 service.

Nearly 15 years later, dozens of firefighters have died and hundreds more are seriously ill with health problems. Howard said there have been rare cancers and chronic health problems found in some victims. Without the funding provided by the Zadroga Act, research on these illnesses would cease, Howard said. ∎

181

AP Wire, September 9, 2015

FLIGHT 93 VISITOR CENTER "TELLS INCREDIBLE STORY OF HEROISM"

By MICHAEL RUBINKAM
The Associated Press

SHANKSVILLE, Pa. (AP)—Gordon Felt knew his brother was sitting directly in front of two of the terrorists who hijacked United Airlines Flight 93. But it "never really hit me," Felt said, until he walked through the new, immersive visitor center at the Flight 93 National Memorial. There it was, the seating chart with his sibling's name on it: Edward Felt, first class, second row.

"It kind of came crashing back," said Felt, whose brother took part in a passenger revolt that brought the plane down in a southwestern Pennsylvania field. "Those feelings that were always there—the emotion, the anger, the sense of loss really are drawn back to the surface."

Sitting on a hill overlooking the crash site near Shanksville, the $26 million visitor center complex will be dedicated and opened to the public on Thursday, one day before the annual 9/11 observances in Pennsylvania, New York and Washington. Victims' family members got a private tour on Wednesday.

Fourteen years in the making, the center uses photos, video, artifacts and interactive displays to tell the story of Flight 93, the only jetliner among the four commandeered by terrorists that failed to reach its intended target on Sept. 11, 2001. Two planes crashed into the World Trade Center towers in New York and one slammed into the Pentagon outside Washington. More than 3,000 people died.

The center's 10 exhibits are laid out chronologically, with visitors learning how the 33 passengers and seven crew members—at least some of them already aware the nation was under attack—voted to charge the cockpit and then fought to regain control of the plane, whose hijackers are believed to have wanted to crash it into the U.S. Capitol.

"You are seeing an incredible story of heroism, a piece of American history playing out in front of you as you are walking through this exhibit that gives perspective on the day," said Felt, president of Families of Flight 93.

One video traces the aircraft's erratic movements in real time, fading to black at the moment of impact. Bits and pieces of the debris field are displayed under glass.

Picking up a handset, visitors can listen to recordings of the voice messages that two passengers and a flight attendant left for family members minutes before plane went down.

"I'm on United 93 and it's been hijacked by terrorists who say they have a bomb," passenger Linda Gronlund, calling her sister Elsa, begins matter-of-factly. "Apparently they have flown

Gordon Felt, whose brother Edward Felt was one of 40 passengers and crew on United Airlines Flight 93 that crashed in a Shanksville, Pa., field 14 years ago on 9/11, leads a media preview of the Flight 93 visitor's center complex at the Flight 93 National Memorial in Shanksville, Sept. 9, 2015. The visitor's center was formally dedicated and opened to the public on Sept. 10, 2015.

a couple of planes into the World Trade Center already and it looks like they're going to take this one down as well."

She breaks down sobbing: "Mostly I just wanted to say I love you and I'm going to miss you."

Other displays trace the recovery and investigation. The center's stark, 40-foot exterior concrete walls are split by a black granite walkway that marks the doomed plane's flight path. Visitors are led through the exhibits to an outdoor platform that offers a commanding view of the crash site and surrounding hills.

Debby Borza, whose daughter, Deora Bodley, 20, was one of the youngest passengers aboard Flight 93, said she hopes the visitor center will inspire.

"The view I come from now is what's available for the visitors, the difference that it'll make in their lives, the courage that they'll find, the fortitude," she said after touring the site. "They'll be moved to take on things that they may have thought were only a dream in their lives."

The money for the visitor center complex was raised from 120,000 private donors, along with contributions from the state and the federal government. Officials project attendance will rise from 300,000 per year to around 500,000. Development of the Flight 93 National Memorial is nearly complete, with only the planned Tower of Voices, a 93-foot structure with 40 wind chimes, still to be built. ∎

LEFT: Visitors to the Flight 93 National Memorial in Shanksville, Pa., participate in a memorial service, Sept. 10, 2015.

BELOW: Ben Wainio, whose daughter, Elizabeth Wainio, was one of the 40 crew and passengers on United Airlines Flight 93, climbs a path to the Flight 93 National Memorial Visitors Center in Shanksville, Sept. 11, 2015.

AP Wire, Monday, July 29, 2019

TRUMP SIGNS SEPT. 11 VICTIMS' COMPENSATION FUND EXTENSION

By JILL COLVIN and JONATHAN LEMIRE
The Associated Press

WASHINGTON (AP)—President Donald Trump on Monday signed a bill ensuring that a victims' compensation fund helping those impacted by the Sept. 11, 2001 attacks never runs out of money, ending years of legislative gridlock as the number of first responders dying of ground zero–related illnesses mounted.

Appearing in the Rose Garden with more than 60 first responders from the 2001 terrorist attacks, Trump signed into law an extension of the fund through 2092, essentially making it permanent.

"You inspire all of humanity," Trump said of the "true American warriors" who rushed to assist victims that day and searched for remains for months after. The president said that the nation has a "sacred obligation" to care for the responders and their families.

The $7.4 billion fund had been rapidly depleting, and administrators recently cut benefit payments by up to 70 percent. The bill passed Congress on a bipartisan basis but only after delays by some Republicans exposed the legislative branch to brutal criticism from activists, including the comedian Jon Stewart.

Dozens of first responders, many gravely ill, would repeatedly travel to Washington to lobby lawmakers to extend the funding every time it needed to be reauthorized. Though their ranks shrunk, as emergency workers died of cancers and other diseases linked to the toxic fumes from the World Trade Center rubble, the fate of the funding had never been permanently guaranteed.

NYPD detective Luis Alvarez appeared gaunt and ill when he testified before Congress last month, urging lawmakers to pass the measure to help his fellow first responders even if it was too late for him. "You made me come down here the day before my 69th round of chemo and I'm going to make sure that you never forget to take care of the 9/11 first responders," Alvarez said.

He died two weeks later.

More than 40,000 people have applied to the fund, which covers illnesses potentially related to being at the World Trade Center site, the Pentagon or Shanksville, Pennsylvania, after the attacks. Stewart, who made the cause a personal passion project, tore into the lawmakers' inaction when he testified alongside Alvarez, creating a moment that was frequently replayed on cable news.

"Hundreds died in an instant. Thousands more poured in to continue to fight for their brothers and sisters," Stewart said before the committee. "They did their jobs with courage, grace, tenacity, humility. Eighteen years later, do yours."

A pair of Republican senators, Rand Paul of Kentucky and Mike Lee of Utah, voted against the measure this month, preventing its adoption from being unanimous. Both cited the need to eliminate unnecessary spending and offset the measure with budget cuts.

Trump did not dwell on that division when he signed the bill. The bill-signing prompted a round of applause from first responders in the Rose Garden as well as Trump's personal attorney, Rudy Giuliani, who was mayor of New York City during the attacks and was widely praised for his leadership in the aftermath of the World Trade Center collapse.

Trump, whose real estate holdings that day included some 20 buildings in Manhattan, played up his own personal connection on Monday to the World Trade Center site. "I was down there also, but I'm not considering myself a first responder," the president said.

But a number of the president's recollections about his own personal experiences that day cannot be verified, including his claims that he sent construction crews to help clear the site, that he had "hundreds" of friends die at ground zero and that he witnessed television coverage of Muslims in the United States cheering the destruction of the iconic skyscrapers.

The ceremony was attended by a handful of lawmakers—all Republican—though a White House official, speaking on condition of anonymity to share planning details, said that all members of Congress had been invited to the event. The invitations went out Friday and Saturday.

But Rep. Carolyn Maloney, D-New York, who sponsored the legislation in the House, said she "never received it. And I looked at all of my emails," she told The Associated Press.

Still, she said she was "just pleased that it was signed into law. It is a great day for America. It is above politics." ■

LEFT: Comedian Jon Stewart stands with New York City first responders during a rally on Capitol Hill in Washington, Sept. 16, 2015. Stewart called for the extension of the Zadroga Heath & Compensation Act that provides health care and compensation to 9/11 first responders and victims.

BELOW: President Donald Trump signs H.R. 1327—Never Forget the Heroes: James Zadroga, Ray Pfeifer, and Luis Alvarez Permanent Authorization of the September 11th Victim Compensation Fund Act—during a ceremony at the Rose Garden of the White House, July 29, 2019.

CHAPTER 6
THE REBUILDING

It was not going to be easy—or be done overnight. But the rebuilding of downtown New York was a vow made by politicians and business leaders of all stripes, and championed by stalwart New Yorkers. The Herculean effort was multifaceted and conceived in a flurry of urban planning, the wrangling of federal funds and emotionally charged debate.

Among the complications: The 16-acre site is largely owned by the Port Authority of New York and New Jersey, which set off jurisdictional conflict between the Port Authority, New York City and New York State. Though the groundwork for revitalization had been laid by the Alliance for Downtown New York, a quality-of-life initiative founded in 1995 to help transform Lower Manhattan from an after-hours ghost town into a bustling hub of life, the plan would need serious revision.

Sept. 11 not only streamlined the plan, it added many priorities to it. The federal government quickly approved $4.55 billion in aid to help rebuild and improve transportation links in lower Manhattan. The funds were part of the $20.9 billion in federal aid that New York was promised to rebuild. Over the summer of 2002, various citizen groups would be called upon to participate in decisions about rebuilding, including the Civic Alliance to Rebuild Downtown New York, a coalition of civic, labor, business and environmental groups and academic institutions committed to ensuring the public had a voice.

Said New York Gov. George Pataki: "The centerpiece of everything we do in Lower Manhattan must be remembering those we lost on Sept. 11 and telling the story of the heroic response of ordinary New Yorkers on that day." Accordingly, the highest priority was building a memorial and museum at ground zero as well as resurrecting the fallen World Trade Center. Under the auspices of the Lower Manhattan Development Corporation and eventually powered by $30 billion in government and private investment, the plan would include not only the reconstruction of office buildings, but new shopping malls, hotels, entertainment venues and a program to attract people to live in neighborhoods near ground zero.

In December 2001, actor Robert De Niro and his partners Jane Rosenthal and Craig Hatkoff announced the creation of the Tribeca Film Festival to help their Lower Manhattan neighborhood rebound. Twenty years later, the annual festival continues to be an integral part of New York's cultural life.

In 2006, in what Pataki called the last major hurdle to revitalization, the Port Authority negotiated a new lease with developer Larry Silverstein, who yielded his rights as landlord to the government agency for the planned 1,776-foot-tall One World Trade Center (also called Freedom Tower) and one of four other planned skyscrapers. The deal was sweetened by the Port Authority's and the city's commitment to each rent 600,000 square feet in the tower. A 10-year plan was now underway.

The opening of the crowning jewel of downtown, One World Trade Center, took place Nov. 3, 2014, and was seen as a symbolic return to normalcy. The giant skyscraper, soaring 104 stories, comprised 3 million rentable square feet with a 55-foot-high lobby. Nearby are dozens of hotels, two shopping malls and myriad entertainment attractions, in addition to the National September 11 Memorial & Museum, an observatory atop the Freedom Center, four other new World Trade Center buildings, a World Trade Center Transportation Hub and Liberty Park.

And as the buildings and the attractions came back, so did the people. The population downtown is more than double what it was before the Sept. 11 attacks.

There is still much to be done. Among the unfinished projects is the St. Nicholas Greek Orthodox Church, which was completely destroyed when the south tower fell. Its reconstruction as a church and shrine is expected to be completed by September 2021. The Ronald O. Perelman Center for the Performing Arts is scheduled to open in 2023. At the site that was 5 World Trade Center, Larry Silverstein has an 82-story structure on the drawing board for a new 2 World Trade Center, and a re-envisioned 5 World Trade Center will be developed in a joint venture by two developers.

Today, construction cranes and skeletal buildings under construction rise as high as the hopes of New Yorkers for the continued reimagining of Lower Manhattan as one of the most visited and beloved urban expanses in the world.

From the vantage point of two decades later, one thing seems clear: That horrifying morning that changed a country forever, and changed the city in ways it is still trying to figure out, did not destroy the neighborhood of Lower Manhattan. From the misery and the heartache and the violence that came from the skies, something new has grown.

A rainbow arcs over the downtown Manhattan skyline and soaring Freedom Tower, Oct. 10, 2016.

AP Wire, Thursday, December 6, 2001

DE NIRO SAYS NEW TRIBECA FILM FESTIVAL WILL HELP WITH DOWNTOWN'S REBIRTH

By KAREN MATTHEWS
The Associated Press

NEW YORK (AP)—Robert De Niro and his business partner Jane Rosenthal announced the creation of a film festival Thursday which they said would help their lower Manhattan neighborhood rebound from the Sept. 11 attacks.

The first annual Tribeca Film Festival will take place May 1–5, 2002 at various downtown venues, said Rosenthal, who co-founded Tribeca Productions with De Niro in 1988.

"This film festival, its programming and the many associated activities will not only commemorate the spirit of the neighborhood as we knew it," she said, "but will also celebrate what is yet to come, the rebirth of downtown, whose future is now more promising than ever."

De Niro and Rosenthal said the festival had long been in the works, but the attacks on the World Trade Center made the project more urgent.

Asked how the festival would help lower Manhattan recover, De Niro said, "We hope it'll help in every way. There are businesses down here that need help, small businesses, everything. And we don't know until we do this where it'll go. It'll take on a life of its own, but it'll take on a good, positive life and it'll definitely help in so many ways."

De Niro and Rosenthal announced the festival in a screening room at their Tribeca Film Center, where they were joined by Gov. George Pataki, state Economic Development Corp. Chairman Charles Gargano, actress Meryl Streep and filmmakers Martin Scorsese and Ed Burns.

"Lower Manhattan is going to be again, as it is today, the financial capital of the world," Pataki said. "But it's also going to be a great place to live and to work and to raise a family. It's going to be a community that's not just financial but also artistic."

Scorsese said the film festival would include a section on archival films.

"The idea is to go back and study the masters," he said. "And it's great if we can have this venue for younger people to see some of these older films in the right aspect ratio and the cleanest

Robert De Niro answers questions during a press conference during the opening of the first Tribeca Film Festival, May 8, 2002.

possible copy." Aspect ratio is the ratio of width to height of a photographic print.

The festival is to include 40 feature-length films, as well as short films, documentaries and student films. The selections will be chosen by a jury of film professionals.

Tribeca, the neighborhood just north of the World Trade Center, has been devastated by the Sept. 11 attacks. Much of the area was behind police barricades for weeks, and local businesses are still trying to cope with drastically reduced foot traffic.

De Niro has lived in the area for 20 years and played a major role in its evolution from a warehouse district to an upscale neighborhood. In addition to locating his film center there, he is a partner in the Tribeca Grill restaurant. His film company has produced recent hits including *Meet the Parents* and *Analyze This*. ■

ABOVE: **Presenters watch a film clip during a press conference for the 2009 Tribeca Film Festival.**

LEFT: **Street scene at the Tribeca Family Festival, part of the Tribeca Film Festival, April 27, 2014.**

AP Wire, Friday, February 15, 2002

FIVE MONTHS AFTER THE SEPT. 11 ATTACKS, BUSINESS FLIGHT CONTINUES IN LOWER MANHATTAN

By *KAREN MATTHEWS*
The Associated Press

NEW YORK (AP)—Five months after the Sept. 11 attack, more than one in four jobs in lower Manhattan has been lost, and half of the businesses whose buildings were destroyed or damaged do not plan to return to the neighborhood, surveys have found.

The surveys solidify the growing sense that the world's financial capital will not be same even as the buildings are repaired or rebuilt.

About 100,000 of the 370,000 jobs that were once in downtown Manhattan have been lost entirely or have been moved to midtown, out of town or out of state, according to the Alliance for Downtown New York.

M. Myers Mermel, chief executive of TenantWise.com, an online commercial real estate firm, said 49 percent of the tenants in destroyed or damaged office buildings say they are leaving

Excavation and construction work at ground zero, March 11, 2002. The towers of the World Financial Center stand in the background.

downtown for good. Those tenants once occupied 17 million square feet.

Many companies that are not leaving outright are decentralizing—or spreading out their employees at different offices—for fear of suffering a devastating loss in another terrorist attack.

"The trend once upon a time was to have the corporate campus, to have everyone in one place," said Valerie Lewis, a spokeswoman for the Alliance for Downtown, a business improvement organization. "9/11 has flipped that around. Now dispersal is in."

Citywide, 94,000 jobs have been lost permanently since the Sept. 11 attack, Mayor Michael Bloomberg said this week as he delivered a delivered a budget address that called for spending cuts and heavy borrowing.

Companies displaced by the attacks include financial giants American Express and Lehman Brothers, joint owners of 3 World Financial Center, a 51-story tower directly across the street from the World Trade Center. Lehman Brothers spokesman Jason Farrago said the lower floors occupied by the investment bank were severely damaged by flying girders. "We have a hole where some of the offices used to be," he said.

Unwilling to wait for the Cesar Pelli–designed tower to be repaired, Lehman Brothers bought a new headquarters at Seventh Avenue and 49th Street and is moving in gradually. The investment bank plans to lease or sell the floors it occupied at the World Financial Center.

American Express will move back, beginning in April. It had about 3,000 employees at 3 World Financial Center and 1,000 at other downtown sites.

Dow Jones & Co. had about 800 employees at 1 World Financial Center. It plans to move about half that number back in once asbestos removal has been completed, spokesman Steven Goldstein said. Other departments, including the *Wall Street Journal*'s copy desk and graphics department, will work out of South Brunswick, N.J., where they have been located since the attacks.

Lewis, of the Downtown Alliance, said an incentive plan announced by Gov. George Pataki last month should help keep businesses in lower Manhattan. She said there is $80 million in state money for small-business grants and $170 million in loans and grants for large businesses that stay in lower Manhattan or seek to locate there.

But Mermel said that even some downtown companies whose buildings were not damaged are leaving or dispersing. He cited the decision by the investment bank Goldman Sachs to move its equities staff to Jersey City, N.J.

"Where it's leading," Mermel said, "is that there is risk of continuing loss of jobs in lower Manhattan." ■

WTC BOOTS MINGLE WITH EASTER FINERY

NEW YORK, April 1, 2002 (AP)—As worshippers sang hymns Sunday in historic St. Paul's Chapel, workers in books dusty from the devastation of the World Trade Center trudged in for hot drinks and then back out to the job a block away.

"The message of Easter is a message of hope, and hope is something to which we cling amid the devastation of ground zero," said the Rev. Lyndon Harris, who delivered the Easter sermon at the 235-year-old Episcopal chapel.

The chapel survived the Sept. 11 terrorist attack with only a few broken windows, and became a sanctuary for workers toiling around the clock at the disaster site.

On Sunday, the work removing debris as parishioners in Easter finery filled the chapel's pews. Police officers, firefighters and workers trickled through the doors and made their way to a table where volunteers served hot drinks. Some stood listening to the hymns and prayers.

Louis Dini, who operates heavy equipment for 12-hour shifts at the trade center site, paused at the chapel before beginning work at 7. a.m. "It was good to be here," he said.

The chapel's role as a relief center was supposed to end Sunday, but at the request of the city, church officials now plan to keep it open until June, when the recovery operation is expected to end. ■

A rescue worker rests in a pew while other first responders pray in St. Paul's Chapel, a sanctuary of consolation after the attacks in New York, Sept. 19, 2001. The chapel, built in 1766 (and the oldest church building in Manhattan) famously became known as "The Little Chapel That Stood" after it survived the collapse of the twin towers, located less than a block away.

AP Wire, Thursday, February 27, 2003

SPIRE, SUNKEN MEMORIAL CHOSEN FOR WTC SITE

By SARA KUGLER
The Associated Press

NEW YORK (AP)—The city intends to fill its vacant skyline with an airy spire that stands taller than any other building in the world and defiantly recalls the year of America's independence with its height of 1,776 feet.

The spire, accompanied by five stark geometrical towers and several smaller cultural buildings, has been picked as the model for redeveloping the site where the World Trade Center once stood, a person close to the process told the AP on condition of anonymity. State and city officials were to announce the decision today.

Architect Daniel Libeskind's design calls for preserving part of the sunken pit that was the foundation of the original 1,350-foot twin towers, where he imagines space for a museum and a memorial to the nearly 2,800 victims who died there on Sept. 11, 2001.

Lee Ielpi, whose son was among the 343 firefighters killed, praised the choice of the Libeskind design, because the sunken space preserves what the families consider hallowed ground. "That area held the largest concentration of the 20,000 body parts that were found," Ielpi said. "That land was consecrated by the blood of the people who were lost that day." Ielpi is among the victims' relatives who have expressed concern about plans to include parking areas in the pit.

The areas would be for memorial visitors, not general public parking, but Gov. George Pataki told planners to "find an accommodation" that the families would approve, the source told the AP. The Libeskind design was chosen over the THINK team's twin 1,665-foot latticework towers, the source told the AP. The choice was made by a committee with representatives of the Lower Manhattan Development Corp., the Port Authority of New York and New Jersey and the offices of Pataki and Mayor Michael Bloomberg. The governor and mayor favored the Libeskind plan, an important factor in the decision, the source said.

LMDC Chairman John Whitehead telephoned Libeskind with the news, the source said, telling the architect that his "vision has brought hope and inspiration to a city still recovering from a terrible tragedy."

Libeskind told the AP he had no comment on the announcement. But he told the LMDC chairman that being selected is "a

Architect Daniel Libeskind, center, presents his winning vision for a new World Trade Center to New York Mayor Michael Bloomberg, left, and New York Gov. George Pataki, right, at a news conference in New York, Feb. 27, 2003.

life-changing experience," according to the source. Libeskind, whose firm is based in Berlin, has estimated the cost of building his design at $330 million. . . .

Planners are expected to focus now on the memorial space, to prepare for a separate competition that begins this spring.

Nine proposals for redeveloping the trade center site were unveiled Dec. 18. The design competition was launched after an initial set of plans, released in July, was criticized as being dominated by office space and bland structures. Two finalists were selected this month, each featuring buildings that would dwarf Malaysia's 1,483-foot Petronas Twin Towers, the tallest in the world. A small number of telecommunications towers would still stand taller than the Libeskind spire. . . .

Libeskind, 57, has said he included the sunken space because he was inspired by the surrounding slurry walls that hold back the Hudson River—what he says are the most dramatic elements to survive the terrorist attack. He wanted to provide a quiet, meditative space for visitors.

The Polish-born Libeskind was schooled in New York. His firm is well known for the design of the Jewish Museum Berlin, an extension to the Denver Art Museum and the Jewish Museum in San Francisco. ■

View of the public meeting organized by the Civic Alliance to Rebuild Downtown New York—a coalition of 85 civic, labor, business and environmental groups and academic institutions—at the Javits Center, New York, July 20, 2002.

THOUSANDS TO WEIGH IN ON FUTURE OF TRADE CENTER SITE

By KATHERINE ROTH
The Associated Press

NEW YORK, July 20, 2002 (AP)—A diverse group of 5,000 New York-area residents converged at the Javits Convention Center on Saturday for the biggest discussion yet about what should be built at the World Trade Center site and what a memorial for those killed on Sept. 11 should entail.

"The events of 9/11 call us all to action, to strengthen the voice of free people here and free people all around the globe," said Carolyn Lukensmeyer, who was serving as emcee for the daylong session.

After singing "America the Beautiful" at 500 tables beneath a half dozen mammoth video screens showing a waving American flag, participants—including many families of those killed in the attacks, survivors, rescue workers and residents of Lower Manhattan—set to work grappling with the most emotional question now facing the city.

"I have to make sure that the memorial will respect the memory of my husband, and that nothing will be built in the places where the towers once stood," said Tessie Molina-Forsythe, 50, of Basking Ridge, N.J., whose husband was killed in the attacks.

Others had decidedly different views. "We want the towers rebuilt just the way they were. Let's not let a bunch of thugs from Afghanistan dictate our urban planning," said Amiad Finkelthal, 40, of the Upper East Side, who said he was one of about 30 participants belonging to Team Twin Towers. . . .

[Participants] sifted through hours of opinions and presentations by architects and city planners. . . . Each group was to vote on the six conceptual plans. Those plans all include more than 11 million square feet of office, retail and hotel space; a transportation hub; and a memorial to the 2,800 people who died. A number of architects and planners complained the plans were unimaginative and family members of victims were outraged that some called for building over the footprints of the twin towers, while redevelopment officials stressed the plans are merely a starting point.

"We don't want to simply reach out to the public, we need to engage them," said Matt Higgins, spokesman for the Lower Manhattan Development Corp., the agency in charge of the redevelopment. . . . [Proposals] are to be narrowed to three by September, with the final plan to be chosen by December. ■

AP Wire, Thursday, September 11, 2003

DEVELOPER LARRY SILVERSTEIN: A REBUILT TRADE CENTER IN 10 YEARS, FREEDOM TOWER FIRST TO RISE

By LARRY MCSHANE
The Associated Press

NEW YORK (AP)—After two tumultuous years, World Trade Center developer Larry Silverstein is looking ahead.

"Within a 10-year time frame, I fully expect to see the site fully developed," Silverstein said in an interview at his Fifth Avenue office where a conference room wall was covered with designs for rebuilding the lower Manhattan site.

"The entire development is going to be unlike anything that one could have envisioned prior to 9-11," the 72-year-old private developer said. Silverstein said he expected rebuilding to proceed without problems—despite an ongoing fight with insurance companies and the concerns of the victims' families.

The cornerstone for the 1,776-foot (532.8-meter) Freedom Tower should be laid next summer, he said, with its steel structure in place by Sept. 11, 2006.

The tower, centerpiece of the redevelopment, will be the first building to be constructed at ground zero. Plans call for a collection of jagged modern buildings with office and retail space, cultural centers, a memorial and transit hub.

Silverstein also reflected on the tumult that followed his July 2001 deal to lease the World Trade Center from the Port Authority of New York and New Jersey, the bistate agency that owns the property. "It's hard to realize that two years have transpired," he said. "It seems as if Sept. 11 was the day before yesterday."

It's certainly not what Silverstein envisioned when he signed the 99-year lease just six weeks before the attack. The deal assured the once little-known developer a key role in redevelopment.

Gov. George Pataki, center, gets a tour of the reconstruction at ground zero by Joseph Seymour, left, executive director of the Port Authority of New York and New Jersey, and World Trade Center developer Larry Silverstein, right, April 24, 2003.

Silverstein has feuded at times with the site architect, Daniel Libeskind, and managed to bring in his own architect, David Childs, to take the lead role in construction of the Freedom Tower. But he offered nothing but praise for both, along with the architect for the site's new commuter rail station, Santiago Calatrava.

"Three gifted architects, world-renowned, with major bodies of work to their credit," he said.

The hardest part of his job, Silverstein said, remains his meetings with the families of the 2,792 victims killed in lower Manhattan. Many of the survivors were quick to offer opinions or complaints about the redevelopment. "It's the single most difficult task in this entire experience," Silverstein said. "Dealing with the families and their pain and their suffering and their grief. Nothing comes close."

The most frustrating part of the past two years? Dealing with the various insurance companies involved with the twin towers, a chore that has landed the two sides in court over how much money is owed Silverstein.

The parties disagree over whether the attacks that collapsed the twin 110-story buildings constituted two separate incidents.

Twenty-one insurance companies are arguing in court that the terrorism was a single "occurrence" as defined in the trade center's policy. If ruled a single occurrence, Silverstein would get $3.5 billion; he believes he's entitled to $7 billion, saying the attacks were separate incidents. ■

NYC, PORT AUTHORITY SIGN ON TO PRICEY RENTS AT WTC SITE

By AMY WESTFELDT
The Associated Press

NEW YORK, Sept. 22, 2006 (AP)—The city and the World Trade Center site's owner joined other governments Thursday in committing to move office workers to ground zero at rents about 50 percent higher than current average prices in downtown Manhattan.

The Port Authority of New York and New Jersey, which owned the twin towers, approved a new lease for developer Larry Silverstein, giving the government agency control of renting out the planned 1,776-foot-tall Freedom Tower and one of four other planned skyscrapers.

Silverstein would build three other towers and rent out office space in one of them to the city and the Port Authority, which leased the twin towers to Silverstein six weeks before they were destroyed on Sept. 11, 2001.

"The last major hurdle toward the completed redevelopment of the World Trade Center site has been overcome today," Gov. George Pataki said Thursday.

After months of bitter, prolonged negotiations over who should build what at ground zero, Silverstein agreed in April to give up his role as landlord of the Freedom Tower and a second planned skyscraper and build and develop the other three towers planned at the 16-acre site. ■

Architect David Childs, left, gestures as he explains the model of the redesigned Freedom Tower to Gov. Pataki, second from left, Larry Silverstein, second from right, and architect Daniel Libeskind, far right, during a news conference in New York to unveil the new plans for the World Trade Center site, June 29, 2005. Ground zero's Freedom Tower was redesigned to address security concerns: It lost the distinctive asymmetrical shape envisioned in earlier plans, officials said, but will rise from a base clad in shimmering metals chosen for both beauty and blast-resistance, and will be topped with an illuminated spire.

AP Wire, Tuesday, December 19, 2006

FIRST STEEL FOR WORLD TRADE CENTER SKYSCRAPER RISES AT GROUND ZERO

By AMY WESTFELDT
The Associated Press

NEW YORK (AP)—Two 25-ton steel columns—one bearing signatures of American steelworkers who helped make it—rose at ground zero Tuesday, a milestone in prolonged efforts to build the skyscraper that will replace the World Trade Center.

As construction workers, politicians and architects applauded, a massive crane lifted the first, 31-foot-high column, which was painted with an American flag and the words "Freedom Tower," and set it over steel bars on the southern edge of the tower's base.

A second column set a few feet away carried the signatures of steelworkers and politicians from Virginia, where it spent time at a steel company before being shipped to New York.

A third column lay on its side, plastered with signatures of New Yorkers and Sept. 11 victims' relatives as well as pictures of some firefighters killed in the 2001 attack. It will be installed in the next few days.

By next spring, 27 of the jumbo steel columns will anchor the skyscraper and rise to street level about 70 feet from the bottom of ground zero.

"Today the steel rises, the Freedom Tower rises from the ashes of Sept. 11, and the people of New York and the people of America can be proud," Gov. George Pataki said.

The 1,776-foot tower, set to open in 2011, is to be the tallest of the five skyscrapers planned to replace the trade center

"Rising from the heart of the World Trade Center site, the Freedom Tower will symbolize the spirit of our city and our nation: inspiring, soaring and undefeated," Mayor Michael Bloomberg said.

Construction workers watch from a ramp as others raise the first of three 25-ton steel columns into position to be bolted into place, marking the beginning of the Freedom Tower's construction at ground zero, Dec. 19, 2006. The columns, signed by families of World Trade Center victims and ground zero workers, were produced in Luxembourg and fabricated in Lynchburg, Va.

THE REBUILDING

Lengthy negotiations over who would build the tower and security concerns have delayed the project. The tower has had more than one design and groundbreaking; politicians laid a granite cornerstone in July 2004 to begin construction, but had to move the building after city police said it was too close to traffic, making it vulnerable to terrorism. Construction began again this spring, after the site's owner renegotiated its lease with a private developer and took over construction.

Gov.-elect Eliot Spitzer, who takes office next month, has said he planned to look again at designs for the tower. Federal and state agencies, including the governor's office, have agreed to occupy half of the building's office space.

The columns installed Tuesday—among the largest in the world—were forged in Luxembourg, then shipped to Lynchburg, Va., where workers welded steel plates onto them so they could be properly set in place. The tower will be built with 45,000 tons of steel, builders say. ■

The Freedom Tower under construction, Nov. 2, 2012.

AP Wire, Monday, November 3, 2014

WORLD TRADE CENTER REOPENS, 13 YEARS AFTER ATTACK

By *VERENA DOBNIK*
The Associated Press

NEW YORK (AP)—The silvery skyscraper that rose from the ashes of the Sept. 11, 2001 terror attacks to become a symbol of American resilience opened for business Monday, as 175 employees of the magazine publishing giant Condé Nast settled into their first day of work there.

The opening of the country's tallest building, One World Trade Center, marked a symbolic return to a sense of normalcy for the site where the twin towers fell more than 13 years ago.

"The New York City skyline is whole again," said Patrick Foye, executive director of the Port Authority of New York and New Jersey, which owns both the building and the World Trade Center site.

Steps away from the new 1,776-foot (541-meter) tower are two memorial fountains built on the footprints of the decimated towers, a reminder of the more than 2,700 people who died.

Condé Nast, publisher of *Vogue*, *The New Yorker* and *Vanity Fair*, is expected to move in about 3,000 more employees by early next year, eventually occupying 25 floors of the $3.9 billion, 104-story tower. Privately, some Condé Nast employees acknowledged that they were nervous about working in a skyscraper that could again be a terrorist target.

Foye countered that it's "the most secure office building in America." And its chief architect, T.J. Gottesdiener, said the high-rise was built with steel-reinforced concrete that makes it as terror attack-proof as possible—much stronger than the original towers that collapsed when the hijacked planes hit. The stairwells are built with a hardened concrete core, and wider to allow firefighters to move while people exit. The building's mechanical systems are also encased in hardened concrete

"If my son told me he had a job in the trade center Tower 1, I would have no qualms about him being there," Gottesdiener said.

One World Trade Center is 60 percent leased. Its eight-year construction came after years of political, financial and legal infighting that threatened to derail the project.

The area has prospered in recent years. About 60,000 more residents now live in the area—three times more than before 9/11—keeping streets, restaurants and shops alive even after Wall Street and other offices close for the day.

Still, it's a bittersweet victory.

"The city and the world were watching us, and we had to do it right, to do it better than before," Gottesdiener said. "And we did it, we finally did it." ∎

RIGHT: **Charles Townsend, CEO of Condé Nast, arrives at One World Trade Center with Patricia Röckenwagner, senior vice president of corporate branding and communications, Nov. 3, 2014, as the World Trade Center reopens for business, with publishing giant Condé Nast as one of the first tenants.**

OPPOSITE: **A dramatic view of the new downtown New York, June 27, 2015; the Freedom Tower, center, towers over the National September 11 Memorial & Museum plaza.**

AP Wire, Tuesday, August 30, 2016

THE NEW DOWNTOWN: LOWER MANHATTAN REBORN 15 YEARS AFTER 9/11

By BETH J. HARPAZ
The Associated Press

NEW YORK (AP)—Fifteen years after the Sept. 11th attacks, Lower Manhattan has been reborn.

The revitalization of the city's downtown, powered by $30 billion in government and private investment, includes not just the reconstruction of the World Trade Center site, but also two new malls filled with upscale retailers, thousands of new hotel rooms and dozens of eateries ranging from a new Eataly to a French food hall, Le District.

The statistics alone are stunning. There are 29 hotels in the neighborhood, compared to six before 9/11. More than 60,000 people live downtown, nearly triple the number in 2000. And last year, the area hosted a record 14 million visitors, according to the Alliance for Downtown New York.

And while there's plenty to do downtown for free, including seeing the 9/11 memorial park, visitors have also shown a willingness to pay relatively steep prices for certain attractions. The 9/11 museum, which charges $24, has drawn 6.67 million visitors since its May 2014 opening. The observatory atop One World Trade Center, which charges $34, has drawn 3 million people in the 15 months since it opened. In comparison, the Statue of Liberty gets about 4 million visitors a year.

"I don't think anyone would have expected that we would have rebounded so robustly, so quickly," said Jessica Lappin, president of the Alliance for Downtown New York. "There's the physical transformation at the site itself, but there's also the neighborhood. There's an energy here. People could have given up after 9/11 and nobody would have blamed them. Instead there has been a tenacity, a dedication that is inspiring."

The Alliance for Downtown New York was founded before 9/11, in 1995, when the "neighborhood was on its heels," Lappin recalled. "The vacancy rate was going through the roof." At the time, downtown was a strictly 9-to-5 area, keyed to the workday rhythms of Wall Street and City Hall, deserted at night and on weekends. Revitalization efforts were just getting underway "when 9/11 hit and changed everything."

But as government funding for disaster recovery began to pour in, private investment followed, spurring a massive rebuilding that continues to this day. For blocks surrounding One World Trade, half-built towers and cranes still clutter the sky, barricades and scaffolding line the streets, and the whine and clatter of jackhammers fill the air. Construction workers in hardhats are as ubiquitous as tourists. The recession hampered efforts to bring businesses back, but Lappin says private sector employment—266,000 workers—is finally nearing pre-9/11 numbers. Condé Nast and Time Inc. have relocated downtown. Group M, one of the world's biggest advertising firms, will move into Three World Trade Center when it's complete.

So far, three towers have been built with plans for more.

The neighborhood is also becoming a shopping destination. Brookfield Place opened last year with luxury retailers like Gucci and Diane von Furstenberg. It also houses Le District, a French food hall with a creperie, cafe, bar and more, as well as Hudson Eats, with outposts of popular local eateries . . .

A second shopping center, Westfield, opened in August inside the Oculus, a striking white structure designed by famed architect Santiago Calatrava. The curves of the Oculus' two ribbed wings are silhouetted by One World Trade rising behind it. Inside the Oculus, retailers range from Apple to Kate Spade to The Art of Shaving. The complex connects to Four World Trade, where the new Eataly NYC Downtown offers a bounty of bread, cheese, coffee, produce, pasta and more. Below ground a massive transit center houses subways and a New Jersey PATH train station. . . . Other downtown attractions include Alexander Hamilton's tomb in the graveyard of Trinity Church, the National Museum of the American Indian and the SeaGlass Carousel, which opened last year near where boats leave for the Statue of Liberty and Ellis Island.

But near the top of many visitors' New York itineraries these days is a pilgrimage to the place where planes turned the twin towers into smoking piles of twisted steel and rubble. The tranquil park formally known as the National September 11 Memorial features tree-lined walkways and reflecting pools in the footprints of the twin towers. Bronze parapets around the pools bear the names of the nearly 3,000 dead.

On Monday, park visitors included three siblings from Barcelona, Arantxa, Meus and Pau Saloni, on their first trip to New York. "It's really sad to see all the names, but it's nice to remember them," said Meus.

Also visiting Monday were Su-Ting Fu and his family, in town from suburban Westchester. "We lived in New York City when 9/11 happened," he said. "But we hadn't come to see this until today. It's nice to see everything they've done to memorialize it, but I also love the greenery, and how it feels very much like a living type of memorial."

Lappin said the neighborhood's rebirth is a fitting tribute to the 9/11 tragedy. "We honor those who were lost, but we also celebrate life and move forward." ∎

BELOW: The September 11 Memorial and Museum seen from an upper floor of 3 World Trade Center, June 7, 2018.

RIGHT: Visitors to the World Trade Center stop to look at *The Sphere* in Liberty Park, Sept. 6, 2017. The 25-foot-high bronze sphere, damaged on 9/11, has been returned to a spot overlooking the rebuilt site. It was made by German sculptor Fritz Koenig in 1971 and originally was situated on the plaza between the twin towers.

WTC HUB OPENS

By KAREN MATTHEWS
The Associated Press

NEW YORK, March 3, 2016 (AP)—New Yorkers and tourists got their first look inside a $3.9 billion transportation hub at the World Trade Center site on Thursday as officials opened one entrance to the cathedral-like pavilion.

The partial opening comes after years of delays and cost overruns. The hub was originally budgeted at $2 billion with a target completion date of 2009. Rising costs have been blamed on factors including architect Santiago Calatrava's demands and the logistical complexity of building it while the Sept. 11 memorial and office towers were also under construction.

"We really hope from the bottom of our hearts that New Yorkers embrace it and love it," said Calatrava, who shook hands with workers.

"I think it's absolutely spectacular," said one New Yorker, Jay Singer, 50. "It's the most amazing steel construction I have seen since I watched the twin towers being built as a small boy."

"I think it's beautiful," said another, Chrissa Chappell, 41, a professor of English at Lehman College in the Bronx. "Maybe it can be an example to the rest of the country."

The structure with its massive steel wings is supposed to evoke a bird in flight. The grand hall, known as the Oculus, is a soaring space with a skylight where the bird's spine would be.

Calatrava and his supporters say the facility will justify its price tag by taking its place as one of New York's most compelling pieces of public architecture. Calatrava called the hub "a monument of faith in this city" during a tour last month. But Patrick Foye, the outgoing executive director of the Port Authority of New York and New Jersey, which owns the trade center site, has criticized the station as "a symbol of excess."

The station is replacing one that was destroyed along with the twin towers in 2001.

When it is completed, the hub will connect Port Authority Trans-Hudson trains to New Jersey with 11 New York City subway lines and ferry service. Shops and restaurants are scheduled to open this summer. ∎

RIGHT: Opening day at the Westfield World Trade Center shopping mall in the Oculus transportation hub, Aug. 16, 2016.

TOP: People walk around the newly opened plaza of the World Trade Center Transportation Hub, Aug. 16, 2016.

AP Wire, Wednesday, September 11, 2019

REBUILDING WORK CONTINUES, 18 YEARS AFTER 9/11

NEW YORK (AP)—Over 18 years, the rubble left by the destruction of the World Trade Center has given way to a gleaming new complex of office towers, a museum, a transit hub and a memorial that draws millions of visitors each year. But though it no longer looks like a construction site, the rebuilding of the World Trade Center is still incomplete. Here's a look at four pieces of the complex that have yet to be finished.

St. Nicholas Greek Orthodox Church and National Shrine

Maybe the most visible sign of unfinished work at the World Trade Center is the unfinished, concrete facade of the St. Nicholas Greek Orthodox Church, perched across the street from the southeast corner of the memorial plaza. Construction on the church, which would replace a small chapel destroyed in the attacks, has been stalled since December 2017 due to financial problems.

The unfinished structure has been wrapped in a protective covering ever since. Designed, like the transit hub, by the Spanish architect Santiago Calatrava, it is intended to become a shrine to the memory of those lost on Sept. 11, 2001, as well as a parish church. Originally budgeted at $20 million, the cost of the Byzantine-inspired church ballooned to $80 million. Greek Orthodox Archbishop Elpidophoros Lambriniadis, who was installed June 22 as the new head of the church in the United States, told The Associated Press he hoped to raise money to resume construction.

Performing Arts Center

A planned performing arts center at the trade center site has long been delayed by disputes over funding and design but is now scheduled to open in 2021. The arts center will be at the northeastern corner of the site and will be called the

The St. Nicholas Greek Orthodox Church and National Shrine at the World Trade Center, under construction, as seen in January 2020. As of this writing construction continues, with the goal of finishing the rebuilding on the church by the 20th anniversary of the terrorist attacks of Sept. 11.

Ronald O. Perelman Center for the Performing Arts. Perelman, a billionaire investor, donated $75 million to make the building happen. Barbra Streisand was named chairwoman of the center's board in 2016. The 138-foot (42-meter), cube-shaped building will be covered with translucent marble.

2 World Trade Center

Four commercial skyscrapers have been built so far to replace the office towers destroyed in the terror attacks. One World Trade Center, originally called the Freedom Tower, now anchors the northwest corner of the site, towering over 7 World Trade Center tucked just behind it.

On the eastern side, two glass towers are complete: 4 World Trade Center and 3 World Trade Center. Yet to be built is 2 World Trade Center, just north of the white wings of the Oculus, the hall that houses a transit hub and shopping mall.

Developer Larry Silverstein plans an 81-story building but has not secured an anchor tenant.

The 2 World Trade Center space now houses mechanical equipment enclosed in a corrugated metal structure covered with graffiti art.

5 World Trade Center

A tower south of the trade center site that housed offices for Deutsche Bank was damaged and contaminated by the Sept. 11 attacks and was later demolished. After years of wrangling by different government agencies over control of the parcel, a formal request for proposals to develop it was released over the summer by Democratic Gov. Andrew Cuomo. Developers can submit plans for either an office building or a mixed-use project that includes housing. ∎

ABOVE: **Architect Daniel Libeskind, left, talks with Ronald Perelman beside a scale model of the Ronald O. Perelman Performing Arts Center at the World Trade Center, during the official design unveiling in New York, Sept. 8, 2016. The cube-shaped center, scheduled to open in 2022 or 2023, will be made out of translucent marble, as seen on the screen behind them. It will have three theaters with moveable walls that could be reconfigured for works of dance, opera, music and theater.**

OPPOSITE: **3 and 4 World Trade Center, overlooking the memorial pools and grove, and the Oculus. 3 World Trade, built on the site of the previous 3 WTC (the Marriot World Trade Center, destroyed on 9/11), opened on June 11, 2018. 4 World Trade, built on the site of the previous 4 WTC (a 9-story office building, also destroyed), opened Nov. 13, 2013.**

"Since 2017, The Associated Press's global headquarters has looked out over the World Trade Center. We see a place where strands of memory, renewal, solemnity and daily life entwine. We see the white roses placed by the names of the dead on their birthdays, and the visitors who come from around the world to pay tribute. We see office workers heading to their jobs and neighborhood residents strolling through. We see a place where 9/11 is still with us every day, but where time has not stood still."

—Jennifer Peltz, AP Newsperson

AFTERWORD

The Falling Man
Is Still You and Me

By RICHARD DREW
AP Photographer

My family calls it "the picture that won't go away." Most newspaper editors refused to print it. Those who did, on the day after the World Trade Center attacks, received hundreds of letters of complaint. The photograph was denounced as coldblooded, ghoulish and sadistic. Then it vanished.

Yet, twenty years later, I still get asked about it. I've been invited on national talk shows, interviewed by foreign TV crews and asked to speak about it at universities across the country. *Esquire* magazine published a 7,000-word essay that hailed it as an icon, a masterpiece and a touching work of art. Entertainer and photo collector Sir Elton John called it "probably one of the most perfect photographs ever taken."

All this for a single frame out of hundreds shot in haste before I was pulled to safety as the second tower of the World Trade Center tumbled toward me.

My fellow photographers called it "the most famous picture nobody's ever seen."

But, in fact, it was seen. Whenever it's mentioned, people say, "Oh, that's the one where the guy looks like he's swan-diving." Or, "That's the one where the guy's body is lined up perfectly with the lines of the World Trade Center." And then there is: "I know—it's the one where, if you turn it upside down, it looks like the guy is sitting on a chair."

I find that ironic. Here's a photograph that was considered too upsetting for readers to look at. Yet people were turning it upside down to take a second look from a different angle.

I look at it from my own angle. I was below the north tower that morning, on the corner of West and Vesey streets. The smoke was so thick, it was tough to see, and tougher to breathe. Rubble was falling, and when I heard the first of a series of loud cracks, I thought it was the sound of concrete debris striking the ground. But I was wrong. It was the sound of human beings hitting the pavement.

I focused on one person falling through the air, and shot eight frames. Then there was a huge noise, like an explosion. I just kept shooting; I thought maybe the roof had collapsed. I had no idea the whole building was falling, because I was too close.

An emergency technician saved my life; he yanked me away. The tower leaned toward us as we ran, and I stopped and shot nine more frames.

Stupid, probably, but when you're in shock, it's like you're on automatic pilot.

It was several days before the trauma had subsided enough for me to realize the magnitude of what had actually happened.

During the first 48 hours, I focused on the technical aspects of the work rather than the people I had photographed. My emotions had completely shut down, I was like a robot. I was operating on adrenalin and did not sleep. My wife says I got up at 4:30 in the morning and started vacuuming the apartment. I'm told my symptoms were consistent with post-traumatic stress syndrome, or PTSD. But I continued to work nonstop, returning to the site of the attack. It was my way of postponing reality. Then on the third day my 3-year-old called me on the phone to tell me she loved me. I started thinking of all the people who, unlike me, had not survived to see their children ever again, and I broke down. I walked five miles home from ground zero, carrying my gear, and went to bed for several days.

To this day, no matter where I am, my daughter calls on September 11 to say she loves me.

◆ ◆ ◆

Watching the tragedy unfold messed me up for a long time. I still take note of every plane I hear flying overhead, wondering if it's friend or foe. But neither the photograph nor the initial reaction to it disturbs me. People ask how I could cold-bloodedly photograph someone dying. I never saw it that way. I made a photographic record of someone living the last moments of his life. And every time I look at it, I see him alive.

I have photographed dying. As a 21-year-old rookie photographer on a supposedly routine assignment, I was standing behind Robert F. Kennedy when he was assassinated. That time, there was no telephoto lens to distance me. I was so close that his blood spattered onto my jacket. I saw the life bleed out of him, and I heard Ethel's screams. Pictures that, shot through my tears, still distress me after 35 years. But nobody refused to print them, as they did the 9/11 photo. Nobody looked away.

It's hard to say why not. The RFK assassination changed the fabric of American history. But then, so did the destruction of the

The Falling Man by Richard Drew, Sept. 11, 2001.

World Trade Center. The Kennedy pictures were more graphic and, in one sense, more personal. We knew him, as a public figure, a brother, a father and a husband.

It took me the better part of a year after Sept. 11 to even address the question. I was fending off PTSD, and I didn't want to think about it. Then The Associated Press sent me to a camp run by former British special forces for training in how to survive in a hostile situation. You'd think simulating being attacked or kidnapped would have increased my anxieties. But I found it comforting. Knowing how to take even a few preventive measures gave me back a sense of control over my destiny.

As my anxieties abated, I continued to wonder why people reacted so differently to the photos of RFK and the World Trade Center.

One editor who objected to my photo said, "Americans don't want to look at pictures of death and dying over their morning cornflakes." I disagree. I think they're fine with it, as long as the victims aren't American.

During the Vietnam War, my friend and colleague Nick Ut took a photograph of a girl who'd been napalmed, running down the road in flames. The picture became an instant icon and won the Pulitzer Prize. But no one in the States worried about getting napalmed. The photo evoked sympathy, not empathy.

In the World Trade Center photo, it's about personal identification. We felt we knew Bobby Kennedy, but we didn't identify with him. We weren't wealthy scions of a political dynasty or presidential candidates. We were just ordinary people who had to show up for work, day after day, more often than not in tall office buildings.

Just like the guy at the World Trade Center.

That's what unsettles people about the picture. We look at it and we put ourselves in the jumper's place. And we ask, "Which option would I choose? Would I wait and pray for help as the flames licked at me, or jump through fresh air and sunlight, to certain death?"

You see, the girl in Nick Ut's picture was on fire. You can see the agony on her face. It's horrifying, but it is not the face of America. The man in my picture is uninjured. He does not look like he's in pain. But you know he is moments from death. And you can't help but think, "That could have been me."

Tom Junod, who wrote the article for *Esquire*, interviewed the families of several victims trying to identify the man he called "9/11's Unknown Soldier." He found their reactions varied according to their own feelings about mortality.

Some were insulted at the suggestion that their relative might have chosen death when he had a family at home (ignoring the fact that death was certain in any case). Others praised his decision to jump as an act of courage (ignoring the possibility that the man might have been forced to leap from the smoke-filled tower in order to breathe).

Though his quest proved fruitless, Junod eventually concluded, as I did, that the point was moot. For we already knew the identity of the man in the picture.

He was you and me. ■

ACKNOWLEDGMENTS

How could I, or anyone, be grateful enough to the first responders of Sept. 11—many of whom lost their own lives while saving others? We are all indebted to their loved ones too, for fostering the virtue of heroism as part of their family values.

If I was ever part of a team effort, this is it! Barbara Berger, executive editor at Sterling Publishing, put her "stamp" on this work, which is why I believe it reads and looks like an important history book, which many will likely regard it as. My partner at The Associated Press, Peter Costanzo, and I loved once again working with her and with the talented Kevin Ullrich—who designed the complex interior and captured the emotions and impact of the day and its aftermath with ink on paper.

We were also privileged to work with the adept senior photo editor Linda Liang and creative director Melissa Farris. Special thanks also to Elizabeth Mihaltse Lindy, senior art director, covers, for the inspirational jacket and case design; Kevin Iwano, production director; and Michael Cea, production editor. Their valuable contributions are evident on every page.

Peter Costanzo and I have worked on several books together. His efforts, along with colleague Ted Anthony and others, to curate the personal recollections featured in this book from the stellar list of AP journalists, make this work something special.

—Les Krantz, Facts That Matter, Inc.

STERLING PUBLISHING WOULD LIKE TO OFFER OUR GRATITUDE to the dedicated correspondents of The Associated Press whose inspiring words and photographs tell the complex story of 9/11 in this book. Special thanks go to: Ted Anthony, David Caruso, Eric Carvin, Richard Drew, Kathy Gannon, Julie Jacobson, Jacqueline Larma, Mark Lennihan, James Martinez, Karen Matthews, Mark Mittelstadt, Peter Morgan, Jennifer Peltz, Suzanne Plunkett, Howie Rumberg, Amir Shah, Karen Testa, and Jerry Schwartz. Additional thanks to Lauren Easton, Michael Fabiano, Molly Gordy, Valerie Komor, Matthew Lutts, Patrick Maks, Francesca Pitaro, Brenda Smiley, Paul Stevens, Sean M. Thompson, and Chuck Zoeller.

We are also grateful to our invaluable partners in developing this project during an extremely difficult year: Les Krantz of Facts That Matter, Inc., who also wrote the insightful chapter opener text and timeline; and Peter Costanzo, Director of Programming & Media Partnerships at The Associated Press. We would not have been able to create this book without you.

Thank you all, for your dedication and expertise.

WE WOULD LIKE TO OFFER OUR VERY SPECIAL THANKS to Robert DeNiro for his moving foreword, which we are so honored to include in our book.

—Sterling Publishing Co., Inc.

The Freedom Tower, far left, soars above the skyline of downtown Manhattan at sunset, busy with trails of traffic, April 16, 2016.

PICTURE AND TEXT CREDITS

Picture Credits

9/11 National Memorial & Museum: Joe Woolhead: 171

Alamy: Louis Champion: 89 bottom; domonabike: 86; *REUTERS:* Jeff Christensen: 91, Kevin Coombs: 67 top, Larry Downing: 69 top, Chip East: 193; William Philpott: 121, Shannon Stapleton: 68; WENN Rights Ltd.: 89 top

The Associated Press: 97, 152; J. David Ake: back endpapers D; Al Jazeera: 93 bottom; Mary Altaffer: 195; Hassan Ammar: 154 top; J. Scott Applewhite: 120, 124, 168; APTN: 4 right; AP Video: 106 inset; Manuel Balce Ceneta: 145; Shawn Baldwin: 17, 36; Diane Bondareff: xiii, 46; Brian Branch-Price: 12, 160; Alex Brandon: 155; Robert F. Bukaty: 42 bottom, 58; Lauren Victoria Burke: 185 top; Arshad Butt: 149; Chao Soi Cheong: 24; Stephen Chernin: 53 top, 163 top; Deshakalyan Chowdhury: 108; Timothy Clary: 166; Jim Collins: 11; Mike Conroy: 96; Jason DeCrow: 143, 174, 175 bottom; Hidajet Delic: 87; Marco Di Lauro: 109; Damian Dovarganes: 49 inset; Richard Drew: 29, 204, 207; Michael Dwyer: 15; Ron Edmonds: front endpapers B; Mel Evans: 210; Mike Faram/Navy Times: 32; Ric Francis: 48 top; Ruth Fremson: 164, 165; Gary Friedman: 76; Hillery Smith Garrison: 92; David Gochfeld: 59, 79; Joshua Gunter/The Plain Dealer; David Goldman: 136, 137; David Guttenfelder: 105, 111 bottom; Janet Hamlin: 139; Steve Helber: 27 top left, 49; Stan Honda: 72 bottom; Tom Horan: 10 right; Daniel Hulshizer: 61 top; Lawrence Jackson: 127; Bridget Jones: 85 top; Caleb Jones: 135 bottom; David Karp: 47, 55, 56 bottom; Carolyn Kaster: 181 bottom; Beth A. Keiser: 44 top, 70, 77 top, 158; Riaz Kham: 1; Charles Krupa: 41 bottom, 67 bottom left; Justin Lane: 176 top, 177; Louis Lanzano: 47 inset; Marty Lederhandler: 28; Mark Lennihan: viii, 23, 54 bottom, 61 bottom, 170, 176 bottom, 178, 198, 201, 202, 203; David Lloyd/The Tribune-Democrat: 13 left; David Longstreath: 2; Shah Marai: 148; Ben Margot: 69 bottom; Joe Marquette: back endpapers C, 129; Enric Marti: 3, 109 inset; Jacquelyn Martin: 139 inset, 147; Pablo Martinez Monsivais: 43 top, 142; Bebeto Matthews: 55 inset, 169, 192; Dimitri Messinis: 99; Joel Meyerowitz: 45; Steve Miller: 10 left, 62; Doug Mills: 7 left, 43 bottom, 64, 65; Jassim Mohammed: 83; Khalid Mohammed: 150; John Moore: 106; Will Morris: 27 bottom; New York City Transit: 72 top; Ferdinand Ostrop: 84; Seth Perlman: 132; Suzanne Plunkett: case cover, 30, 31; Portland Police Department: 4 left; Gene J. Puskar: 67 bottom right, 146, 182, 183; Chad Rachman: 42 top; Adam Rountree: 154 bottom; Angela Rowlings: 60; Mohammad Sajjad: 111 top left; Gulnara Samoilova: 16, 37; Amy Sancetta: 6, 14; Ivan Sekretarev: 94 inset; Amir Shah: 101, 111 top right; Brendan Smialowski: 153; Robert Spencer: 56 top; Jennifer Szymaszek: 128; Carmen Taylor: 7 right; Elaine Thompson: 48 bottom, 144; Martial Trezzini: 82; Bernadette Tuazon: 41 top; Tomas Van Houtryve: 126; Dana Verkouteren: 135 top; Alejandra Villa: 179 bottom; Richard Vogel: 110; Evan Vucci: 133, 173; Susan Walsh: 172; Seth Wenig: 179 top; Kathy Willens: 44 bottom, 74, 159, 162, 163 bottom, 191, 194, 196; Ed Wray: 104; Heesoon Yim: 13 right

FBI: 26, 33, 114, 116, 117

FEMA: 71 bottom; Andrea Booher: front endpapers A, 53, 54 top, 118 top, 119 bottom; back case cover

Getty Images: Keith Bedford: 188; E+: ferrantraite: 199; iStock/Getty Images Plus: EXTREME-PHOTOGRAPHER: 208, Pawel Gaul: 197, Tomas Sereda: 186, Ultima_Gaina: x

Library of Congress: vii; David Finn: 57; Carol M. Highsmith: ii, iv, 5, 20, 80, 180, 181 top

National Archives: David Bohrer: 9 right; George W. Bush Presidential Library: Eric Draper: 8, 9 left, 18, 89, 93 top, 102, 115, Tina Hager: 19 left, Paul Morse: 19 top right, 90; Capt. Charles G. Grow: 107

National Park Service: 34, 116 left

Shutterstock.com: Mark Lennihan/AP: 190; Julian Makey: 85 bottom; Mihai_Andritoiu: 205

US Navy: Scott Guereck: 112

USA TODAY NETWORK: © The Journal News: 27 top right

The White House: Chuck Kennedy: 175 top; Pete Souza: 151

Courtesy of Wikimedia Commons: Department of Defense: 167, Robert D. Ward: 77 bottom; FEMA: Andrea Booher: 38, 71 top, 73, Gene Corley: 119 bottom, Michael Rieger: xiv; Hamid Mir: 131; National Archives: Records of the White House Photo Office: 19 bottom right; National Park service: 35 inset; US Navy: Aaron Ansarov: 130, Terry Cosgrove: 94, Shane T. McCoy: 122, 123, Richard L. Oasen: 125, Brandon W. Schulze: 156, Eric J. Tilford: 75, Jim Watson: 118 bottom; The White House: Joyce N. Boghosian: 185 bottom, Pete Souza: 140

Text Credits

x: Foreword, "When New York Came Back to Life," by Robert De Niro; a version of this account previously appeared in *The International Herald Tribune*, 2011.

xii: Preface, "The Day the Sky Fell," by Mark Mittelstadt; a version of this account previously appeared in *APME News*, 2002.

30: "It's Not Safe, It's Not Safe," by Suzanne Plunkett; a version of this account previously appeared in *The Guardian*, 2006.

50: "9/11: Memory and Beyond," by Richard Pyle; a version of this account previously appeared in *NPPA Magazine*, 2011.

110: "With New Experiences, a Reporter Evolves," by Ted Anthony; a version of this account previously appeared in *The South Central Review*, 2002.

206: Afterword, "The *Falling Man* Is Still You and Me," by Richard Drew; a version of this account previously appeared in *The Los Angeles Times*, 2003.

Three police officers look out over the Hudson River toward One World Trade Center and the Lower Manhattan skyline from Jersey City, N.J., Sept. 11, 2013. Behind them is the *Empty Sky* memorial, which honors New Jersey's victims in the 9/11 attacks.